CALL TO ARMS

GREAT MILITARY SPEECHES

JULIAN THOMPSON

PUBLICATION DATE: June 2009
DO NOT REMOVE
FILE COPY

Quercus

CONTENTS

INTRODUCTION

'For if the trumpet give an uncertain sound, who shall prepare himself to the battle?'

THE FIRST EPISTLE OF ST PAUL TO THE CORINTHIANS 14:8

It is D-Day, 6 June 1944, on Omaha Beach, Normandy. The pathetic remnants of the leading US assault troops huddle beneath the sea wall; leaderless, sea-sick, shocked and shattered. Fierce German artillery and machine gun fire has mowed down successive waves of follow-up troops, and now the survivors find themselves penned into an ever-shrinking beach by the remorselessly rising tide. The surf, whipped into a bloody foam, slowly rolls corpses back and forth on the waterline from which wounded men crawl. Soldiers whose landing craft sank before hitting the beach cling to obstacles protruding above the water, as bullets ping off them or whine viciously overhead. The assault has stalled. By 8.30 a.m. there is no room on the beach, and the Navy beach master halts the landing of reinforcements. Disaster stares General Omar Bradley, the overall American commander, in the face. The deadlock is broken by Brigadier General Norman Cota moving among the groups nearest to him, shouting: 'There are only two kinds of people on this beach: those who are already dead and those who are going to die. Now let's get the hell out of here!'. Others follow his example; painfully slowly, but with gathering momentum, the soldiers fight their way out of the death trap.

Commanders and leaders communicate with those whom they lead in order to get across a message. I use the broad term 'communicate' advisedly, since the message can be conveyed by a variety of media. It may take the direct form of a commander standing in his stirrups and shouting 'charge' or delivering a pre-battle speech; alternatively, it may be transmitted by signal (as Nelson famously did before Trafalgar), in an order of the day, an address by a politician or a radio broadcast. Some of the rousing exhortations I have included here were made to thousands; others were heard by just one person. Certain addresses were well thought through and tailored to fit a particular circumstance, while others were delivered almost as an aside in the heat of the moment. That is why I decided to call the book *Call to Arms* and discarded my original title *Battle Speeches*, which I felt placed too great an emphasis on the carefully crafted address. The leaders and commanders I have chosen range from heads of state and politicians, through generals and admirals, and down the chain of command to non-commissioned officers; their audiences vary in size accordingly.

Likewise, some of the calls to arms presented here are long, and some extremely short. In a number of instances, the leader made only one memorable speech, or at least only one that was recorded for posterity; in such cases, the entries devoted to them are necessarily brief. For others, I have had to choose from a large body of speeches, some very long. In every case, I have tried to set the scene for the reader by sketching the historical context in which the address was given. Sometimes I have included a short biography of the commander in question. My apologies in advance to those military history buffs who are already well acquainted with this information, and may therefore find it extraneous – or perhaps rather too abridged.

Such are the vagaries of war that the speech, order or communication, however stirring, did not always lead to success on the battlefield. Equally, a few of the utterances were not geared to a specific impending engagement: General Douglas MacArthur's farewell address to the cadets at West Point, for example. A commander may address large numbers of men simultaneously; thus, with the aid of loudspeakers, General George Patton was able to speak to a whole division. But at another time and place, the same commander might make a memorable comment to a few staff officers, or just one subordinate or aide. I included several such remarks because they added colour to the picture I was trying to paint of the commander's milieu. In making my selection, I also wanted to cover as wide a spectrum as possible of commanders and their different (sometimes highly individual) styles and modes of communication. Yet, for all their diversity, one common factor shines through: a good leader always tailors his, or her, call to arms to the circumstances, and to the people being 'called'.

I am sometimes asked what makes a man stand and fight rather than either run away or cower and try to save his skin. Deep down within a soldier, what really counts in the last resort is the close proximity of his mates, his buddies, his *copains*, his *Kameraden*; he does not want to let them down. Some of the leaders here appealed directly to that instinct, such as Captain Danjou of the French Foreign Legion at Camerone in 1863, or Sergeant Daly of the US Marines at Belleau Wood in 1918.

At the next level up, involving perhaps several hundred men, leaders may recognize that disaster, or defeat, can only be turned around if they step down several rungs on the command ladder and intervene personally; for example, David Farragut at New Orleans in 1862, Norman Cota at Omaha Beach in 1944, or Walton Walker in Korea in 1950.

Others, commanding many thousands of troops, and only able to do so by a written order of the day, must choose words that will strike a chord with their soldiers or sailors, appealing to their *ésprit de corps*. Like Admiral Cunningham's terse message 'Stick it out. Navy must not let Army down' during the darkest moments in the evacuation of Crete. Or Montgomery before the Battle of Alam Halfa: 'We will fight the enemy where we now stand; there will be no withdrawal and no surrender.'

Above all the 'call' must ring true, for fighting men have an unerring nose for bullshit. Cromwell's practical advice – 'aim for their shoelaces' – surely made his men grin, and was perfectly attuned to the occasion. As was Drake's menacing address to his fainthearted crews during his circumnavigation of the world, 'But if any of you turn back take very good care of one thing. Keep out of my way, for if I find you on the open sea, as God is my witness, I'll sink you'.

JULIAN THOMPSON 2009

ALEXANDER THE GREAT

'What of the two men in command? You have Alexander, they – Darius!'

ALEXANDER ADDRESSING HIS TROOPS BEFORE THE BATTLE OF ISSUS, 333 BC

Alexander was born in 356 BC. His father, Philip, king of Macedon, taught him the art of war, while Aristotle tutored him in philosophy. Alexander first commanded in battle at the age of 16, and succeeded his father at 20. His story is extraordinary: a young man with little money and deeply in debt, surrounded by older, jealous noblemen at home and hostile states, first had to establish his dominance in his own country, followed by mastering the rest of Greece. He then decided to set out to conquer the world with an army he could not pay. He spent the next 11 years fighting; first against Greek city-states, and subsequently against the Persians. Although frequently outnumbered, he never lost a battle.

The army Alexander inherited from his father was well-trained and disciplined. Its core was the infantry phalanx, armed with 5.5-metre (18-ft) spears. His phalanxes were so well drilled that, despite their heavy weapons, they could change formation and direction more swiftly than any of their opponents. Light infantry, slingers and archers supported the phalanxes, usually operating on the flanks and ahead of the heavy infantry in the manner of skirmishers in later armies. Engineers and siege machines also formed part of the Macedonian army. But the main striking component was a heavy cavalry force, known as the Companions, led by Alexander in person.

FROM GREECE TO ASIA MINOR

For two years after inheriting the throne of Macedonia, Alexander concentrated his energy in bringing the Greek city-states under his control. His destruction of the city of Thebes presaged the tactics used against towns and cities during his conquests outside Greece. He issued an ultimatum: instant, unconditional surrender. When he was not immediately obeyed, there was no second chance, Alexander followed up with a swift, violent attack. All citizens were massacred, including women and children. He was equally savage and ruthless on the field of battle.

Having subdued Greece, Alexander invaded Asia Minor in 334 BC. At Granicus he fought his first battle against the occupying Persians. He never returned to Macedon or Greece. Here he established a concept of operations that in outline form he would hold to in future. It was evident in his three

most famous victories: Issus (333 BC), Gaugamela (331 BC) and the Hydaspes river (326 BC). He had a flair for designing a battle plan that appeared to concede advantages of terrain to his opponents, which led them on by imbuing them with a false sense of security. Alexander arrived at his strategy for battle after a painstaking assessment of the terrain following detailed reconnaissance, rather than a flash of inspiration; surprise and deception are more often achieved by the former than the latter. A further important ingredient in such a formula is boldness combined with good training.

Having lured his enemy into opening up a gap, or exposing a flank, Alexander would lead his heavy cavalry in a shattering armoured onslaught at a point in the enemy line personally selected by him. After breaking through, he would lead his horsemen in a turning movement to trap a selected portion of the enemy against the advancing infantry phalanxes. When the enemy broke and fled, Alexander pursued and destroyed them.

The number of wounds on his body testified to his reckless courage, which saw him almost lose his life on several occasions. Before the Battle of Issus, he addressed his men, harking back to Granicus:

> Remember that already danger has often threatened you and you have looked it triumphantly in the face; this time the struggle will be between a victorious army and an enemy already once vanquished. God himself, moreover, by suggesting to Darius to leave the open ground and cram his army into a confined space, has taken charge of operations on our behalf. We ourselves shall have room enough to deploy our infantry, while they are no match for us either in bodily strength or resolution; and will find their superiority in numbers of no avail. Our enemies are the Medes and Persians, men who for centuries have lived soft and luxurious lives; we of Macedon for generations past have trained in the hard school of danger and war. Above all we are free men and they are slaves. There are Greek troops, to be sure, in Persian service – but how different is their cause from ours! They will be fighting for pay – and not much of it at that, we, on the contrary, shall fight for Greece, and our hearts will be in it. As for our foreign troops – Thracians, Paeonians, Illyrians, Agrianes – they are the best and stoutest soldiers in Europe, and they will find as their opponents the slackest and softest of the tribes of Asia. And what, finally, of the two men in supreme command? You have Alexander, they – Darius!
>
> The victory this time will not be over the mere underlings of the Persian King, or the Persian cavalry along the banks of the Granicus, or the 20,000 foreign mercenaries, it will be over the fine flower of the Medes and Persians and all the Asiatic people which they rule. The Great King is there in person with his army, and once the battle is over, nothing will remain but to crown our many labours with the sovereignty of Asia.

Having reminded them of what they had so brilliantly accomplished together – including drawing attention to conspicuous acts of individual bravery – he went on to say:

> Remember Xenophon and his force of 10,000, a force that cannot be
> compared with ours in strength or reputation – a force without the support of
> cavalry such as we have, from Thessaly, Boeotia, the Peloponnese, and
> elsewhere, a force without archers or slingers except a small contingent from
> Crete and Rhodes hastily improvised by Xenophon under pressure of
> immediate need – nevertheless he defeated the King of Persia at the gates of
> Babylon and successfully repelled all the native troops who tried to bar his
> way to the Black Sea.

When he had finished, his officers pressed forward to clasp his hand and express their appreciation of what he had just said. Alexander's first order was that the men should eat, and a reconnaissance party should be sent out to establish the route forward.

Alexander's army consisted of at least 40,000 horse, foot and supporting arms (increasing to three times that strength later in India). Without modern means of getting the message across simultaneously to large bodies of troops such as microphones, or orders of the day that could be read out, Alexander probably addressed his soldiers by units, and sometimes chose to stress different points, depending on his audience. In all his major battles Alexander had between 12,000 and 14,000 men just in the phalanx, the basic infantry unit in a phalanx being the 256-man 'Syntagma'. With the advantage of height when mounted on a horse, it would be possible to make oneself heard to between 2000 and 3000 men at a time, in a tight formation, and provided the conditions were right: a light wind in the right direction, and not too much external noise. So it is highly likely that the speech quoted above was given in parts, and tailored to suit the type and composition of the unit to whom it was addressed. Alternatively, it may have been delivered to just the commanders for them to pass on to their units.

ONWARD TO INDIA

Alexander's campaigning after the Battle of Issus (in present-day Turkey) took him to Egypt, and on to what is now Iraq, where he defeated the Persians again at Gaugamela. Here, having extensively reconnoitred the ground, he returned and summoned his commanders, telling them:

> There is no need for me to encourage you to do your duty; your past deeds,
> and the courage you have shown in the past is inspiration enough. Every
> officer of whatever rank, whether commanding a company, a squadron, a
> brigade, or an infantry battalion, should urge the men entrusted to his
> command to their utmost efforts; for we are about to fight, not as before, for
> Syria or Phoenicia, or Egypt, but this time the issue at stake is the sovereignty

Alexander (far left) is shown defeating Darius III of Persia (centre) at the Battle of Issus on a mosaic found in the ruins of the Roman town of Pompeii

of the whole Asian continent. There is no need for me to rouse you, my officers, to valour, when that valour is already within you. Let me remind you to preserve discipline in the hour of danger – to advance, when called upon to do so, in utter silence; to watch the time for a hearty cheer, and, when the moment comes, to roar out your battle cry and put the fear of God into the enemy's hearts. All must obey orders promptly and pass them on without hesitation to your men; and finally, every one of you must remember that upon the conduct of each of you depends the fate of all; if each man attends to his duty, success was assured; if one man neglected it, the army will be in peril.

Alexander inflicted a crushing defeat on Darius at Gaugamela, but the Persian king hastily fled the scene and evaded capture. After the battle, Alexander marched through Persia (Iran), and what are now Turkmenistan, Uzbekistan, Afghanistan and Pakistan as far as the Punjab, the land of the five rivers. Having crossed the River Indus at Hund, in May 326 BC, he encountered the local ruler, Porus, on the River Hydaspes (now the Jhelum), somewhere near the modern railway bridge at Haranpur. Here, in a battle deemed by Napoleon to be Alexander's most brilliant, he defeated Porus. Alexander continued his march and crossed the Ravi. At this point, the Macedonians began to express doubts about continuing. Some of the veterans were over 60 years old and, tough as they were, felt that pressing on was pointless. Nevertheless, this is exactly what they did. Finally, at the River Beas, last but one of the great rivers of the Punjab, Alexander, under pressure from his army, decided to turn back, and headed southwest towards the coast near present-day Karachi. The exchange of words between him and his commanders illustrates that he fulfilled one of the requirements of a good general: having the acumen to recognize when he should retreat, and the courage to do so. He started by addressing his senior officers thus:

I observe, gentlemen, that when I would lead you on a new venture you no longer follow me with your old spirit. I have asked you to meet me that we may come to a decision together: are we, upon my advice, to go forward, or, upon yours, to turn back?

If you have any complaint to make about the results of your efforts hitherto, or about myself as your commander, there is no more to say. But let me remind you: through your courage and endurance you have gained possession of Ionia, the Hellespont, both Phrygias, Cappadocia, Paphlagonia, Lydia, Caria, Lycia, Pamphylia, Phoenicia, and Egypt; the Greek part of Libya is now yours, together with much of Arabia, lowland Syria, Mesopotamia, Babylon, and Susia; Persia and Media with all the territories formerly controlled by them or not are in your hands; you have made yourselves masters of the lands beyond the Caspian Gates, beyond the Caucasus, beyond the Tansis of Bactria, Hyrcania, and the Hyrcanian sea; we have driven the Scythians back into the desert; and Indus and Hydaspes, Acesines and Hydraotes flow now through country which is ours. With all that you have accomplished, why do you hesitate to extend the power of Macedon – your power – to the Hyphasis and the tribes on the other side? Are you afraid that a few natives who may still be left will offer opposition? Come, come! These natives either surrender without a blow or are caught on the run – or leave their country undefended for your taking; and when we take it, we make a present of it to those who have joined us of their own free will and fight at our side.

For a man who is a man, work, in my belief, if it is directed to noble ends, has no object beyond itself; none the less if any of you wish to know what limit may be set to this particular campaign, let me tell you that area of country still ahead of us, from here to the Ganges and Eastern Ocean, is comparatively small. You will undoubtedly find this ocean is connected with the Hyrcanian Sea [The Caspian], for the great Stream of Ocean encircles the earth. Moreover I shall prove to you, my friends, that the Indian and Persian Gulfs and the Hyrcanian Sea are all three connected and continuous. Our ships will sail round from the Persian Gulf to Libya as far as the Pillars of Hercules [Straits of Gibraltar], whence all Libya to the eastwards shall soon be ours, and all Asia too, and to this empire there will be no boundaries but what God himself has made for the whole world.

But if you turn back now, there will remain unconquered many warlike peoples between the Hyphasis and the Eastern Ocean, and many more to the northward and the Hyrcanian Sea, with the Scythians, too, not far away; so that if we withdraw now there is a danger that the territory that we do not securely hold may be stirred to revolt by some nation or other we have not yet forced into submission. Should that happen, all that we have done and suffered will have proved fruitless – or we shall be faced with the task of doing it over again from the beginning. Gentlemen of Macedon, and you, my friends and allies, this must not be. Stand firm; for well you know that hardship and danger are the price of glory, and that sweet is the savour of a life of courage and of deathless renown beyond the grave.

Are you not aware that if Heracles, my ancestor, had gone no further than Tiryns or Argos – or even than the Peloponnese or Thebes – he could never have won the glory that changed him from a man into a god, actual or apparent? Even Dionysus, who is a god indeed, in sense beyond what is applicable to Heracles, faced not a few laborious tasks; yet we have done more: we have passed beyond Nysa and we have taken the rock of Aornos which Heracles himself could not take. Come, then; add the rest of Asia to what you already possess – a small addition to the sum of your conquests. What great or noble work could we ourselves have achieved had we thought it enough, living at ease in Macedon, merely to guard our homes, accepting no burden beyond checking the encroachment of the Thracians on our borders, or the Illyrians and Triballians, of perhaps such Greeks as might prove a menace to our comfort?

I could not have blamed you for being the first to lose heart, if I your commander, had not shared in your exhausting marches and your perilous campaigns; it would have been natural enough if you had done all the work merely for others to reap the reward. But it is not so. You and I, gentlemen, have shared the labour and shared the danger, and the rewards are for us all. The conquered territory belongs to you; from your ranks the governors of it are chosen; already the greater part of its treasure passes into your hands, and when all Asia is overrun, then indeed will I go further than the mere satisfaction of your ambitions: the utmost hopes of riches or power which each one of you cherishes will be far surpassed, and whoever wishes to go home will be allowed to go, either with me or without me. I will make those who stay the envy of those who return.

A long silence followed. Alexander invited comment; the officers present did not want to give an unprepared reply, yet they were still not happy. Eventually, Coenus plucked up courage, and began by conceding that Alexander had not demanded unreasoning obedience. He said that he spoke on behalf of the common soldiers, since the officers had already received much reward for service and it was in their interests to support Alexander. Other parts of the army, including Greeks, had been sent home, or allowed to stay and settle in the newly founded towns. Only a dwindling band of Macedonians had served from beginning to end. The old campaigners should be allowed to go, and be replaced by younger men. Coenus ended by saying:

> If there is one thing above all others a successful man should know, it is when to stop. Assuredly for a commander like yourself, with an army like ours, there is nothing to fear from any enemy; but luck, remember, is an unpredictable thing, and against what it may bring no man has any defence.

LEADING BY EXAMPLE

Coenus's words were greeted with applause, and even tears, proof of how reluctant most men were to prolong the campaign. After two days, and offering sacrifices in the hope of good omens, Alexander announced that he had decided to withdraw. As his biographer Arrian said, this was 'the only defeat he had ever suffered'. Alexander then made preparations for his voyage downriver to the Indian Ocean.

On the journey down the Ravi, Alexander besieged and assaulted the town of Multan. His troops held back; they had probably had enough. Alexander pressed on, and found himself cut off on the walls with three of his senior officers, with the scaling ladders smashed behind him. Lesser men would have jumped back down again. Not Alexander; instead, he leapt down into the fort and fought single-handed until his soldiers hammered sections of the broken ladder into the mud walls, swarmed up and came to their king's aid. By now he had taken an Indian arrow in the chest, but killed his assailant before collapsing. In revenge the Macedonians massacred every man, woman and child in Multan.

In the autumn of 326 BC, Alexander, having recovered from his wound, set off to return to Babylon (Iraq), the centre of his empire. He took the main body overland through the Makran Desert and southern Iran. A column under Craterus went north through the Helmand Valley and Kandahar, while another group travelled by sea, sailing all the way to the head of the Persian Gulf. Alexander's march nearly ended in disaster thanks to a lack of water and food. At one point the portion of the army led by Alexander was trudging through the sand under a blazing sun. Alexander like all his men was tormented by thirst, but marched on foot at the head of his men, leading by example. A party of light infantry having gone ahead to find water, found a tiny trickle in a watercourse that was almost dried up. They scooped up what they could in a bladder and brought it back to the main body. Tipping the water into a helmet, they handed it to Alexander. He thanked them for the present, and in full view of everyone, tipped it out on the ground. He was adamant that he would not drink if his men could not.

UNREST IN THE RANKS

By February 324 BC Alexander was back in Susa (Shushtar). He had been away six years in some of the wildest and most forbidding terrain in the known world. From Susa, Alexander moved to Opis,

A Persian manuscript illumination showing Alexander battling Darius

north of Babylon. By now he had decided to send his Macedonian veterans home. At the same time, he introduced Iranians into his army dressed in Macedonian equipment and trained in Macedonian tactics. Similarly, he recruited Iranians into the Companions. The Macedonians took grave exception to this, and on arrival at Opis, they mutinied, refusing to go home. Perhaps after ten years of plundering the riches of southern Asia, the prospect of a shepherd's hut in Macedonia did not appeal. What is more, most of them had acquired Asian or Iranian 'wives', and they did not relish returning to Macedonian wives they had left behind a decade earlier, especially with their 'foreign' women and bastard children. They had no intention of leaving all the good pickings they had accumulated, and those that they foresaw in the future, to a crowd of upstart Iranians. Like all élite troops throughout history, such as today's marines or paratroopers, they regarded interlopers with contempt. Alexander had perfectly good reasons for wanting to recruit in Iran, which had a far larger population than Macedonia. His intention was to replenish his army in preparation for further conquest. But the Macedonians did not see it that way.

The veterans marched on Alexander's palace, shouting, jeering and calling for the discharge of every man in the army, although this may not actually have been what they had in mind. They suggested that on his next campaign he should take his father, the god Ammon, with him; a jibe at Alexander's expense alluding to the fact that, while in Egypt several years before, he had announced that he was the son of this local deity. Alexander received them standing on a platform. After listening to them for a while, he jumped down in a fury, pointing out the ringleaders, and ordering their arrest. The 13 men in question were marched off and executed without delay. Although the mutineers could have killed him when he was in their midst, they desisted; they still needed him. Having climbed back onto the platform, Alexander then addressed the seething mob:

> My countrymen, you are sick for home – so be it! I shall make no attempt to check your longing to return. Go whither you will; I shall not hinder you. But, if go you must, there is one thing I would have you understand – what I have done for you, and in what coin you will have repaid me.
>
> First I will speak of my father Philip, as it is my duty to do. Philip found you a tribe of impoverished vagabonds, most of you dressed in skins, feeding a few sheep on the hills and fighting feebly enough to keep them from your neighbours – Thracians and Triballians and Illyrians. He gave you cloaks to wear instead of skins; he brought you down from the hills into the plains; he taught you to fight on equal terms with the enemy on your borders, till you knew that your safety lay not, as once, in your mountain strongholds, but in your own valour. He made you city dwellers; he brought you law; he civilized you. He rescued you from subjugation and slavery, and made you masters of the wild tribes who harried and plundered you; he annexed the greater part of Thrace, and by seizing the best places on the coast opened your country to trade, and enabled you to work your mines without fear of attack. Thessaly, so long your bugbear and your dread, he subjected to your rule, and by humbling the Phocians he made the narrow and difficult path into Greece a broad and easy road. The men of Athens of Thebes, who for years had kept watching for the moment to strike us down, he brought so low – and by this time I was working at my father's side – that they who once exacted from us either our money or our obedience, now in their turn looked to us as the means of their salvation. Passing into the Peloponnese, he settled everything there to his satisfaction, and when he was made supreme commander of all the rest of Greece for the war against Persia, he claimed the glory of it not for himself alone, but for the Macedonian people.

These services which my father rendered you are, indeed, intrinsically great; yet they are small compared with my own. I inherited from him a handful of gold and silver cups, coin in the treasury worth less than 60 talents and eight times that amount of debt incurred by him; yet to add to this burden, I borrowed a further sum of 800 talents, and, marching out from a country too poor to maintain you decently, laid open for you at a blow, and in spite of Persia's naval supremacy, the gates of the Hellespont. My cavalry crushed the satraps of Darius, and I added all Ionia and Acolia, the two Phrygias and Lydia to your empire. Miletus I reduced by siege; the other towns all yielded of their own free will – I took them and gave them you for your profit and enjoyment. The wealth of Egypt and Cyrene, which I shed no blood to win, now flows into your hands; Palestine and the plains of Syria and the Land between the Rivers are now your property; Babylon and Bactria and Susa are yours; you are masters of the gold of Lydia, the treasures of Persia, the wealth of India – yes and of the seas beyond India, too. You are my captains, my generals, my governors of provinces.

From all this which I have laboured to win for you, what is left for myself except the purple and the crown? I keep nothing for my own; no one can point to treasure of mine apart from all this which you yourselves either possess, or have in safe keeping for your future use. Indeed, what reason have I to keep anything, as I eat the same food and take the same sleep as you do? Ah, but there are epicures among you who, I fancy, eat more luxuriously than I; and this I know, that I wake earlier than you – and watch, that you may sleep.

Perhaps you will say that, in my position as your commander, I had none of the labours and distress which you had to endure to win for me what I have won. But does any man among you honestly feel that he has suffered more for me than I have suffered for him? Come now – if you are wounded, strip and show your wounds, and I will show mine. There is no part of my body but my back, which has not a scar; not a weapon a man may grasp or fling the mark of which I do not carry upon me. I have sword cuts from close fights; arrows have pierced me, missiles from catapults bruised my flesh; again and again I have been struck by stones or clubs – and all for your sakes: for your glory and gain. Over every land and sea, across river, mountain, and plain I led you to the world's end, a victorious army. I married as you married, and many of you will have children related by blood to my own. Some of you have owed money – I have paid your debts, never troubling to inquire how they were incurred, and in spite of the fact that you earn good pay and grow rich from the sack of cities. To more of you I have given a circlet of gold as a memorial for ever and ever of your courage and of my regard. And what of those who have died in battle? Their death was noble, their burial illustrious; almost all are commemorated at home by statues of bronze; their parents are held in honour, with all dues of money or service remitted; for under my leadership not a man among you has ever fallen with his back towards the enemy.

And now it is in my mind to dismiss any man no longer fit for active service – all such should return home to be envied and admired. But you all wish to leave me. Go then! And when you reach *home, tell them that Alexander your King, who vanquished Persians and Medes and Bactrians and Sacae; who crushed the Usii, the Arachotians, and the Drangae, and added to his empire Parthia, the Chorasmian waste, and Hyrcania to the Caspian Sea; who crossed the Caucasus beyond the Caspian Gates, and Oxus and Tanais and the Indian Stream, which none but Dionysus had crossed before him, and Hydaspes and Acesines and Hydraotes – yes, and Hyphasis too, had you not feared to follow; who by both mouths of the Indus burst into the great sea beyond, and traversed the desert of Gadrosia, untrodden before by any army; who made Carmania his own, as his troops swept by, and the country of the Oreitans; who was brought back by you to Susa, when his ships had sailed the ocean from India to Persia – tell them, I say, that you deserted him and left him to the mercy of barbarian men, whom you yourselves had conquered. Such news will indeed assure you praise upon earth and reward in heaven. Out of my sight!*

At the end of his address, Alexander jumped down from the platform and walked to his palace. There he remained for three days, handing out commands to Persian officers and creating new élite units formed from Persian troops. Hearing this the Macedonians marched to the palace and begged Alexander's forgiveness. Alexander was touched and relented. A Macedonian officer told him that what really hurt was being told that he had made Persians his kinsmen 'Persians kiss you, but no Macedonian has yet had this honour'. Alexander replied that henceforth every one of them was his kinsman. The Macedonians returned to camp singing. Eventually some 10,000 Macedonians were sent back home with full pay plus a bonus equivalent to 15 years' pay. Alexander's handling of the mutiny showed that he had neither lost his touch nor his astonishing presence. Lesser men would have been murdered by their guards, or found themselves faced with open revolt in their camp.

HANNIBAL

❛We will either find a way or make one.❜

HANNIBAL, 218 BC

This was Hannibal's answer to his generals' claim that crossing the Alps with an army was impossible. He duly proceeded to do just that, leading 20,000 infantry, 6000 cavalry and 40 elephants over the Alps into Italy in 218 BC, in 15 days.

Hannibal (247–182 BC) was born in Carthage in what is now Tunisia. He started learning his profession as a soldier at the age of ten in his father's campaign against the Romans in Iberia (most of what is now Spain). This First Punic War (264–241 BC; from the Latin term *Punicus* – literally 'Phoenician' – used to denote the Carthaginians) ended in disastrous defeat for Carthage. In 221 BC, Hannibal returned to become commander of all Carthaginian forces in Iberia. The Romans responded by declaring war on Carthage, so initiating the Second Punic War (218–202 BC). To forestall a Roman attack on Spain, Hannibal decided to take the war to the enemy by crossing the Alps.

On arrival in northern Italy he found a Roman army waiting for him on the River Trebia, a tributary of the Po. Hannibal addressed his soldiers, apprehensive at facing the Romans on their home ground:

We have nothing left in the world but what we can win with our swords. Timidity and cowardice are for men who can see safety at their backs – can retreat without molestation along some easy road and find refuge in the familiar fields of their native land; but they are not for you: you must be brave; for you there is no middle way between victory or death – put all hope of it from you, and either conquer, or, should fortune hesitate to favour you, meet death in battle rather than in flight.

In bitter winter conditions, Hannibal defeated the Romans, who lost about two-thirds of their army. However, icy conditions foiled Hannibal's attempts to follow up his victory.

Two years later, Hannibal inflicted his most crushing defeat on the Romans at Cannae in southern Italy. Hannibal spent the next 14 years in Italy, but never succeeded in capturing Rome or destroying the Roman state. The Roman reaction was to send Scipio to Spain, to destroy the Carthaginian base, including New Carthage (Cartagena). Having successfully completed his mission, Scipio was duly dispatched to Africa, where he defeated a Carthaginian army in the interior of what is now Tunisia. Hannibal was recalled to Carthage and defeated by Scipio (soon to be dubbed 'Africanus') at the Battle of Zama in 202 BC.

Hannibal advised his countrymen to make peace, before going into exile in Syria. There he committed suicide by taking poison rather than fall into the hands of an advancing Roman army.

SCIPIO AFRICANUS

'Come with me instantly sword in hand, if you wish to save our country. The enemy's camp is nowhere more truly in the place where such thoughts can rise!'

PUBLIUS CORNELIUS SCIPIO, QUOTED BY LIVY IN *THE HISTORY OF ROME*, BOOK XXII

Scipio was born to a patrician family in *c*.237 BC, and first came to notice at the Battle of the Ticinus River in 218 BC against the Carthaginian general Hannibal, where he rescued his father and escaped the subsequent catastrophe. After surviving the crushing defeat by Hannibal at Cannae two years later, he returned to Rome to learn that Lucius Caecilius Metellus and other senior Roman politicians were holding a meeting at which they were advising surrender. Sword in hand, Scipio burst into the room and, uttering the words above, persuaded them to continue to resist.

In the battles that followed, Scipio lost his father-in-law, brother, uncle and eventually his father. After a successful period of command in Spain, where he conquered all the territories overrun by the

Carthaginians, he returned to Rome as consul. In Spain, he had trained his army hard, specializing in a double outflanking manoeuvre, which relied on highly disciplined and well-drilled troops. He also realized that the key to defeating the Carthaginian army lay in aggressive manoeuvre tactics. What mattered was defeating the enemy, not conquering ground.

Rather than remain in Italy and fight Hannibal, who was still ravaging the north of the country, Scipio invaded North Africa, the Carthaginian homeland. There he defeated their forces at Campi Magni. The Carthaginians sued for peace, but the negotiations collapsed, possibly deliberately undermined by Scipio. At this juncture Hannibal was recalled to Africa, exactly what Scipio wanted.

They met at Zama where battle was joined. Scipio addressed his soldiers:

> Go therefore, to meet the foe with two objects before you, either victory or death. For men animated by such a spirit must always overcome their adversaries, since they go into battle ready to throw away their lives.

Hannibal was short of cavalry, and attempted to wear down the Roman infantry, beginning with a charge of his elephants. He held his veteran infantry in reserve, and his cavalry on the flanks. The Roman infantry disrupted and disorientated the elephants by shouting, and opening up lanes in their formation, down which the elephants charged, enabling the Romans to attack them in the rear. When the Carthaginian cavalry tried to take a hand, they were driven from the battlefield by the Roman cavalry. The Roman infantry advance pressed back the Carthaginians, but they did not break. Eventually the battle was decided by the Roman cavalry, who returned from their pursuit of the Carthaginian horse and attacked Hannibal's army in the back. In the ensuing slaughter, Hannibal lost about 20,000 men to Scipio's 2000.

Scipio returned to a hero's welcome in Rome, where the title of 'Africanus' was bestowed on him by a grateful senate.

JULIUS CAESAR

'Let us march on and go where the gods'
omens and our enemies' crimes summon us.
The die is cast.'

JULIUS CAESAR AT THE CROSSING OF THE RUBICON 11 JANUARY 49 BC,
QUOTED BY THE BIOGRAPHER SUETONIUS

In 49 BC the Roman senate ordered Julius Caesar (102–44 BC) to return to Rome as a private citizen, without his army. Caesar chose to defy them and crossed the Rubicon, the boundary between Cisalpine Gaul and Italy, at the head of his troops, thus initiating 13 years of civil war that ended only when his adopted nephew Octavian brought lasting peace to the empire. Caesar cleared Italy in 66 days, driving the consul Pompey and his supporters into exile. Having defeated Pompey's forces in Spain, he pursued them to Greece, and despite being outnumbered two to one, defeated them again at the Battle of Pharsalus in 48 BC. At a key moment in this battle, Caesar personally led a cavalry charge.

Pompey fled to Egypt, where he was assassinated. Arriving shortly afterwards, Caesar completed the destruction of Pompey's army. After embarking on an affair with Queen Cleopatra of Egypt, he attacked and defeated her enemy King Pharnaces of Pontus in 47 BC, reporting his victory in the phrase often wrongly associated with his invasion of Britain earlier in his career: '*veni, vidi, vici*' ('I came, I saw, I conquered').

Julius Caesar came to notice as a soldier at the age of 42 as the commander of a small army in Spain in 60 BC. Like many Romans of the patrician class, he was both a politician and a soldier, following both professions from early manhood. Already a consummate politician, he proved himself an outstanding general during an eight-year campaign in Gaul, subduing the whole country, and advancing the Roman frontier to the Rhine.

Like many distinguished commanders he was an excellent trainer of soldiers, and an early exponent of the dictum, 'train hard, fight easy'. Although all his troops admired him immensely, he had an especially close relationship with the Tenth Legion, with whom he had first soldiered in Spain. They accompanied him to Gaul, and eventually to Britain in 55 BC. The first landing there would have stalled but for the standard bearer of the Tenth, who plunged into the surf and showed the way to the rest of the legion.

The commentaries written by Caesar on the Gallic War and the Civil War are some of the best sources for the military history of the period, and contain many examples of his ability to inspire his men in battle. Unfortunately, he does not quote directly what he said; for example, regarding an encounter with the Helvetii, a Celtic tribe from southern Germany and Switzerland, he writes:

> *I first of all had my own horse taken out of the way and then the horses of the other officers. I wanted the danger to be the same for everyone and for no one to have any hope of escape by flight. Then I spoke a few words of encouragement to the men before joining battle.*

Afterwards, Caesar commented with satisfaction on the conduct of his troops: 'In the whole of this battle, which lasted from midday until the evening, not a single man was seen to turn and run.'

Caesar was very close to his soldiers, treating them well. He addressed them as 'comrades', and used his skill as an orator to make telling battle speeches. Before a extremely close-run battle against the Belgic tribe of Nervii in present day Flanders, he says: 'I only gave the orders that were most essential, and then ran down to address the troops where I could first find them'.

Caesar recorded the siege of Avaricum (Bourges), which ran into difficulties, thus:

> *I used to speak to the men of each legion while they were working. I would tell them that, if they found their privations unbearable, I was quite ready to raise the siege, but one and all they would beg me not do do so. They had now, they said, served under me for many years without ever disgracing themselves or ever failing to finish any task to which they had set their hands; they would count it as a disgrace if they were to abandon this siege, which they had begun.*

At the Sambre in 57 BC, Caesar saw the Twelfth Legion faring badly, with many of its centurions out of action, the standard bearer dead and the standard itself captured. He could see that the legion was about to break, and so, seizing a shield off a rear rank man, he pushed into the front line and called on the centurions by name, ordering the line to advance and open out to give freer play with their swords. All the men were heartened by the sight of their general leading from the front, and they tried their utmost in his presence.

A year after his return to Rome from North Africa in 45 BC, Caesar was assassinated by political rivals. Despite his commentaries being somewhat economical with the truth at times, they are brilliant examples of clear Latin prose. One criticism is that Caesar tends to be self-aggrandizing, mentioning his own name over 700 times in the two accounts. However, this cannot detract from the fact that, along with Alexander, he was without doubt the greatest soldier of the classical period.

HARALD HARDRADA

'Forth we go in our lines
Without our armour, against the blue blades.
The helmets glitter: I have no armour.
Our shrouds are down in those ships.'

HARALD HARDRADA, 1066

King Harald Hardrada of Norway (1015–66) composed this verse just before the Battle of Stamford Bridge on 25 September 1066. He and many of his men had no armour because as his poem informs us, it, along with many of his men, had been left in his ships in the Humber at Riccall, 9 miles (15 km) from the City of York and some 15 miles (24 km) from Stamford Bridge.

Harald had come to claim the throne of England. The Englishman Harold Godwinson had been crowned king when Edward the Confessor died in January 1066. But there were other claimants, including William, duke of Normandy, waiting with his ships at the mouth of the River Dives in northern France for a favourable wind to take him to England. Harald Hardrada's claim was thin, but such a minor matter did not deter this formidable soldier from an attempt to seize the English crown by force, just as he had taken the Norwegian throne in 1047. He also had a useful ally in Harold Godwinson's brother, Tostig, lately the earl of Northumbria. One year previously, Edward the Confessor had exiled Tostig, after the people of his domain had petitioned the king to remove him. Tostig, believing that his brother Harold Godwinson had played a leading role in his dismissal, bore him a grudge.

Harald and Tostig sailed up the River Humber and left their ships at Riccall before marching north to York. About a mile outside the city, on the River Ouse at Fulford, the Norsemen met Edwin of Mercia and Morkere, Tostig's replacement as earl of Northumbria, with their Englishmen drawn up in battle array. Initially, the English pushed back Harald's right, and the Norsemen fell back in disorder. Harald had a blast blown on the horn, unfurled his battle standard, 'Land-Ravager', and his men counter-attacked in berserk rage. The English broke, ran into the river and marsh, and were slaughtered. The 12th-century Icelandic poet Snorri Sturluson vividly recalls the scene:

Waltheof's fighters, bitten with weapons,
There lay dead, deep in the marshes,
So that the war-keen Norsemen
Could cross on corpses only.

Waltheof, earl of Huntingdon, was not actually there, but no matter. The battle lasted under an hour, and York was theirs for the taking. The city was spared the usual sacking that followed a Norse victory, as Harald wanted it as an interim capital until he took London. He and his army withdrew to their ships to celebrate victory. In the meantime he demanded 500 hostages. The date and place agreed for the handover was Monday 25 September at Stamford Bridge, 7 miles (11 km) east of York, where the road crosses over the River Derwent.

THE BATTLE OF STAMFORD BRIDGE

In his *Heimskringla*, which recounts the lives of the Norse kings, Snorri Sturluson wrote that on Monday, after King Harald Hardrada had breakfasted, he had the landing signal blown. He and Tostig took two-thirds of their army to Stamford Bridge, leaving one-third under the king's son, Olav, to look after the ships. It was a fine, warm morning and Harald, convinced that there would be no more fighting, told his men to leave their chain-mail in the ships. Some rode, most walked, in a merry throng, carrying helmets, shields, spears and swords.

After arriving at the bridge, the Norsemen wandered about on both sides of the river. A crowd was spotted on the York road. But instead of a meek bunch of hostages, it was an army. Snorri recorded: 'the army grew greater the nearer it came, and it looked like a sheet of ice when the weapons glittered'. The army belonged to King Harold of England, who had marched up from the south, taking a mere week to cover the 200 miles (320 km) from London to York, nearly 30 miles (48 km) per day. When Tostig suggested withdrawing to the ships, collecting the rest of the men and the armour, and fighting there, Harald disagreed. Instead, he sent three men back to the ships on horseback to bring the rest of the army to join them.

Harold of England rode forward and, having established that his brother was there, they met between the armies. Tostig refused Harold's offer of one-third of the kingdom to change sides. When Tostig asked what Harold would offer the king of Norway, he replied: 'six feet of English earth – or a bit more as he is such a big man'.

Harold of England attacked. The battle started on the York side of the river, fought dismounted with swords, spears and the great battle-axes so beloved of both Norsemen and Englishmen. The Norsemen were forced back across the bridge and the river itself. For a while the bridge was held by a giant Norseman, one of the few who had brought his armour with him. Finally, an English soldier found a swill-tub, floated under the bridge, and drove his spear through a gap in the planks, under the Norseman's mail byrnie and up into his groin.

Crossing the bridge, the English charged the Norse battle line, which broke under the savage attack. Harald Hardrada burst out of the Norse line in a berserker rage cutting down all who confronted him, but was soon hit in the throat by an arrow; it is not recorded who fired the fatal shot. Tostig went down fighting. The men from the boats at Riccall arrived breathless, having run in their mail. Some threw off their mail, and hurled themselves into the mêlée. Few escaped. Seventy years later the battlefield was still heaped with bones.

A week later, as Harold Godwinson's army was sitting down to a victory feast, a messenger arrived: William 'the bastard' duke of Normandy had landed at Pevensey.

SALADIN

'Victory over God's enemy.'

SALAH AL-DIN IBN AYYUB, 1187

Thus proclaimed the renowned Saracen commander to his troops assembled between Damascus and Tiberias. A few days earlier, Saladin (1137–93) had destroyed a detachment of Templars north of Nazareth, and the defeat of these greatly feared and hated military-religious knights was a boost to the morale of his men. Keen to follow up his success before his vassals and allies returned home at the end of the fighting season in the autumn, he announced:

> The opportunity now before us may well never arise again. In my view the Muslim army must confront all the infidels in an organized battle, we must throw ourselves resolutely into the jihad before our troops disperse.

In his determination to inflict a decisive defeat on the Crusaders, or Franks as he called them, Saladin set a trap. He took Tiberias, and besieged the citadel occupied by the wife of Count Raymond of Tripoli. Deliberately holding back from taking the citadel, which he could easily have done, he waited.

On 3 July 1187, a Frankish army under King Guy of Jerusalem set out to relieve Tiberias, exactly as Saladin had hoped. All day, small detachments of Saladin's forces harassed the Franks. Although some of the Frankish army managed to drink at some springs on their route, the majority forged on through the dust and heat of a blistering hot afternoon. Showers of arrows killed their horses, and Guy, hoping to evade Saladin, turned off his original route, heading for some wells at Hattin nearly 4 miles (6 km) away, and a day's march from Lake Tiberias.

MASSACRE AT THE HORNS OF HATTIN

The Franks covered about another mile before setting up camp for the night; both men and horses were frantic with thirst. Guy, having rejected advice from experienced campaigners to mount an immediate attack on Saladin's camp only around a mile off, set off before first light, marching in infantry squares with his cavalry in the centre of each square. Saladin deployed his troops on all sides of the marching Franks, subjecting them to a storm of arrows. As the Frankish army stumbled forward, weak with thirst and hunger, Saladin's cavalry and hordes of foot deflected them from their route to Hattin. Raymond of Tripoli broke clear with much of the vanguard cavalry, but the main body of Franks crumbled under repeated attacks. Eventually, Guy, with around 150 knights and some infantry, established a defensive position west of some hills known as the Horns of Hattin near the village of that name, pitching tents in preparation for a last-ditch stand.

Saladin's men pressed home their attacks, but the Franks, fighting with the fury of desperation, threw back every assault. Urging his men on, Saladin shouted 'Satan must not win' and his troops renewed their asssault, buckling the Frankish line, and leaving only Guy's tent intact. Saladin's son thought that they had succeeded in breaking the Franks at last and screamed with joy. His father turned and reprimanded him: 'Silence! We will have crushed them only when that tent on the hill has fallen!' At this, the tent collapsed, and Saladin dismounted, thanking God and weeping for joy.

Not content with his victory, Saladin then announced:

> I think that when God grants me victory over the rest of Palestine I shall
> divide my territories, make a will stating my wishes, then set sail on this sea
> for their far off lands and pursue the Franks there, so as to free the earth of
> anyone who does not believe in God, or die in the attempt.

Although Saladin went on to capture Jerusalem, he died in Damascus in 1193, having concluded a treaty with Richard I of England, one of the leaders of the Third Crusade. This agreement preserved part of the Frankish kingdom and assured Christian pilgrims access to Jerusalem.

KING HENRY V

'Once more unto the breach, dear friends, once more;
Or close the wall up with our English dead.'

'*In peace there's nothing so becomes a man / As modest stillness and humility: / But when the blast of war blows in our ears, / Then imitate the action of the tiger; / Stiffen the sinews, summon up the blood, / Disguise fair nature with hard-favour'd rage; / Then lend the eye a terrible aspect; / Let pry through the portage of the head / Like the brass cannon; let the brow o'erwhelm it / As fearfully as doth a galled rock / O'erhang and jutty his confounded base, / Swill'd with the wild and wasteful ocean. / Now set the teeth and stretch the nostril wide, / Hold hard the breath and bend up every spirit / To his full height. On, on, you noblest English. / Whose blood is fet from fathers of war-proof! / Fathers that, like so many Alexanders, / Have in these parts from morn till even fought / And sheathed their swords for lack of argument: / Dishonour not your mothers; now attest / That those whom you call'd fathers did beget you. / Be copy now to men of grosser blood, / And teach them how to war. And you, good yeoman, / Whose limbs were made in England, show us here / The mettle of your pasture; let us swear / That you are worth your breeding; which I doubt not; / For there is none of you so mean and base, / That hath not noble lustre in your eyes. / I see you stand like greyhounds in the slips, / Straining upon the start. The game's afoot: / Follow your spirit, and upon this charge / Cry "God for Harry, England, and Saint George!"*'

WILLIAM SHAKESPEARE, *HENRY V* (ACT 3, SCENE 1)

There is no evidence that Henry V (r. 1413–22) ever delivered the famous speech that Shakespeare ascribes to him at the siege of Harfleur, which began on 17 August 1415. The 'breach' certainly existed, made by the 78 cannon Henry had brought with him, firing gun-stones at the walls. With 10,000 gun-stones and such a weight of artillery, the English kept a continuous bombardment throughout the daylight hours. The walls of Harfleur crumbled under the impact of the cannon balls, some of which, according to a contemporary chronicler, the monk of St Denis, were as big as millstones – very likely a gross exaggeration. At night the defenders did their best to repair the breach with timber, stones, baskets of earth and anything else that came to hand, including dung.

What is beyond dispute is Henry's leadership. He is recorded as moving among his army by day and night, praising good work and correcting poor performance. The scene in Shakespeare's play where Henry disguises himself and fraternizes with the common foot-soldiers ('a little touch of Harry in the night'), is certainly credible; rumours abounded at the time that the king personally reconnoitred the town to find the best ways in. True or not, this would have endeared him to his men.

The defenders of Harfleur refused to countenance surrender, until Henry ordered an all-out assault on 18 September. At dawn that day 14 burgesses from Harfleur came out with a message for the duke of Clarence offering to surrender if the king of France did not come to their rescue by 22 September. Historians have queried why the offer was made to Clarence, and not Henry, who was the only commander on the English side who could have agreed any terms. It is possible that the assault had already started on the south side of the town, led by Henry, and that after a few hours resistance there, some townspeople opened the gate on the north side, where Clarence was in command. The evidence points to the surrender being initiated by the inhabitants of Harfleur, not by the commander of the garrison, Raoul de Gaucourt. Henry wrote to the lord mayor of London:

> It was our full purpose to make an assault upon the town on Wednesday the 18th day of this month of September; but those within the town had perceived it, and made a great instance, with means which they had not employed theretofore to have conference with us. And to avoid the effusion of human blood on the one side and on the other, we inclined to their offer, and thereupon we made answer unto them, and sent to them the last conclusion of our will; to the which they agreed, and for the same we do render thanks unto God, for we thought they would not have so readily agreed to the said conclusion. And on the same Wednesday there came by our command out of the said town the Sieurs de Gaucourt, d'Estouteville, de Hacueville, and other lords and knights, who had the governance of the town, and delivered hostages; and all those were sworn upon the body of Our Saviour that they would make unto us full deliverance of our said town.

It had been suggested that Henry's command to de Gaucourt to come out to him is evidence that the surrender was offered by the citizens, without the knowledge of the garrison commander. This is entirely plausible. According to the custom of the time, if Harfleur had fallen to an assault, the town with all its inhabitants and contents would have been the property of the attackers. The men would have been killed, the women raped, everything portable looted, and what could not be carried away destroyed. Against that prospect, notions of chivalry and knightly honour, however important to the aristocratic commanders, would have weighed little in the reckoning of the ordinary folk.

Henry struck a deal with de Gaucourt. One more request for help could be sent to the king of France, or his son, the *dauphin*. If no assistance arrived by 22 September, the town would yield. Meanwhile a truce was imposed. No help came, and the surrender took place on the agreed date.

By now a large part of Henry's army had dysentery. Indeed, had the siege not been brought to a successful conclusion, he might have been forced to abandon it for lack of soldiers to continue. He sent as many as possible of his sick home to England in some of the ships he had used to blockade Harfleur. Having left a garrison of 300 men-at-arms and 900 archers to garrison Harfleur, Henry set out with the remainder, some 900 men at arms and 5000 archers, to march to Calais. He could have gone by sea, but chose to march through northern France. His reasons were twofold: first, he wanted to proceed through Normandy and Ponthieu to make the point that this was part of his ancient inheritance, the kingdom of France, the very reason for him being there; second, he hoped to tempt the king of France's eldest son, the *dauphin*, into engaging him in battle. A decisive defeat of the heir to the French throne would establish him, Henry, as the rightful successor to the mad King Charles VI of France. To take an army, many of whom were still suffering from dysentery, on a trek through enemy territory was highly risky, and nearly ended in disaster.

As well as putting words into the mouth of Henry V, which in all likelihood he did not utter, Shakespeare (in his play *Henry IV* about Henry's father) also incorrectly portrays the prince as a recalcitrant, stroppy youth. In fact by the time Henry, prince of Wales, was 14 he was fighting against a rebellion in Wales. Aged 16 he fought in the battle of Shrewsbury, against the rebel Henry Percy 'Hotspur', where he was wounded by an arrow that pierced his face and lodged against the back of his skull. This was removed without anaesthetic. By the time the Welsh campaign and 'Hotspur's' rebellion had ended, Henry was a seasoned soldier. He read avidly when time allowed, played several musical instruments, including the harp, and also composed music.

VICTORY AT AGINCOURT

Henry left Harfleur on 8 October intending to cross the Somme at the ford at Blanche Taque between Abbeville and the mouth of the river. His great-grandfather, Edward III, had crossed here on the way to his great victory at Crécy, 69 years before. The French, judging that this is what Henry intended, were waiting for him. As the English marched along the south bank of the Somme, searching for unguarded crossing places, they were shadowed by the French on the north bank. Henry had to march nearly 80 miles (130 km) inland before he found an undefended ford connecting the villages of Béthencourt-sur-Somme and Voyennes on each side of the river. Having crossed and continued his march towards Calais for another 80 or so miles (130 km), on 24 October he found the route blocked at Azincourt (Agincourt) by a huge French army. The *dauphin* was not there, having been kept back at Rouen by his father. Neither were there any senior princes of the blood present who could have assumed overall command of the French army. Instead, command was exercised by committee, a council of war, headed by Constable d'Albret and Marshal Boucicaut. Neither had the authority to impose their plans on the other nobles present.

Anticipating battle, the English army deployed; the French, who outnumbered Henry's army by about three to one, followed suit. Henry expected to be attacked by the huge French army without delay. But there was disagreement among the council about what to do next. Some wanted to let the English go, and, having seen them leave France, retake Harfleur.

The English, thinking that the battle would start at any moment quickly disengaged from the line of march and assembled into fighting formation. Henry walked through the ranks encouraging the men. Meanwhile the priests heard the confessions of many who were convinced they were about to die. One of the chaplains reported:

*A certain knight, Sir Walter Hungerford, expressed a desire to the king's face
that he might have had, added to the little company he had with him, ten
thousand of the best archers in England who would have been only too glad to
be there. 'That is a foolish way to talk' the king said to him, 'because by the
God in Heaven upon Whose Grace I have relied and in Whom is my firm
hope of victory, I would not, even if I could, have a single man more than I
do. For these I have with me are God's people, whom He deigns to let me
have at this time. Do you not believe,' he asked 'that the Almighty, with these
his humble few, is able to overcome the opposing arrogance of the French who
boast of their great number and their own strength?'*

This conversation was recorded in the *Gesta Henrici Quinti* ('The Deeds of Henry V') written in 1416–17 probably by a priest in Henry's household. It may be, then, that in his play *Henry V*, Shakespeare used the exchange between Hungerford and Henry as the basis for Henry's response to Westmoreland. Shakespeare has Henry deliver these lines just before the battle, which, as will be related, actually took place on the day after the conversation with Sir Walter. Westmoreland, in the play, having said:

*Oh that we now had here
But ten thousand of those men in England
That do no work today!*

Henry replies:

*What's he that wishes so?
My cousin Westmoreland? No, my fair cousin:
If we are mark'd to die, we are enow
To do our country loss; and if to live,
The fewer men, the greater share of honour.
God's will! I pray thee, wish not one man more.*

*By Jove, I am not covetous for gold,
Nor care I who doth feed upon my cost;
It yearns me not if men my garments wear;
Such outward things dwell not in my desires:
But if it be a sin to covet honour,
I am the most offending soul alive.
No, faith, my coz, wish not a man from England:*

*God's peace! I would not lose so great an honour
As one man more, methinks, would share from me
For the best hope I have. O, do not wish one more!
Rather proclaim it, Westmoreland, through my host,
That he which hath no stomach to this fight,
Let him depart; his passport shall be made
And crowns for convoy put into his purse:
We would not die in that man's company
That fears his fellowship to die with us.
This day is called the feast of Crispian:
He that outlives this day, and comes safe home,
Will stand a tip-toe when the day is named,
And rouse him at the name of Crispian.*

(continued on page 34)

(continued from page 33)

He that shall live this day, and see old age,	This story shall the good man teach his son;
Will yearly on the vigil feast his neighbours,	And Crispin Crispian shall ne'er go by,
And say 'To-morrow is Saint Crispian:'	From this day to the ending of the world,
Then will he strip his sleeve and show his scars.	But we in it shall be remember'd;
And say 'These wounds I had on Crispin's day.'	We few, we happy few, we band of brothers;
Old men forget: yet all shall be forgot,	For he to-day that sheds his blood with me
But he'll remember with advantages	Shall be my brother; be he ne'er so vile,
What feats he did that day: then shall our names.	This day shall gentle his condition:
Familiar in his mouth as household words	And gentlemen in England now a-bed
Harry the king, Bedford and Exeter,	Shall think themselves accursed they were not here,
Warwick and Talbot, Salisbury and Gloucester,	And hold their manhoods cheap while any speaks
Be in their flowing cups freshly remember'd.	That fought with us upon Saint Crispin's day.

With the approach of darkness, the French started to break ranks in order to cook supper and bed down for the night. The English remained in battle order until well after nightfall, before standing down. Even then the king enforced silence within the English ranks. It rained heavily during the night, turning the heavy clay soil in the freshly ploughed fields between the two armies into a sticky quagmire.

At first light both armies shook out into their formations. The famous 1943 film starring Laurence Olivier as Henry V depicts the French knights being lifted up by cranes on to their horses before the battle. This is artistic licence. Most of the French men at arms at Azincourt attacked on foot. Even those that did ride would have been able to mount a horse unaided. Evenly distributed over a man's body, armour weighed less than one-third of the load carried by marines and soldiers in the Falklands War of 1982. An armoured knight, trained since boyhood, could spring into the saddle or climb a ladder in a siege, unaided.

The English men-at-arms all fought on foot, including their king. Some days before, Henry had ordered all archers to cut and point a stake, which they carried with them. These were hammered into the ground to form a bristling hedge in front of the line of archers. While he waited for the battle to begin, Henry rode up and down the English line on a small grey horse, talking to his men, encouraging them by his presence. It is at this stage in the play that Shakespeare has Henry rebuke Westmoreland for wishing that ten thousand more men could join them.

Then the waiting began. Who would move first? Finally, Henry decided to take the initiative and provoke the French into a charge. He ordered the line forward. Stakes were pulled up, and the army advanced. When the English were within long bowshot of the French, the line halted, stakes were hammered in again. The English flanks were now protected by woodlands at Azincourt and Tramecourt. The French plan to outflank the line would now not be possible.

Illumination in a late medieval chronicle, showing the Battle of Agincourt

At last the French acted, with a charge by some 420 mounted men-at-arms, followed by men on foot. The horses churned up the muddy ground, making it very difficult for the mass of armoured men marching along behind to keep their balance. The 5000 English archers loosed off volleys of arrows, which literally darkened the sky. Scores of horses were hit. Some fell, throwing their riders into the mud, and tripping horses in the next rank. Knights were pinned to their saddles by arrows.

Riderless horses galloped back over their own men following on foot, trampling them. The few horses that reached the English line were impaled on the stakes.

The French were unable to retaliate for their crossbowmen had been deployed in rear and did not have a clear line of sight to the English, and in any case their rate of fire was much slower. Now the dismounted men-at-arms came under the flail of the English arrows. Heads down to avoid arrows coming in through the slits in their helmets, the men-at-arms slipped and slid towards the English line; sometimes brought to a complete halt by having to pull one foot, or both feet, out of the clinging mud. Some fell and were trampled by horses, or lay wallowing in the mud, often tripping up their fellows in the next rank. The English archers ran out, felled the men-at-arms with the leaden mallets they used to hammer in their stakes, and slipped daggers and swords through the visors of the fallen men-at-arms, killing them in droves. The battle lasted three hours; by the end the French were lying in heaps and mounds. Almost the whole nobility among those Frenchmen present had been killed, including three dukes, eight counts, a viscount, an archbishop and four marshals. Several hundred French noblemen including two dukes, three counts and Marshal Boucicaut were prisoners of the English. The exact figures for French men-at-arms killed will never be known. The best guess is around 3000, plus about 100 barons. The heralds did not bother to count the number of cross-bowmen and lowly soldiers. The only noblemen among the English dead were Edward, duke of York and Michael, earl of Suffolk, plus a few men-at-arms and about 100 archers. For the English, it was a crushing victory.

The significance of Shakespeare's rendering of the speeches by Henry V is that this has served to preserve the spirit, if not the substance of them for posterity. They have become part of the English, and later British, heritage. At the height of the Second World War, Winston Churchill asked the renowned actor Laurence Olivier to make a film about Agincourt, which he hoped would be a powerful piece of propaganda to help prepare the United Kingdom for the coming assault on the beaches of Normandy in mid-1944.

JOAN OF ARC

'In God's name go bravely.'

JOAN TO HER TROOPS BEFORE ATTACKING THE BRIDGE OVER THE
RIVER LOIRE AT ORLÉANS, 1429

Joan of Arc (1412–31) first stepped onto the world's stage in 1429 when she travelled to Chinon in the Loire Valley to see Charles, claimant for the throne of France, to persuade him to send her to raise the English siege of Orléans. Charles was the son of Charles VI, king of France at the time of the Battle of Agincourt. Henry V followed up his success at Agincourt by defeating the French in a series of battles, eventually forcing Charles VI to sign the Treaty of Troyes in 1420. This treaty disinherited the *dauphin* Charles, and Henry of England became heir to Charles VI and regent of France. The treaty was not accepted outside the lands controlled by the English.

Charles VI was still alive when Henry V died in 1422, leaving his nine-month-old son Henry. English commanders acting on behalf of the infant Henry VI managed to extend the territory under their control as far as the Loire, and in 1428 laid siege to Orléans.

Joan was born in 1412 in the village of Domrémy, and at the age of 13 began to hear 'voices' from saints. When she was taken in to see the *dauphin*, she announced her divine mission:

> *I bring you news from God, that our Lord will give you back your kingdom, bringing you to be crowned at Rheims, and driving out your enemies. In this I am God's messenger. Do you set me bravely to work, and I will raise the siege of Orléans.*

Among all the highly glamourized and fictional accounts of Joan there is no indication why the French commanders should have agreed to allow her to go to Orléans, let alone to take command. The story is further embellished by religious propaganda surrounding her canonization in 1920 by a pope endeavouring to revive Roman Catholicism in France. All that aside, the fact remains that she succeeded in convincing the *dauphin* that she was genuine, and she was allowed to go to Orléans. Here her influence was more inspirational than tactical, when attacking the bridge over the River Loire at Orléans, she cried out exhortations such as:

> *Courage! Do not fall back: in a little the place will be yours. Watch! When the wind blows my banner against the bulwark, you shall take it.*

And attacking an outwork fortress:

> *In God's name go bravely*

And to the English commander on the bridge:

> *Gladsdale, Gladsdale, yield to the King of Heaven. You have called me 'whore'. I pity your soul and the souls of your men.*

THE LEGEND OF THE MAID OF ORLÉANS

What is undeniable is that her appearance inspired the French soldiery, whose morale was low after repeated defeats at the hands of the English. How much credence can be given to reports that Joan turned up at Orléans clad in a suit of brilliant white armour, mounted on a black war-horse, and with a lance in her hand, which she learned to wield with grace and skill, is arguable. These accounts go on to say that she wore a small battle-axe and a consecrated sword, marked on the blade with five crosses, which she had received at the shrine of St Catherine at Fierbois. A page is said to have carried her banner, which she caused to have made and embroidered as her 'voices' demanded. It was white satin, strewn with fleur-de-lis, and on it the words 'Jhesus Maria'. At some later time, after her first appearance, Joan carried her banner herself in battle, saying that although she loved her sword, she loved her banner 40 times as much, and loved to carry it because it could not kill anyone.

She was not the heaven-sent general that she may have appeared at the time, and as such has been enshrined in French mythology ever since. The raising of the siege of Orléans may have seemed miraculous to her contemporaries, but an unbiased appraisal of the tactical situation persuades us otherwise. The English had only 5000 men to besiege a large town, divided in half by the large River Loire. The siege lines were thin, and the English lacked a commander with the genius of Henry V. The English withdrew from Orléans on 8 May 1429.

Inspired by her example, the French went on to win the Battle of Patay on 18 June 1429, and on 17 July, Charles was crowned at Rheims. This was a major setback to English claims in France, and provided a focus for French efforts to expel them. Against the advice of his council, and inspired by Joan, Charles marched on Paris, which had been occupied for ten years by the English. The attack, led by Joan, failed and Charles retired back to the Loire Valley.

Joan returned to attempt to capture Paris and at Compiègne on 23 May 1430, she was captured by Burgundian allies of the English. They in turn ransomed her to the English, who handed her over to be tried for heresy by a religious court, which they controlled. By now Charles VII, the new king of France, had distanced himself from Joan, fearful that he might be accused of gaining his throne by heresy or through intercession by the devil – a rumour that the English enthusiastically put about.

Initially tried on charges of witchcraft, Joan was told she would be executed on a charge of heresy, hearing voices and wearing men's clothing. At first Joan admitted to her crimes and errors, but several days later, clad in men's clothing she recanted. On 31 May 1431, she was burned at the stake in the market place in Rouen. Charles VII did nothing to save her.

The ten-year-old Henry VI of England was crowned king of France in Paris on 16 December 1431. Unlike his father, he was a poor soldier, and the next 20 years saw the steady reduction of English power in France. After her death Joan remained an inspiration to the French, and by 1453 only Calais remained in English hands. It is a tribute to Joan's personality and courage that in a mere six months she should have exerted so much influence.

In 1456, Charles VII ordered a retrial that rehabilitated Joan, and probably not coincidentally, removed any remaining taints of witchcraft on his accession to the throne. Her national festival is celebrated in France to this day on the second Sunday of May.

SULTAN MEHMET II

B y the mid-1400s, successive waves of Turkish conquest had reduced the Byzantine empire to a toehold on the eastern shore of the Bosphorus: the city of Constantinople. The Ottoman Turks had nearly taken it several times. In 1451, Sultan Mehmet II (r. 1451–81) decided to eliminate the last traces of Byzantium. Having isolated Constantinople by building fortresses on the approaches, he began the siege on 6 April 1453, with 80,000 troops and 120 ships.

The Byzantine emperor, Constantine XI, sought help from Western Europe, even intimating that he would end the religious schism between the Greek Orthodox Church and Rome as the price for assistance. Venice and other Western states initially promised help but did nothing. The defenders of Constantinople consisted of 7000 men, including some individual volunteers from Western Europe, and 26 ships with which to defend 14 miles (23 km) of walls, both facing inland and to seaward; all commanded by Giustiniani Longo, a Genoese mercenary. An inlet known as the Golden Horn offered a potential route into the heart of the defences from the Bosphorus. However a floating boom at its mouth closed it off, and the walls along its shore were unguarded. On the landward side of the city, the walls were exceptionally thick by the standards of the time, but still unable to withstand the shock of recoil of a large cannon, so the Byzantines were unable to mount guns of any size on them.

ORBAN'S MIGHTY SIEGE GUNS

Mehmet on the other hand had in his employ a Hungarian cannon maker, called Orban (or Urbanus), whose services the Byzantines had rejected as too expensive. Orban claimed to be able to manufacture cannon capable of knocking down the walls of any city, and was immediately hired by the Sultan. He cast what was probably the largest gun of its time. The barrel was 8 metres (27 ft) long and the bore big enough to take a man's body. It fired a 544-kilogram (1200-lb) ball up to a mile. In addition to this massive piece, Mehmet had several other large cannon, some designed and built by Orban. Constantinople's walls were of medieval design, flat-faced and ill-suited to withstanding cannon fire.

Before the siege got under way, Mehmet addressed his troops:

> *The city and the buildings are mine; but I resign to your valour the captives and the spoil, the treasures of gold and beauty; be rich and be happy. Many are the provinces of my empire: the intrepid soldier who first ascends the walls of Constantinople shall be rewarded with the government of the fairest and most wealthy; and my gratitude shall accumulate his honours and fortunes above all measure of his own hopes.*

Mehmet's cannon succeeded in breaching the outer set of landward walls, but his troops failed to gain entrance to the city. The Turks were frustrated by technology: their giant cannon took hours to reload, and in the interval between shots, the defenders had sufficient time to make temporary repairs to the breaches. Mehmet's answer was to have some of his galleys dragged overland and launched on the Golden Horn. The Byzantines tried to burn them, but failed. By forcing the Byzantines to man the additional stretch of wall along the Golden Horn, some 4 miles (6.4 km), Mehmet forced Longo to spread his troops too thinly. Outnumbering the Byzantines by over ten to one, he could afford to use attritional tactics, wearing down his enemy who could not replace losses.

Still, the Turks could not penetrate the defences. Mehmet's grand vizier actually suggested closing down the siege. But Mehmet was made of sterner stuff:

> *I have decided to engage successively and without halt one body of troops after the other, until harassed and worn out the enemy will be unable to further resist.*

His persistence paid off. On 28 May, the giant cannon eventually breached the inner wall. At 1.30 in the morning the Janissaries, the picked infantry of the Ottoman empire, smashed through the flimsy repairs to the breach. Having gained control of a section of wall, the city was theirs.

JEAN DE LA VALETTE

'And even if this siege, contrary to my expectation, should end
in a victory for the enemy, I declare to you all that I have resolved that
no one in Constantinople shall ever see a Grand Master of our Holy
Order there in chains, if, indeed, the very worst should happen and
all be lost, then I intend to put on the uniform of a common soldier
and throw myself sword in hand into the thick of the enemy and
perish there with my children and my brothers.'

JEAN DE LA VALETTE, 15 AUGUST 1565

This was the defiant response that Jean de la Valette (c.1494–1568), Grand Master of the
Order of the Knights Hospitaller, gave when addressing his brothers in arms on 15 August
1565 after being told that the Turkish besiegers of Malta intended to drag him to Constantinople in
chains. As a strictly celibate member of a religious order, Valette had no children; his 'children and his
brothers were his fellow knights'.

The Knights of the Order of St John of the Hospital of Jerusalem, to give them their full title,
were the last surviving military order of the three that had been established during the Crusades: the
other two being the Templars and the Teutonic Order. Beginning as a nursing order in the 11th
century, they soon took upon themselves the duties of defending pilgrims to the Holy Land.

After the fall of Christian strongholds in Palestine, the Knights of St John settled in Rhodes.
In Palestine they were primarily hospitallers with soldiering as a second profession. Based in
Rhodes, they became soldiers first and hospitallers second. In effect, they became Christian corsairs,
commerce raiders or pirates. They were tough, battle-hardened and ruthless. Being a Christian military
monastic order did not deter them from owning slaves, whom they used to row their galleys. Nor
do some of their activities bear too close a scrutiny. Edward Gibbon's remark that 'the Knights
neglected to live but were prepared to die, in the service of Christ', contained more than a grain
of truth. The Turks loathed and feared them in equal parts.

In 1522, after a five-month siege, the Turks ejected the knights from Rhodes, and they settled
in Malta around the two major inlets on the east coast. They built forts to protect the two main

harbours, Marsamuscetto and Grand Harbour.
Fort St Elmo was sited on the point of the spit of
land between the two, and on the southeast side
of Grand Harbour, they built St Michael on
Senglea, and St Angelo and Castile on Birgu.

Although as early as the 14th century there
were several branches of the Order, the Military
Knights had become pre-eminent. To be a
Military Knight, a candidate had to prove noble
birth on both sides of his family, back for four
generations. After acceptance, a young knight
would serve for three or more years in one of the
Order's galleys on what were known as 'caravans',
expeditions to attack Muslim ships and territory
for booty. After a further period spent on duty in
the 'Convent' in Malta, a knight was free to
return to his estate and other obligations in
Europe if he so wished, but could be recalled at
any time by the Grand Master, who also ranked
as a cardinal in the Roman Catholic Church.

Jean Parisot de la Valette, a descendant of the
counts of Toulouse, joined the order at the age
of 20 and never returned to his estates. Tall, with
a commanding presence, hardened by years of
fighting and roving the Mediterranean, Valette
was 71 years old when the Turks attacked Malta,
although he neither looked nor acted his age. He
had fought bravely throughout the Turkish siege of Rhodes. At the age of 47 he had spent a year as
a slave on the oar bench of a Turkish galley, after losing his ship in action against Barbary corsairs.
He was lucky; an exchange of prisoners between the knights and the corsairs secured his release, or
he might have spent the rest of his life in a Turkish galley as some of his fellow knights did.

In May 1565, a Turkish fleet sent by Sultan Suleiman the Magnificent arrived off Malta tasked
with eliminating the threat posed to Turkish aspirations by the garrison of this island, which
dominated the narrows between Sicily and North Africa. Commanded jointly by Mustafa Pasha
and Kapudan Piali Pasha, 130 Turkish galleys and 50 vessels landed 30,000 troops at Marsasirocco,
in the south of the island, some distance away from Grand Harbour. Valette commanded some 500
knights, and about 2300 infantry, of whom about 1000 were normally employed as marines on the

war galleys, plus 4000 local Maltese. Valette detached 52 knights and 600 men to garrison Fort St Elmo under command of the 70-year old Luigi Broglia, with Juan de Guaras as second-in-command. Before the Turks landed and his own men took up their positions, Valette addressed them, knowing that he would never see some of them again:

> *It is the great battle of the Cross and the Koran, which is to be fought. A formidable army of infidels are now on the point of investing our island. We, for our part, are the chosen soldiers of the Cross, and if Heaven requires the sacrifice of our lives, there can be no better occasion than this. Let us hasten then, my brothers, to the sacred altar. There we will renew our vows and obtain, by our Faith in the Sacred Sacraments, that contempt for death which alone can render us invincible.*

Having ordered all the wells in the area near the harbours to be poisoned, Valette sent his few cavalry to the city of Mdina in the centre of the island. He ordered them to harass the Turkish foraging parties and attack their lines of communication with their base at Marsasirocco, but not to try to engage the far superior numbers of enemy cavalry. At the same time a message asking for help was sent to the pope, and to Garcia de Toledo, the viceroy of Sicily.

After they had marched across from the south of the island, the Turks concentrated their efforts on taking Fort St Elmo. With that in their hands, they could take their galleys into Marsamuscetto harbour, thus shortening their lines of communication considerably. The Turkish artillery, which was considerably more powerful than Valette's, pounded St Elmo.

THE RIGOURS OF THE GREAT SIEGE

After two days, Luigi Broglia sent his second-in-command, La Cerda, by boat to tell Valette that he needed reinforcements. The Turks could take the fort only from landward, and provided he had enough men to man the guns, he believed that he could hold out. La Cerda was a rare exception to most knights, a person whom a historian of the order later described as 'one whom fear made eloquent'. He painted a desperate picture of the state of the garrison. When asked by Valette how many casualties they had taken, he was evasive, saying: 'St Elmo, Seigneur, is like a sick man worn out and at the end of his strength. He cannot survive without a doctor's aid and help.'

'Then I myself will be your doctor,' replied Valette coldly eyeing La Cerda. 'I will bring others with me and if we cannot at any rate cure your fear, we will at least make sure that the fortress does not fall into the hands of the enemy.'

He said that he would cross to St Elmo that very night and hold the fortress with a band of volunteers. His council dissuaded him from going himself, but others volunteered. Eventually, Valette sent 50 knights and 200 soldiers across. After they had left, Valette told his council that St Elmo was probably doomed, but must hold out as long as possible to gain time for a rescue operation from Sicily.

A few days later on hearing that relief was delayed, Valette told his council:

> *We now know that we must not look to others for our deliverance. It is only upon God and our own swords that we may rely. Yet this is no reason why we should be disheartened. Rather the opposite, for it is better to know the truth of one's situation than to be deceived by specious hopes. Our Faith and the Honour of our Order are in our own hands. We shall not fail.*

By 7 June the situation at Fort St Elmo seemed hopeless; viewed from across the harbour it looked like a volcano erupting in fire and smoke under the fire from Turkish guns and mortars. Help from Sicily was no closer, and Valette was advised by some of his council to evacuate the fort. His response was unequivocal: 'We swore obedience when we joined the Order. We swore also on the vows of chivalry that our lives would be sacrificed for the Faith whenever, and wherever, the call might come. Our brethren in St Elmo must now accept that sacrifice.'

Those listening were in no doubt that Valette would, if necessary, give his life too when the moment came. They also knew he was right, every fort must hold out if there was to be a chance of driving the Turks from Malta.

On 8 June, Valette received a letter from the garrison of St Elmo, which informed him that the enemy held key parts of the fort, had mined under the ramparts and dominated even the open space within the ramparts by fire. The garrison could not post sentries because snipers picked them off within minutes of their being posted. The garrison had no shelter except the chapel. Signed by 53 knights, the letter ended:

> *Since we can not longer efficiently carry out the duties of our Order, we are determined – if your Highness does not send us boats tonight so we can withdraw – to sally forth and die as Knights should. Do not send reinforcements, since they are no more than dead men. This is the most determined resolution of all those whose signatures Your Most Illustrious Highness can read below.*

Valette knew that the fort could not hold for long, but the suicidal course of action proposed would hasten the end not prolong it. He sent three knights across as a 'commission' with orders to report on the state of the fort's defences, saying to one of them:

> *The laws of Honour cannot necessarily be satisfied by throwing away one's life when it seems convenient. A soldier's duty is to obey. You will tell your comrades that they are to stay at their posts. They are to remain there, and they are not to sally forth. When my commissioners return, I will decide what action is to be taken.*

On their return two of the commissioners said that the condition of the fort was hopeless, but one was more optimistic, and volunteered to return with reinforcements. Valette agreed, and the knight was allowed to find 600 volunteers to go over to St Elmo, although the Grand Master had no intention of allowing so many valuable men to be lost in what he knew was a hopeless venture. Valette sent over this message:

> *A volunteer force has been raised under the command of Chevalier Constantino Castriota. Your petition to leave St Elmo for the safety of Birgu is now granted. This evening as soon as the relieving force has landed, you may take the boats back. Return my Brethren, to the Convent and Birgu, where you will be in more security. For my part, I shall feel more confident when I know that the fort – upon which the safety of the island so greatly depends – is held by men whom I can trust implicitly.*

STIFFENING THE DEFENDERS' RESOLVE

The knights at St Elmo, reading his sarcastic words, saw themselves dishonoured and disgraced before the Order and the chivalry of Europe. Within minutes of reading Valette's letter, they sent a note across with a Maltese swimmer informing the Grand Master that they would obey his orders. They would not sally forth. They would stay and die at St Elmo. The Grand Master cancelled orders for Castriota's relief force to join the St Elmo garrison.

The garrison held out for another three days, falling on 23 June, after 31 days of siege, only a few Maltese soldiers, good swimmers, escaped to tell the tale. There is no record of any knights surviving, although it is thought that five were taken prisoner, probably by Corsairs for ransom. But they either died of wounds or spent the rest of their lives as galley slaves, for nothing more was ever heard of them.

St Elmo had fulfilled Valette's hopes and more. The Turkish commander, Mustafa Pasha, looking across at the grim walls of St Angelo across Grand Harbour, cried: 'Allah! If so small a son has cost us so dear, what price shall we have to pay for so large a father'.

Mustafa ordered that the headless bodies of the St Elmo garrison commanders be fixed on stakes overlooking Grand Harbour. The other knights were beheaded and their bodies nailed to crosses. Some of these were floated across to St Angelo during the night, the eve of the feast of St John, patron saint of the Order. Dawn on 24 June revealed the headless bodies of four knights lying on the rocks below St Angelo. Valette gave orders for all Turkish prisoners to be beheaded. Their bodies were thrown in the harbour, and their heads fired from cannon across at the Turks.

This was a double message from Valette: to the Turks, 'we can be as ruthless as you, and will stick at nothing to win'; and to his own people, 'there is no turning back, it is better to die in battle than like this'. He addressed the council:

*And what could be more fitting for a member of the Order of St John to lay
down his life in defence of his Faith? We should not be dismayed because the
Moslem has at last succeeded in planting his accursed standard on the ruined
battlements of St Elmo. Our brothers – who have died for us – have taught
him a lesson, which must strike dismay throughout his whole army. If poor,
weak, insignificant St Elmo was able to withstand his most powerful efforts
for upwards of a month, how can he expect to succeed against the stronger
and more numerous garrison of Birgu? With us, must be the victory.*

The same message was relayed to the garrison at Mdina, where every morning one Turkish prisoner
was hanged from the walls.

Having dragged some of their ships overland on rollers from Marsamuscetto into the head of
Grand Harbour, the Turks now prepared to attack Birgu from the land and seaward, a move that
initially took the knights by surprise. Before the first week in July was out, the bombardment began.
The attacks which followed in the glaring heat of July and August, were repulsed with huge loss to
the Turks: some 10,000 casualties with nothing except St Elmo to show for it. Mustafa vowed:

*By the bones of my fathers – may Allah brighten their tombs – I swear that
when I take these citadels I will spare no man. All, I shall put to the sword.
Only their Grand Master will I take alive. Him alone I will lead in chains –
to kneel at the foot of the Sultan.*

The Grand Master's response is recorded at the head of this chapter. On hearing that the
promised relief force would probably never come, Valette stoically announced to his council:

*Let no man think that there can be any question of receiving honourable
treatment, or of escaping with his life. If we are beaten we shall all be killed.
It would be better to die in battle than terribly and ignominiously at the hands
of the conqueror.*

The next day, a huge mine was exploded breaching the walls of the Castile bastion of Birgu, and
the cry went up, 'withdraw to St Angelo!' Valette, without waiting to put on a cuirass, grabbed a pike
from a nearby soldier, and rushed to meet the Turks pouring into the breach. Knights and Maltese
soldiers rushed to join him as he hurled himself up the pile of rubble towards the Turkish invaders.
A grenade burst near, wounding him in the leg, but he staggered on, and the enemy began to fall
back. Some of his staff now appeared and begged him to withdraw for his own safety:

*I will not withdraw as long as those banners still wave in the wind. I am
seventy-one. And how is it possible for a man of my age to die more gloriously
than in the midst of my friends and brothers, in the service of God.*

THE FINAL SHOWDOWN

Only when the breach was cleared did Valette consent to have his leg dressed. With the breach made, the Turks attacked again, and this day, 19 August, was the crisis point of the siege. Valette's own nephew was killed with another knight, Polastron, trying to destroy the Turkish siege tower. His body was brought in, and Valette looking down at his face, said to knights who tried to comfort him:

> All the Knights are equally dear to me. I look upon all of them as my
> children. The death of Polastron moves me as much as that of my nephew.
> These two young men have only gone before the rest of us by but a few days.
> For if the relief from Sicily does not come, and we cannot save Malta, we must
> all die. To the very last man – we must bury ourselves beneath these ruins.

The following day, the Turkish siege tower, whose attempted destruction had cost the life of Valette's nephew, was shattered by chain shot. On 23 August, after further furious attacks had taken their toll of the garrison, the council advised Valette to order a withdrawal, abandon Birgu town, and pull back to St Angelo on the end of the spit on which the town stood. Valette replied:

> I respect your advice, my brethren – but I shall not take it. And these are my
> reasons. If we abandon Birgu we lose Senglea, for the garrison there cannot
> hold out on its own. The fortress of St Angelo is too small to hold all the
> population as well as ourselves and our men. And I have no intention of
> abandoning the loyal Maltese, their wives, and their children to the enemy. St
> Angelo's water supply, even supposing we can get all the people within its
> walls, will not be adequate ... No, my brothers, this and this only is the place
> where we must stand and fight. Here we must all perish together, or finally,
> with the help of God succeed in driving off our enemy.

The courage of Valette was what held the weary knights and soldiers together. Wherever danger threatened he seemed to be there, his already white beard covered with dust, his expensive, once glittering armour dull and dented. That very day, the relief force sailed from Sicily.

The rest is quickly told. Another Turkish attack on 1 September failed. On 7 September the relief force landed in the north of the island. Mustafa, with half his men dead, sick or wounded, ordered the besieging force to withdraw and embark. He attempted one more throw, landing part of his force at St Paul's Bay to attack the relief force. The attack failed, and the withdrawal to the ships was accompanied by a great slaughter of the Turks.

The indomitable Jean de la Valette is buried in the Cathedral of St John, in the city of Valetta, named after him.

Francis Drake

'The wind commands me away. Our ship is under sail.
God grant we may live so in His fear as the enemy may
have cause to say that God doth fight for her majesty
as well abroad as at home.'

FRANCIS DRAKE TO QUEEN ELIZABETH'S SECRETARY OF STATE SIR FRANCIS WALSINGHAM, 2 APRIL 1587

When Francis Drake (1539–95) set out in 1577 on the voyage that was to take him round the world he was 38 years old. The son of a tenant farmer in Devon, as a boy he served on a coaster, learning the art of pilotage (coastal navigation). When the master of the vessel died, he left it to Drake, still in his late teens. In 1563, Drake sold his coaster, and signed on as an officer in one of the ships owned by his cousin John Hawkins, who had pioneered the triangular trade between England, West Africa and the West Indies, then exclusively Spanish territory: the Spanish Main.

When Columbus first returned to Spain, the Portuguese claimed that he had merely visited a part of their dominion of Guinea in Africa. Spain and Portugal accordingly asked the Spanish pope Alexander VI to settle the dispute. Completely ignorant of the extent of the new discoveries, he complied by drawing an arbitrary north–south line of demarcation in 1494 (the Treaty of Tordesillas), effectively dividing the 'New World' and most of what is now Southeast Asia, the Far East and the Pacific, between Portugal and Spain. Naturally, other countries, including the French, and especially the Protestant Dutch and English, ignored this papal apportioning of the major part of the world.

FROM SLAVER TO PRIVATEER

During the four years Drake was involved in this trafficking he taught himself the then relatively new techniques of deep-sea navigation, involving a sound knowledge of geography, mathematics and astronomy. Throughout the 1560s English printing presses were publishing a stream of navigational manuals translated from Spanish and Portuguese. Among the most notable was *Bourne's Almanack* (1567) followed a few years later by his *Manual*. Hawkins's encroaching on the hitherto Spanish monopoly of the trade to the West Indies, which included opportunistic plundering of Spanish settlements and ships, to the Spanish nothing less than piracy, led to what today we would call a 'life-changing experience' for Drake. In 1568, Drake, by now in command of the 50-ton *Judith*, along with five other ships commanded by Hawkins in the *Minion*, ran into the tail of a hurricane in the southern part of the Gulf of Mexico. Hawkins put into San Juan de Ulua, off Vera Cruz to refit and revictual his ships before sailing for England. Two days later, 12 Spanish ships appeared off the anchorage. Hawkins made a deal with the Spanish, allowing both fleets to use the haven. The Spanish, reluctant to miss such a golden opportunity to destroy the English 'pirate' Hawkins, reneged on the agreement and attacked the English ships. Only the *Judith* and the *Minion* survived the fierce battle, and the ensuing storm they encountered outside the anchorage. After a harrowing voyage, both eventually arrived in England; of the 400 men who sailed with Hawkins, 70 returned home.

The experience at San Juan de Ulua left Drake with a fanatical hatred of Spain, and he focused his energies on mounting expeditions to plunder King Philip's American dominions. Following two reconnaissance voyages to the West Indies, he set out on a much longer foray involving raids all along the east coast of Central America, most notably Nombre de Dios which was the storehouse for all the gold from Peru brought across the Isthmus of Panama. The raid on Nombre de Dios failed because Drake was badly wounded. So, with the help of the Cimarrons – ex-slaves who had escaped from the

Spanish who had intermarried with the indigenous tribes in the Isthmus – he turned his attention to raiding Spanish mule treasure-trains crossing the Isthmus of Panama. In the course of one of these expeditions, Drake climbed a tall tree from which he sighted the Pacific Ocean. He realized that if he could take ships into the Pacific, he could dominate the route along which the treasure from Mexico and Peru was transported to the Isthmus and prevent it reaching Spain.

On his return to England, rich thanks to his capture of booty from mule trains, he spent much time garnering support among Queen Elizabeth's advisers to persuade her to charter a voyage to the Pacific, led by him. Eventually the queen agreed that a blow be directed at the source of Spanish New World treasure. To protect the queen, this objective was not committed to writing; instead, the charter defined the purpose of the expedition as being to discover the Terra Australis and establish English colonies on such coasts of South America as were not claimed by any other Christian prince.

The secrecy surrounding the object of the enterprise nearly led to its downfall. John Wynter and Thomas Doughty, respectively second and third in command, were wholeheartedly in favour of a voyage of discovery. But they neither shared Drake's loathing of Spain, nor his penchant for piracy. This was to cause considerable strain at senior command level as the expedition progressed.

Drake left Plymouth on 13 December 1577. His flotilla consisted of the 100-ton, heavily armed and fast *Pelican* (Drake's flagship for most of the expedition), the *Swan*, a 50-ton supply ship, the 15-ton *Christopher*, the 80-ton *Elizabeth* and the 30-ton *Marigold*. Later in the voyage, Drake renamed the *Pelican* the *Golden Hind*.

During his passage down the coast of West Africa, Drake snapped up three Spanish fishing vessels. His motives for this action are easily explained. Their captains' charts, or their rutters, might contain valuable information about the Atlantic routes. (A rutter was a notebook kept by every ship's master with navigational and pilotage information about routes he had sailed and places he had visited. A master might inherit another man's rutter, or steal it, for the information it contained. A rutter containing sailing directions to destinations of importance to a particular nation was jealously guarded by the owner, rather as a top secret national intelligence document would be today.) The fresh fish they carried was a useful addition to the rations in Drake's flotilla. It is likely that Drake also wanted to impress his merciless sense of purpose towards Spain on his men. Although these fishing vessels were hardly an impressive catch, everyone, especially the gentlemen who had invested in the expedition, were happy to share the profits from the voyage, which most accepted were likely to be the fruits of pillage. There were exceptions: both Wynter and Doughty entertained lofty ideals for the expedition, and began to look askance at Drake's motives, as well as his obsessive loathing of Spain, which he never bothered to conceal.

Off the Cape Verde Islands, Drake captured the Portuguese merchant ship, the 100-ton *Santa Maria*, renamed the *Mary*. Drake gave command of the *Mary* to Doughty, the senior gentleman. In the 16th century, a 'gentleman' would often command a ship, leaving the navigation and all responsibility for seamanship matters to the master.

Engraving (1626) of the clash on 1 March 1579 between Drake's Golden Hind (right) and the Spanish treasure ship Nuestra Señora de la Concepción – also known crudely as the Cacafuego ('fire-shitter')

DRAKE VERSUS DOUGHTY

Trouble in the flotilla surfaced soon after clearing La Brava in the Cape Verde Islands on 2 February 1578, and persisted throughout the next four months of the voyage, including weeks spent in the roasting heat of the doldrums. While the mariners did all the difficult and dangerous work, the gentlemen relaxed on the afterdeck, playing cards and gossiping. The gulf between gentlemen and mariners was especially wide in the *Mary*. The crew hated Doughty, suspecting him of pilfering from the ship's cargo; in effect taking a share of the crew's loot.

Thomas Doughty, arrogant, sophisticated, well-educated, self-regarding and the acknowledged leader of the gentlemen adventurers in the flotilla, was a well-connected courtier who had been secretary to Sir Christopher Hatton, one of the queen's advisers. Initially he and Drake had been friends; Doughty admired Drake the man of action, while Drake valued Doughty's contacts.

As the flotilla headed southwest Doughty became the focus for dissent among the gentlemen. Drake removed him from command of the *Mary* and sent him to the *Swan*, where he openly mocked Drake behind the admiral's back. The matter came to a head when the flotilla, now reduced to the *Pelican*, *Elizabeth*, *Marigold* and *Mary*, anchored in St Julian's Bay, about 200 miles (320 km) north of the eastern entrance of the Magellan Strait, on 20 June 1568. Drake knew that soon he would have to reveal to his men that they were about to go through the Strait, but not to Terra Australis or the Moluccas. Instead, they were heading for the rich pickings among the ill-defended Spanish settlements on the west coast of South America. Doughty and Wynter, with their well-known opposition to piracy, might lead a mutiny, which would result in the expedition returning home, or heading straight across the Pacific.

On an island in the middle of St Julian's Bay, Drake had Doughty tried in front of a jury of 40 men. Despite Doughty's eloquent defence, Drake's force of personality was sufficient to secure a verdict of guilty, and the death sentence. On 2 July 1568, Doughty was beheaded on what many of Drake's sailors came to call 'The Island of Blood'.

The *Mary* was broken up to provide material for huts to accommodate the crews while work was carried out on the other ships. In the bitter southern hemisphere mid-winter, morale plummeted. All most could talk about as they ate their meagre rations round the campfires was returning home. The most garrulous were John Audley and Edward Worrall, who said they were determined to head for home. Furthermore they claimed that Captain Wynter would be amenable to taking them in the *Elizabeth*, despite the chances of Wynter taking such drastic action being highly unlikely. After Doughty had been so ruthlessly disposed of, no one wanted to confront Drake. Although even the gentlemen were thoroughly subdued, they were still idle and useless, the object of the mariners' dislike and a potential source of discord. Drake decided that the incipient insubordination must be checked before it took hold on his men.

On 11 August he ordered his crews mustered by ships' companies in front of his tent. Drake sat in his great chair at the entrance. According to John Cooke, not a Drake supporter, who wrote down the speech after the event, he spoke thus:

> *My masters, I am a very bad orator, for I was not brought up to be a scholar, but I want every one of you to listen very carefully to what I am going to say. Write it down, if you wish, for I am ready to answer for every every word before her Majesty when we return safely to England.*
>
> *We are, all of us, far from our own country, our families and friends. We are in the midst of enemies and we are few in numbers. Every man here is precious; he cannot be replaced for ten thousand pounds. Yet some of you seem determined to die for you plot mutiny and spread discord and you know well what I must do to such men as that. God's life! I say there must be an end to plots and grumblings. There will no more dissensions between sailors and gentlemen, I am thoroughly sick of your squabbles. You will all work together in harmony, gentleman with mariner and mariner with gentlemen. There must be good order and discipline, that's why the gentlemen are here and all seamen will respect and obey them. But I have no room for any*

gentleman who doesn't care to get his hands dirty or won't take a pull on a rope next to a brother mariner. Let us prove that we are united and not give our enemies the satisfaction of seeing us destroy ourselves by our own arguments. If there are any here who want to go home, let him speak up now.

He gestured towards the harbour:

There is the Marigold. I don't need her. I victual her and send any deserters home with letters explaining to the backers of this voyage why they have run away.

The crew murmured, and many turned to gaze at John Audley and Edward Worrall. Drake paused, before continuing in a menacing tone:

But if any of you do turn back take very good care of one thing. Keep out of my way for if I find you on the open sea, as God is my witness, I'll sink you. Now, who is for going home?

He coolly eyed the ranks of dispirited men, shivering with cold. If one man stepped forward many would follow. But if the potential ringleaders quailed at the prospect of confronting Drake, no man would subsequently be able to claim that he remained against his will. No one moved.

Is there any man here who did not come on this voyage of his own free will? Who do you look to for your wages?

You sir. We look to you, the crew replied.

Will you take your wages now, or wait for your full share of the venture when we get home?

We will wait, was the mumbled reply.

Good now we all know where we stand. Master Wynter, John Thomas, Thomas Hood, William Markham, Nicholas Anthony [the Captains and Masters of the Pelican, Elizabeth, and Marigold], you are all dismissed your posts. Is there any reason why I should not dismiss you if I choose? Did I not put Thomas Doughty to death, who was my closest friend? Does anyone say that I had no right to do that?

Some people who want to discredit me say that Master Hatton sent me on this voyage; others that my master is Sir William Wynter or Master Hawkins. These are foolish stories conceived in idle brains which have nothing else to think about.

I work with the Earl of Essex and Sir Francis Walsingham. I have had a private interview with the Queen, who invited me to help her be revenged on the King of Spain. Together we decided that this would be best achieved by a surprise attack on his American possessions. The Queen has a stake of 1,000 crowns in this venture. You see I have been open and plain with you. I have her Majesty's commission and you and I are here at her bidding. Think what it will mean if our enterprise fails. We shall be the laughing stock among our enemies in Spain and Portugal and we shall bring shame upon our own country.

Now by the authority vested in me, I restore every man to his office. Furthermore, I swear on my word as a gentleman that there will be no more killings. Although some of you deserve to die. Stand forth Edward Worrall and John Audley.

The two stumbled forward. Drake called them rogues and boasters. They fell on their knees and craved his forgiveness. Drake forgave them and told them to return to their ship's company. They were broken, no longer potential ringleaders, now no one would follow them. Drake concluded:

Well then my masters, I have done. Remember this one thing: if any man says he has come on this voyage to serve Francis Drake, he will get no thanks from me. We are all here to serve Her Majesty. She it is who set this voyage forth and she expects every one of us to serve her faithfully until our journey is ended.

This was arguably Drake's supreme test, and he triumphed. The expedition was coming apart. Many lesser men would have failed to win round their crews. Thomas Cavendish, the second Englishman to attempt a voyage round the world, died in the same waters because he was unable to exert his will and stamp out mutiny and dissent.

THE RETURNING HERO

Drake sailed on. Having battled through the Magellan Strait, and emerged at the western end, he was blown 300 miles (480 km) south towards Antarctica. He lost the *Marigold* 200 miles (320 km) southwest of Cape Horn on 30 September 1578. A week later the *Elizabeth* became separated from the *Golden Hind*, passed back through the Magellan Strait, and returned to England alone. Drake in *Golden Hind* finally clawed his way free of the gales raging around the southern tip of South America. He pillaged the Spanish settlements along the western coast of South and Central America, captured the treasure ship *Cacafuego*, sailed as far north as Trinidad Bay north of San Francisco and, after crossing the Pacific, called at the Philippines, Moluccas, Celebes and Java. He came home round the Cape of Good Hope, arriving in Plymouth on 28 September 1580. He returned a fabulously wealthy man, to be knighted by his queen, who was also enriched by his success.

QUEEN ELIZABETH I OF ENGLAND

'My loving people, we have been persuaded by some, that are careful of our safety, to take heed how we commit ourselves to armed multitudes, for fear of treachery; but I assure you, I do not desire to live to distrust my faithful and loving people. Let tyrants fear; I have always so behaved myself that, under God, I have placed my chiefest strength and safeguard in the loyal hearts and good will of my subjects. And therefore I am come amongst you at this time, not as for my recreation or sport, but being resolved, in the midst and heat of the battle, to live or die amongst you all; to lay down, for my God, and for my kingdom, and for my people, my honour and my blood, even the dust. I know I have but the body of a weak and feeble woman; but I have the heart of a king, and of a king of England, too; and think foul scorn that Parma or Spain, or any prince of Europe, should dare to invade the borders of my realms: to which, rather than any dishonour should grow by me, I myself will take up arms; I myself will be your general, judge, and rewarder of every one of your virtues in the field. I know already, by your forwardness, that you have deserved rewards and crowns; and we do assure you, on the word of a prince, they shall be duly paid you. In the mean my lieutenant general shall be in my stead, than whom never prince commanded a more noble and worthy subject; not doubting by your obedience to my general, by your concord in the camp, and by your valour in the field, we shall shortly have a famous victory over the enemies of my God, of my kingdom, and of my people.'

ELIZABETH I, ADDRESSING HER TROOPS AT TILBURY ON THE EVE OF THE SPANISH ARMADA

On 18 July 1588, Elizabeth I, queen of England (1533–1603), visited the English army assembled at Tilbury ready to repel the expected invasion by Spanish troops carried across the Channel by the Armada. Mounted on a horse, she addressed the troops with the words opposite.

Although there is little doubt that her speech inspired those who heard it, this remarkable and courageous woman was not required to put her words into action. The Armada had a running fight with the English fleet all the way up the English Channel from Plymouth to Gravelines, and on 30 July nearly ended up by being driven onto the Zealand Banks off the Dutch coast. At the last moment the wind backed, a miracle to the Spanish and a frustration to the English. This allowed the Spanish to claw their way back out to open sea, but the wind and positioning of the English fleet was such that the Armada was unable to work its way back to Dunkirk to pick up the soldiers for the invasion of England, and so headed out into the North Sea. Off May Island in the mouth of the Firth of Forth, the English admiral, Lord Howard broke off the pursuit, consigning the Spanish to 'the winds of Hell and the wrath of God'.

GUSTAVUS ADOLPHUS

'HARK! I hear the drum: Forward in God's name! Jesu! Jesu!'

GUSTAVUS ADOLPHUS, KING OF SWEDEN, LEADING HIS ARMY INTO
BATTLE AT LÜTZEN, NOVEMBER 1632

Gustavus Adolphus (1594–1632) was trained as a soldier from childhood by his father, King Charles IX of Sweden, and succeeded him at the age of 16, to command the army against a Danish invasion in 1611. He is famous as one of the great innovators of the military art as well as being a great general. Sweden had many enemies: the Danes, the Grand Duchy of Muscovy (Russia), and most dangerous, Poland, which in his time encompassed what are now the Baltic States, Belarus and the Ukraine. His early battles were fought against these three enemies, before his campaigns in Germany during the Thirty Years' War, for which he is better known.

Although, along with his contemporaries, Gustavus Adolphus employed some mercenaries, mainly Protestant Dutch, English and Scots, he built up a professional army of Swedes led by dedicated and skilled officers. His tactical innovations included inculcating far better discipline than his opponents, which allowed him to control his infantry, fire in mass and manoeuvre more flexibly. He overhauled his artillery, which played an increasingly important part in his success. He restored shock action to his cavalry by training them to charge with the sword, and not merely acting as mounted pistoleers as was the current practice in Europe.

In 1630, he led his army into Germany to come to the aid of the faltering Protestant cause in the Thirty Years' War, which had begun in 1618. He went on to win a series of victories over the Spanish and Habsburg armies that supported the Catholic cause in Germany. His most brilliant victory at Breitenfeld in September 1631 cost his opponent, the count of Tilly, the leading Habsburg general, a third of his army. At their next encounter, Lech, Tilly was defeated again, being killed in the battle.

The Swedish army also defeated Tilly's successor, Albrecht von Wallenstein, at Lützen. But Gustavus Adolphus was killed leading a cavalry charge.

OLIVER CROMWELL

'I have not the particular shining bauble or feather in my cap for crowds to gaze at or kneel to, but I have power and resolution for foes to tremble at.'

OLIVER CROMWELL IN A RESPONSE TO A PETITIONER, 28 JULY 1656

Cromwell (1599–1658) began his soldiering at the advanced age of 43. While a member of Parliament for Huntingdon he threw in his lot with the Parliamentary side against King Charles I. He quickly proved how able he was and became one of England's greatest generals – feared and respected, as he himself was well aware.

He was also a consummate trainer of troops. For instance, the advice that he famously dispensed to them to aim at the enemies' shoelaces was given in the knowledge that soldiers new to battle almost invariably shoot high. Cromwell commanded a troop of horse in his first major engagement, Edgehill in 1642, a Parliamentary defeat. There he saw that the quality of individual soldiers was a key factor in deciding success or defeat; speaking to his cousin John Hampden, he compared the Parliamentary troops unfavourably with their Royalist opponents:

> Your troopers are most of them old decayed serving men, tapsters, and such kind of fellows, and their troopers are gentlemen's sons, younger sons, and persons of quality. Do you think that the spirit of such base and mean fellows will ever be able to encounter gentlemen that have honour, and courage, and resolution in them? You must get men of a spirit that is likely to go on as far as gentlemen will go, or else, I am sure you will be beaten still.

The next year he raised his regiment, subsequently to become famous as the 'Ironsides'. Seeking recruits he expounded his view that:

> I would rather have a plain russet-coated captain that knows what he fights for, and loves what he knows, than which you call a gentleman and is nothing else.

This appears to contradict his words to Hampden, and is cited by anti-monarchists to this day as evidence that Cromwell had become an egalitarian or social reformer. He most certainly was not; although his way of talking to his soldiers, his practical jokes and humour and his love of horses endeared him to his men, he brooked no ill-discipline. He rarely hesitated to shoot mutineers, whether officers or soldiers. It has become fashionable to portray the English Civil War as a conflict fought between the nobility and gentry (the Royalists) against the common people (the Parliamentarians). This is a distortion caused by ascribing the beliefs held by 21st-century Hampstead socialists to mid-17th-century squires. The divide was between those who supported the king and those who backed Parliament, and between Catholics and Anglicans on the one hand and Presbyterians and Independents, of whom Cromwell was one, on the other.

Cromwell recruited his troopers from among yeoman farmers, or freeholders in towns – in other words, from a higher social class than most cavalry privates of the day (and for a very long time thereafter). For officers he tried to find members of the gentry, preferably people he knew, or their sons. Failing this, he looked lower down the social ladder for men he could trust. In essence he was seeking the sort of thinking, fighting officers and men that make up the bulk of the British army today.

TRUSTING IN GOD

The Battle of Marston Moor, on 22 July 1644, was the largest engagement ever fought on British soil. Here the Parliamentary army under the earl of Manchester and Sir Thomas Fairfax combined with the Scots under the earl of Leven. Cromwell commanded the left wing of the Anglo-Scottish Allied Army. The battle started in the late afternoon. At 7 p.m., as the Allied infantry were about to advance, a huge thunderstorm broke above the heads of the two armies, soaking the powder of Royalist musketeers manning a ditch in advance of their main position. Cromwell merely said:

Put your trust in God, my boys, and keep your powder dry.

They did, and the battle was an Allied victory – thanks in no small part to Cromwell, who took his cavalry round the back of the Royalist line under the cover of darkness. Night attacks were rarely attempted at that time, especially by cavalry, as the risks were too great. Cromwell's success in pulling off this daring manoeuvre was a tribute to his skill both as a trainer and as a commander in the field.

He played a leading part in the defeat of the Royalists at Naseby the following year as second-in-command to Fairfax, and commander of the cavalry. 'I truly think he that prays and preaches best will fight best', claimed Cromwell. Perhaps he was right for after Naseby he said:

> When I saw the enemy drawn up and march in gallant order towards us, and we a company of poor ignorant men, to seek how to order our battle, the General having commanded me to order all the horse, I could not, riding alone about my business, but smile out to God in praises in assurance of victory, because He would by things that are not, bring to naught things that are. Of which I had great assurance – and God did it.

Thereafter Cromwell led his own armies, campaigning in England, Scotland and Ireland, winning every battle, and living up to his precept:

> Not only strike when the iron is hot, but make it hot by striking.

FREDERICK THE GREAT

'The world does not rest as securely on the shoulders of Atlas as Prussia relies on her army.'

FREDERICK THE GREAT AFTER THE BATTLE OF HOHENFRIEDBERG, 4 JUNE 1745

After Napoleon had defeated the Prussian army at Jena in 1806, he visited the tomb of Frederick the Great (1712–86), saying to his officers: 'If he were alive, we would not be here in Prussia'. Frederick had a terrible upbringing at the hands of a boorish father, who ordered his son's best friend to be executed for encouraging him to run away from home. Frederick's experiences as a child and young man left him with a damaged personality. He loved music, art and philosophy, and corresponded regularly with the French writer and thinker Voltaire. Yet there were aspects of his character that he shared with a later German leader who held him in deep admiration: Adolf Hitler. Frederick was certainly a warmonger and, as the quotation above hints, actively pursued a policy of making war as a means of diplomacy. He once wrote to Voltaire:

It is the fashion these days to make war; and presumably it will last a while yet.

Frederick came to the throne aged 28, inheriting a magnificently trained army and a full treasury. As an absolute monarch he was untrammelled by obligations or royal duties, except when he chose to exercise them. The state functioned as his executive arm. He had an intellectual and logical approach to war, and his expertise in the art of war fighting was the mastery that a man of intellect achieves in any area of study to which he applies his mind. In another letter to Voltaire, he noted:

> *Troops always ready to act, my now well-filled treasury, and the liveliness of my disposition – these are my reasons for making war on Maria Theresa* [the empress of Austria].

STRIKE HARD, STRIKE FIRST

Before Germany was unified, nearly 90 years after Frederick's death, Prussia had no natural barriers against invasion, and was surrounded by potential enemies: Austria and Russia, with long contiguous borders. France, also an enemy, lay farther off, but could still make war on Prussia through alliances with other German states. Prussia therefore relied entirely on its army to defend itself, and the best way to do this was to use its mobility to forestall enemy attacks before they could gather momentum. Whenever he could, Frederick took the offensive and if possible in someone else's territory. He once summed up his guiding strategy:

> *Our wars must be short and active. Those who lead the Prussian armies must be clever and careful, but must try to bring the issue to a decision.*

This meant taking risks, and Frederick was fully prepared to do so. As he explained to his officers:

> *A general, who with other nations would be regarded as being rash or half mad, would with us be only acting by established rules.*

In this way he set the tone for his Prussian, and later German, successors, who usually strove to fight short wars, but on occasion were frustrated in this aim by faulty strategy. Frederick was not only a general but also a monarch, and since he answered to no one, could shrug off his occasional mistakes.

He was not averse to breaking the accepted rules and fighting in winter, in an age when most armies went into winter quarters. The practice of building barracks to house soldiers was still in its infancy; troops were billeted in villages and towns. The large number of horses and mules that accompanied 18th-century armies needed large quantities of fodder, and to avoid stripping a locality bare, an army would be spread widely over the countryside. Even as an opponent started to move to his winter quarters he might be vulnerable, and if one pretended to be about to do the same, one might catch them unawares. Hence Frederick's instruction to his generals:

> *The best stratagem is to lull the enemy into security at the time when the troops are about to disperse and go into winter quarters, so that by retiring [pulling back as if about to do likewise], you may be enabled to advance on them with good purpose. With this view [in mind], the troops [your troops] should be so distributed as to assemble again very readily, in order to force [attack] the enemy's quarters. If this measure succeeds, you may recover in a fortnight the misfortunes of a whole campaign.*

Frederick's ruthlessness is demonstrated by another of his instructions to his generals on the subject of gathering intelligence:

> *There is another way to gain intelligence of the enemy when milder methods fail, though I confess it to be an harsh and cruel practice. We find a rich citizen who has a large family and good estate, and allow [plant on] him a man who understands the language of the country dressed as a servant, whom we force him to take along with him into the enemy's camp, as his valet or coachman, under pretence of complaining of some injuries which he has received; he is to be threatened also at the same time, that if he does not return after a certain period, and bring the man with him, that his house shall be burned, and his wife and children hacked to pieces.*

Frederick, also addressed his soldiers in a forthright way when required. He always aimed for a decision early in the battle to avoid protracted fire-fights, which were expensive in manpower and ammunition. He counted on his well-trained infantry to break the enemy by shock. Prussian infantry was renowned for its ability to manoeuvre quickly around the battlefield. Plenty of practice with live ammunition enabled them to fire and reload faster than their opponents. His infantry was trained to advance at a steady pace in a remorseless 'moving wall', which few adversaries could withstand. At the Battle of Prague, on 6 May 1757, he shouted:

> *By push of bayonets – no firing until you see the whites of their eyes.*

Frederick's tactics did not always work, and he sometimes lost. At the Battle of Kölin, in 1757, when his Guards hesitated, Frederick shouted:

> *Rascals, would you live forever?*

At another point in the Battle of Kölin, Moritz of Dessau, commanding the Prussian centre, disagreed with Frederick about attacking. Frederick dashed up to Moritz, and flashed out his sword, the only time he ever drew it in battle, and in a thunderous voice said:

> *And will he obey orders then?*

Before the Battle of Leuthen, Frederick announced:

> *I shall attack them* [the Austrians] *even if they stood on the steeples of Breslau.*

And in a typically forthright speech prior to the same battle, he encouraged his officers thus:

> *Gentlemen, the enemy stands behind his entrenchments armed to the teeth. We must attack him and win, or else perish. Nobody must think of getting through in any other way. If you don't like this you may resign and go home.*

Frederick could also be flippant on occasion. After the very confused Battle of Zorndorf, he turned to one of his officers and said:

> *That was a diabolical day. Did you understand what was going on?*

> *Your Majesty,* the officer replied, *I had a good grasp of the preliminary march, and the first arrangements for the battle. But all of the rest escaped me. I could make no sense of the various movements.*

> *You were not the only one, my dear friend. Console yourself, you weren't the only one,* said Frederick ruefully.

While again at Hochkirk, after Lord Keith remarked that:

> *If the Austrians leave us unmolested in this camp, they deserve to be hanged,* Frederick replied, *It is to be hoped that they are more afraid of us than the hangman.*

Frederick's strategy of blunting his enemies by forcing battle eventually exhausted his resources. After the death of his arch-enemy, Empress Elizabeth of Russia in 1762, he fought no more battles until his death 24 years later.

GEORGE WASHINGTON

'The Parliament of Great Britain hath no more right to put their hand in my pocket, without my consent, than I have to put my hands in yours for money.'

GEORGE WASHINGTON, IN A LETTER DATED 20 JULY 1774

The views aired on taxation by George Washington (1732–99), a member of the Virginia aristocracy, would have chimed with those of his English forebears who had lived on land in Northamptonshire given to them in the time of Henry VIII. Washington's great grandfather emigrated in 1657, and George was born in 1732, the son of the owner of over 4000 hectares (10,000 acres) in Virginia and 50 slaves. From his youth he was a keen soldier, but until the American Revolution – or War of Independence, as the conflict is known in the United States – did all his soldiering in the militia.

During the French and Indian War (1754–63), after leading an unsuccessful foray into the Ohio Valley in 1754 at the head of a Virginia militia company, he served on the staff of General Braddock as a lieutenant colonel. He was present at the British defeat at Fort Duquesne (present-day Pittsburgh) at the hands of the French and their Native American allies, and led the survivors to safety. Although still only 23 years old, Washington was appointed to command all the troops of his native state, Virginia. He married a wealthy widow, who brought a further 6000 hectares (15,000 acres) to add to his already large estate of Mount Vernon, as well as a large number of slaves. Washington also tried to obtain a regular commission in the British army, but was rejected.

Shortly after one of the early battles of the American Revolution, Bunker Hill (19 June 1775) Washington was appointed by the Continental Congress to command their army. On his arrival at Boston, he was unimpressed by what he found, remarking with the hauteur of a Virginian grandee:

> I dare say our men would fight very well (if properly officered), although they
> are an exceedingly dirty and nasty people; had they been properly conducted
> at Breed's [Bunker] Hill or those that were there properly supported, the
> regulars [The British] would have met with a shameful defeat, and a much
> more considerable loss than they did. Such a dearth of public spirit, and want
> of virtue, such stock-jobbing and fertility in the low arts to obtain advantages

of one kind or another in this great change of military arrangements, I never saw before and pray God I may never be witness to again. It is among the most difficult tasks I ever undertook in my life to induce these people to believe that there is, or can be, danger until the bayonet is pushed at their breasts; not that it proceeds from any uncommon prowess, but rather from an unaccountable kind of stupidity in the lower class of these people which, believe me, prevails but too generally among the officers of the Massachusetts part of the army who are nearly of the same kidney as the privates.

INSPIRED LEADERSHIP

Washington did not express these views publicly, knowing that what was needed was good leadership, and a well-administered and properly paid regular army. This objective is clearly evident in his address to one of his regiments in December 1776:

My brave fellows, you have done all I asked you to do, and more than could be reasonably expected; but your country is at stake, your wives, your houses, and all you hold dear. You have worn yourselves out with fatigues and hardships, but we know not how to spare you. If you will consent to stay only one month longer, you will render that service to the cause of liberty, and to your country, which you probably never can do under any other circumstances. The present is emphatically the crisis, which is to decide our destiny.

Most of the regiment stepped forward and volunteered, but his army was still woefully under strength. He issued a general order to his army:

Let us therefore animate and encourage each other, and show the whole world that a Freeman contending for liberty on his own ground is superior to any slavish mercenary on earth.

The irony that these words were penned by a slave-owner was probably lost on most of his army. The term 'mercenary', was an allusion to the fact that the soldiers in the British army were paid. His own soldiers would have welcomed regular pay. This was an obligation that the Continental Congress met more in the breach than the observance, and when they did pay they did so months in arrears and in paper money. Little wonder, then, that the majority of the inhabitants of the rebellious Thirteen Colonies preferred to billet British troops who paid in gold; rather than the Continental soldiers who proffered paper, or just took what they wanted without recompense.

Like Cromwell before him, Washington realized that enthusiastic officers who could lead were what was lacking in the Continental Army. Their officers made no effort to ensure that their men were reasonably clothed. Some joined their soldiers on plundering expeditions, one acted as the

Washington (pointing) is seen preparing the final assault during the siege of Yorktown in this 1836 painting by Louis-Charles-Auguste Couder

company barber, another was convicted of selling his company's blankets. Washington told Congress there was an urgent need for: 'gentlemen and men of character to come forward as officers, as well for reliable men to be enlisted as soldiers for longer than the short terms previously considered appropriate'.

Congress eventually agreed to raise an army of 60,000 men enlisted for three years or the duration of the war. But armies are not created in a matter of weeks, and there was much to be done. Washington gave a wonderful example of leadership when he crossed the Delaware river on Christmas Day 1776. He could give no rousing pep talks beforehand, lest his enemy learn of his plans. In the freezing cold and dark, after crossing the river, he entreated his men: 'Soldiers, keep by your officers. For God's sake keep by your officers!' His success at Trenton, followed by victory at Princeton, were the only bright spots in a disastrous year. At Princeton, when all seemed to be going badly with his troops running before the British bayonets, Washington galloped forward on his white horse, and put a stop to the rout. When the British guns fired, Colonel Fitzgerald thought his general would be killed, and not bearing to see it pulled his hat over his eyes. When he saw Washington sitting in his saddle unharmed, he burst into tears, saying:

Thank God, your Excellency is safe.

Bring up your troops my dear Colonel, the day is our own, Washington replied.

FROM DIRE STRAITS TO FINAL VICTORY

The next year, 1777, was scarcely better. Defeated at Brandywine, Washington had to abandon Philadelphia to save his army, which did not endear him to Congress, who were forced to flee their capital city. Washington's army spent the winter of 1777–8 at Valley Forge, where he had no means to pay or clothe his men. Holding his army together was one of his greatest feats, mostly by the power of his personality, but he built a gallows to show that if necessary he would hang men for indiscipline.

The intervention of France in 1778 saved the revolution. Spain also later joined in the war on the side of the American rebels. Neither did so out of any love for the colonists, but in the hope of regaining territory lost in the previous war against Britain; one in which Washington had taken part on the British side. Washington was perfectly aware of what motivated the French in particular, warning that Canada won with the help of France would become French again:

> *It is a maxim founded on the universal experience of mankind that no nation is to be trusted further than it is bounded by its interest; and no prudent statesman or politician will venture to depart from it.*

The capitulation of the British garrison at Yorktown brought the war to a successful conclusion for Washington and the rebellious colonies. This was made possible by the only major French naval victory over the British since 1690. The temporary loss of mastery of the sea, resulting from the Battle of the Virginia Capes in September 1781, meant that the British garrison could not be resupplied or reinforced. When the British commander, General Lord Cornwallis, asked for terms, Washington replied:

> *An ardent desire to spare the further effusion of blood will readily incline me to listen to such terms for the surrender of your post and garrisons of York [town] and Gloucester [Point] as are admissible.*

Washington was not a great field commander, losing as many battles as he won. But he held the new nation's army together, and in the end the colonists gained their independence. It bears repeating that without the French, the outcome would have been very different. The greatest compliment paid to Washington was by George III, who called him the 'most distinguished character of his age'. Yet this was not in recognition of his qualities as a military commander but for his refusing a third term as president of the United States of America.

FIELD MARSHAL PRINCE ALEXANDER SUVOROV

Alexander Vasilevich Suvorov (1729–1800) never lost a battle. The son of a Russian general, Suvorov was admitted to the Semenovsky Guards as a private soldier, at the age of 12. After service as a non-commissioned officer he was commissioned when he was 24. He was small, wiry and ugly, but revered by his troops whom he addressed as 'brother'. His time in the ranks enabled him to empathize with his soldiers, something that many Russian senior officers found beyond them. His men admired his eccentric ways, and knew how to respond to his banter. He once asked a soldier how far it was to the moon. The soldier, knowing that Suvorov hated the answer, 'I don't know', paused, and replied, 'For Suvorov, two campaigns!'.

A RISING STAR

By the time he was promoted to commanding an army, he had fought in several campaigns in three wars as a regimental, brigade and divisional commander. In his fourth war, the Second Russo-Turkish War (1787–92), he notched up three victories, the most notable being at Rymnik, on 22 September 1789. On being told before the battle that the Turks outnumbered him four to one, he responded coolly:

> That's all right. The greater the enemy, the more they will fall over one
> another, and the easier it will be for us to cut through. In any case, they're
> not numerous enough to darken the sun for us.

His victory at Rymnik earned him the title of count.

At Izmail in 1790, he put in a six-pronged attack, inflicting some 26,000 casualties on the Turks, and opening the way to the Danube and Constantinople. He exhorted his subordinate commanders:

> Do not delay in the attack. When the foe has been split off and cut down,
> pursue him immediately and give him no time to assemble or form up. Spare
> nothing. Without regard for difficulties, pursue the enemy by day and night
> until he has been annihilated.

Suvorov followed his own remorseless advice again in the combined land/sea attack on Izmail the next year, massacring nearly all the city's 40,000 inhabitants in the ensuing fighting. Four years later Empress Catherine the Great promoted him to field marshal as a reward for capturing Warsaw.

However, when the empress died, her son Tsar Paul I stripped Suvorov of his rank and sent him into exile, as part of his paranoid determination to dispense with all his mother's favourites and close advisers. But when Russia joined Austria and Britain in an alliance against France in 1798, Paul realized that he needed his most experienced generals back, and Suvorov was recalled. Although by this time he was nearly 70 years old, his energy was undiminished, and he set about training a joint Russo-Austrian army with the objective of removing the French from northern Italy. Napoleon had won a series of stunning victories there, before leaving to campaign in Egypt. The French forces in northern Italy were commanded by three leading French generals: Moreau, Macdonald and Joubert. Suvorov defeated them in a series of battles. His energy and the speed with which he moved during this campaign, which recovered all the territory won by Napoleon in his 1796–7 campaign, are summed up in the following succinct orders issued by Suvorov:

> *Pursue the last man to the Adda, and throw the remains into the river.*

> *Only pursuit destroys a running enemy. A strong pursuit gives no time for the enemy to think, take advantage of victory, uproot him, cut off his escape.*

On his way to defeating Macdonald and faced with the Tidone and Trebbia rivers, he advised:

> *In cases of obstacles arising, don't be too distracted by them. Time is more valuable than anything else – one must know how to save it. Often our previous victories remained without results because of insufficient men. The fastest of rules is that conviction that after an enemy defeat everything is over, whereas the fact is that it is necessary to try for even greater success.*

Eventually Suvorov was forced to abandon Italy when one of his subordinates lost at Zurich to Masséna. With no support, Suvorov fought his way back north across the Alps against considerable odds, in the process fighting and winning a battle in the St Gothard Pass. In spite of Suvorov saving the Russian army, the emperor Paul, jealous of his popularity, stripped him of his rank. Worn out by his last campaign, Suvorov died a few months later and was buried without ceremony.

At Paul's death, Suvorov was instantly restored as the hero of the Russian people. He still retains this status, despite the Soviet rewriting of history. Indeed even under Stalin, his portrait hung in many a senior commander's office, and still does today. His spirit of attack was a model for the Red Army in the Second World War and in its strategic doctrine thereafter.

THE DUKE OF WELLINGTON

'I can do the business.'

ARTHUR WELLESLEY, 1ST DUKE OF WELLINGTON BEFORE THE BATTLE OF WATERLOO, 1815

Field Marshal the duke of Wellington (1769–1852) was a past master of the laconic phrase and the biting remark. He was neither given to long speeches, nor to self-consciously polishing his ego. It is unlikely that he gave much thought to the notion that his remarks might be recorded for posterity. One of his young officers wrote home from Portugal about him:

> Although not the language of the Marlboroughs … it is very much this modern
> Hero's style of addressing his generals and is found to answer equally well.

Arthur Wellesley, first duke of Wellington, was the fourth son of an impoverished Irish peer. At 18 he was commissioned into the 73rd Regiment of Foot, and in six years, by a rapid succession of purchase and exchange, obtained the colonelcy of the 33rd Regiment of Foot, but saw no active service. He remedied this in the campaign under the duke of York in Flanders in 1794–5. Wellesley's handling of the 33rd was noted as being competent and he briefly commanded a brigade. Viewed as a whole, the campaign was a disastrous affair, but as Wellesley remarked:

> I learned what not to do, and that is always something.

The breakthrough in Wellesley's career came in 1796. His elder brother, Richard, now Lord Mornington, was appointed governor general of India. At the same time Wellesley was posted there, purely coincidentally, with the 33rd Foot. Thanks to his brother's influence, Arthur Wellesley, promoted to major general, was given command in Mysore. In 1799, he defeated Tippu Sultan, the ruler of Mysore, after the siege of his stronghold at Seringapatam. The siege did not start well, with a disastrous night attack, accompanied by unnecessarily heavy fatalities among Wellesley's force, including the brother of a great friend. Twelve of his men taken prisoner were subsequently found with nails driven into their skulls. This episode taught him two lessons: firstly to keep the vivid imagination that made him such an intuitive commander under strict control, and secondly, in his own words, that:

> The only thing I am afraid of is fear.

Four years later he won the Battle of Assaye with an army of 7000 men and 22 guns against the Maratha Confederacy with 40,000 men and 100 cannon. He returned to England in 1805 to a knighthood.

A brief expedition to Denmark in 1807 preceded six years of campaigning in Portugal and Spain beginning the following year. Now a lieutenant general, Wellesley won the first of his battles in Portugal at Vimiero, against Marshal Junot: one of the many French generals he was to defeat. Here he established his reputation for an almost uncanny ability to arrive at the crucial spot of the battle at just the right time; and for calling out to regiments or commanding officers by name. He launched the 20th Light Dragoons in a counter-attack at a critical stage of the battle with the shout of:

Now, 20th! Now!

At Vimiero Wellesley was actually the second-in-command to Lieutenant General Sir Harry Burrard, one of several lieutenant generals senior to him, either in, or about to arrive in, Portugal. Burrard appeared at Vimiero before the end of the battle, but allowed Wellesley to continue what he had begun. Wellesley, spotting that Junot's men were exhausted and ripe for a counter-attack followed by pursuit by the combined British-Portuguese army, cantered across to Burrard, saying:

> *Sir Harry, now is your chance. The French are completely beaten; we have a large body of troops that have not yet been in action. Let us move on Torres Vedras* [the line of hills overlooking Lisbon]. *You take the force here straight forward; I will bring round the left with the troops already there. We shall be in Lisbon in three days.*

Burrard disagreed, and ordered the army back to camp. The next day, an even more senior lieutenant general, Sir Hew Dalrymple, arrived. Then followed an episode that nearly finished Wellesley for good. Along with Burrard and Dalrymple, he acquiesced in an agreement known as the Convention of Sintra that allowed the defeated French, with all their impedimenta, to evacuate Portugal in ships provided by the British. The press in Britain howled their derision, and cartoons lampooned Wellesley along with Burrard and Dalrymple.

IN COMMAND IN THE PENINSULAR WAR

Fortunately, Wellesley had friends in high places, and April 1809 found him in Portugal, in command. Stung by the earlier criticism, he announced:

> *I shall do the best I can with the force given to me, and if the people of England are not satisfied they must find someone else who will do better.*

One of his first tasks was to stamp his discipline on his army, and to ensure that his orders were obeyed. Wellesley realised that the British must pay for everything, not pillage and loot, and respect women and the Catholic Church. In all of the foregoing, the French were conspicuous by behaving in the opposite manner, thus earning them the undying hatred of the Portuguese and Spanish people.

Montgomery was to say that there was too much 'bellyaching' in the British army that he took over in the Western Desert in 1942 (his phrase for questioning orders). Wellesley found the same in 1809. To a brigadier who complained that he was suffering from rheumatism, Wellesley snapped:

> *And you wish to go to England to get cured of it. By all means. Go there immediately!*

Likewise, a major who requested leave to save his fiancée's heart from breaking was told:

> *We read occasionally of desperate cases of this description, but I cannot say that I have ever yet known a young lady dying of love. They continue, in some manner, to live and live tolerably well. Some have even been known to recover so far as to be inclined to take another lover, if the absence of the first has lasted too long.*

Wellesley brusquely dismissed the objections of a Portuguese nobleman who complained about British officers being quartered in his house:

> *It is not very agreeable for anyone to have strangers quartered in his house, nor is it very agreeable to us who have good houses in our own country to be obliged to seek for quarters here. We are not here for our own pleasure.*

Having defeated Marshal Jourdan at Talavera in July 1809, Wellesley was forced to withdraw back into Portugal for logistic reasons, remarking about adverse comment in the press in England:

> *They may do as they please. I shall not give up the game here as long as it can be played.*

THE DUKE OF WELLINGTON

Yet Wellesley's talents had in the interim been recognized in his elevation to the title of Viscount Wellington of Talavera.

At the Battle of Busaco in September 1810, Marshal Masséna attacked Wellington up a steep hill and in columns, usually a mistake against the British infantry in line. Throughout the fighting Wellington seemed to be everywhere regardless of bullets and balls thudding round him as he peered through his telescope, giving orders in a calm voice, such as those to Major General 'Daddy' Hill:

> *If they attempt this point again, Hill, you will give them a volley and charge*
> *with the bayonet, but don't let your people follow them too far down that hill.*

An officer who overheard him remarked: 'He had nothing of the truncheon about him, nothing important, foul-mouthed or fussy; his orders on the field are all short, quick, clear and to the purpose'.

A year later, at Fuentes de Oñoro, worried staff officers rushed to convey the news to Wellington that Masséna was in the process of carrying out a flanking attack, and what was more, his whole army was in the field. Wellington merely said:

> *Oh! They are all there are they? Well, we must mind a little what we are*
> *about.*

Masséna lost the battle.

In 1812, Wellington advanced out of Portugal and moved on the city of Salamanca, which Marshal Auguste Marmont had abandoned on the approach of the British. Wellington entered the city on 27 August. However his main purpose was not served by taking it; above all, he wanted to destroy Marmont's army. Even when an opportunity to attack Marmont presented itself, Wellington was not satisfied that he would achieve the desired result. He expressed his frustration to his aide-de-camp:

> *Damned tempting, I have a great mind to attack 'em.*

Yet his iron self-control asserted itself and he refrained from making a precipitate move.

For two weeks the armies manoeuvred for position. Marmont then started heading southwest, threatening Wellington's line of communication with Portugal. For a while the two armies marched parallel to each other, but Wellington had most of his men out of sight behind high ground, with the exception of the 3rd Division under his brother-in-law Ned Pakenham. Wellington, sitting on his horse, watched the French moving across his front and outpacing his men. Marmont was so keen to head off Wellington that he allowed a big gap to open up between his divisions, who were strung out in columns. Wellington, eating a chicken leg, burst out:

> *By God that will do!*

Turning to General Alva, his Spanish liaison officer he said:

Mon cher Alva, Marmont est perdu.

He then galloped up to Pakenham, and spurred him on with the words:

*Ned, d'ye see those fellows on the hill, throw your division into column, have
at them and drive them to the devil.*

Pakenham's division crushed the French infantry at the head of Marmont's army, and the coup de grâce was administered by General Le Marchant – British despite his name – at the head of three regiments of Dragoons. Though Le Marchant himself was killed, sabre in hand, at the culmination of the charge, Wellington was full of admiration, saying to Lieutenant General Cotton, who commanded his cavalry division:

*By God, Cotton, I never saw anything so beautiful in all my life. The day
is yours.*

The British attack ended with the destruction of three French divisions, a quarter of Marmont's army. A Frenchman was moved to say that Wellington had beaten 40,000 men in 40 minutes.

ASTUTE GENERALSHIP

Although Wellington, now a marquis, advanced and entered Madrid, the French combined two armies in an attempt to defeat him. Faced with overwhelming enemy numbers, and recognizing that he must preserve Britain's only army, Wellington now manifested one of the characteristics of the great general he was: the intelligence to realize that he must retreat, and the courage to do so. He pulled back into Portugal behind the great fortresses of Ciudad Rodrigo and Badajoz, which he had captured at great cost the previous year.

His soldiers showed their disapproval of this tactical withdrawal by outbreaks of indiscipline. The final straw came on 17 November. The 3rd Division had startled a herd of black pigs, who scattered across their front. The hungry soldiers embarked on a raucous pig hunt, in the course of which two British dragoons were wounded, while some of the division were snapped up by French forces in pursuit of the retreating British. Having hanged two of the 3rd Division for 'the shameful and unmilitary practice of shooting pigs in the woods', Wellington issued an order to his senior commanders:

*I must draw your attention in a very particular manner to the state of discipline of the troops. I am
concerned to have to observe that the army under my command has fallen off in this respect in the
late campaign to a greater degree than any army with which I have ever served, or of which I have
ever read. Yet this army has met with no disaster; it has suffered no privations which but trifling
attention on the part of the officers could not have prevented, and for which there existed no reason
whatever in the nature of the service. Nor has it suffered any hardships excepting those resulting from
the necessity of being exposed to the inclemencies of the weather at a moment when they were most severe.*

It must be obvious, however, to every officer, that from the moment the troops commenced their retreat from the neighbourhood of Burgos on the one hand, and from Madrid on the other, the officers lost all command over their men. Irregularities and outrages of all descriptions were committed with impunity, and losses have been sustained which ought never to have occurred. Yet the necessity for retreat existing, none was ever made in which the troops made such short marches; none on which they made such long and repeated halts; and none on which the retreating armies were so little pressed on their rear by the enemy.

I have no hesitation in attributing these evils to the habitual inattention of the officers of the regiments to their duty, as prescribed by the standing regulations of the Service, and by the orders of this army.

I am far from questioning the zeal, still less the gallantry and spirit, of the officers of the army. Unfortunately, inexperience has induced many to consider that the period during which an army is on service is one of relaxation from all rule, instead of being, as it is, the period during which of all others every rule for the regulation and control of the conduct of the soldier, for the inspection and care of his arms, ammunition, accoutrements, necessaries, and field equipments, and his horse and horse appointments; for the receipt, issue and care of his provisions; and the regulation of all that belongs to his food and the forage for his horse, must be most strictly attended to by the officers of his company or troop.

These are the points then to which I most earnestly intreat you to turn your attention, and the attention of the officers of the regiments under your command. The Commanding Officers of regiments must enforce the orders of the army regarding the constant inspection and superintendence of the officers over the conduct of the men of their companies in their cantonments; and they must endeavour to inspire the non-commissioned officers with a sense of their situation and authority, and the non-commissioned officers must be forced to do their duty by being constantly under the view and superintendence of the officers. By this means the frequent and discreditable resource to the authority of the provost, and to punishments by the sentence of courts martial, will be prevented, and the soldiers will not dare to commit the offences and outrages of which there are too many complaints, when they well know that their officers and their non-commissioned officers have their eyes and attention turned towards them.

The Commanding Officers of regiments must likewise enforce the orders of the army regarding the constant, real inspection of the soldiers' arms, ammunition, accoutrements, and necessaries, in order to prevent at all times the shameful waste of ammunition, and the sale of that article and of the soldiers' necessaries. With this view both should be inspected daily.

In regard to the food of the soldier, I have frequently observed and lamented in the late campaign, the facility and celerity with which the French soldiers cooked in comparison with those of our army. The cause of this disadvantage is the same with that of every other description, the want of attention of the officers to the orders of the army, and the conduct of their men, and the consequent want of authority over their conduct. Certain men of each company should be appointed to cut and bring in wood, others to fetch water, and others to get the meat, etc to be cooked. If this practice were daily enforced, and a particular hour for seeing the dinners and for the men dining named, as it ought to be, equally as for parade, cooking would no longer require the inconvenient length of time which it has lately been found to take, and soldiers would not be exposed to the privation of their food at the moment at which the army may be engaged in operations with the enemy.

I repeat, that the great object of the attention of the General and Field Officers must be to get the captains and subalterns of the regiments to understand and perform the duties required from them, as the only mode by which the discipline and efficiency of the army can be restored and maintained during the next campaign.

Wellington later admitted that he regretted this outburst, but 1812 had been a fine year for him and the alliance against France: all Spain south of the Tagus had been liberated, while in far-away Russia, Napoleon was about to embark on his disastrous retreat from Moscow. Morale in Wellington's army quickly recovered in warm winter quarters with plentiful cheap wine and tobacco. Wellington, however, still had something to say about the quality of some of the officers under his command, for at that time, the senior staff of a British general in the field were chosen for him by the War Office, or Horse Guards as it was known from the building in which it was situated. Writing to an officer on the staff of the War Office in his usual forthright manner, Wellington remarked:

I have received your letter announcing the appointment of Sir William Erskine, General Lumley and General Hay to this army. The first I have generally understood to be a madman; I believe it is your own opinion that the second is not very wise; the third will, I believe, be a useful man. Colonel Sanders who was sent away from Sicily for incapacity and whom I was very glad to get rid of from hence last year, has lately come out again. I have been obliged to appoint him a Colonel on the Staff because he is senior to others and I wished to prevent him from destroying a good regiment. Then there is General Lightburne, whose conduct is really scandalous. When I reflect upon the characters and attainments of some of the General Officers of this army and consider that these are the persons on whom I rely to lead columns against the French generals and who are to carry my instructions into execution, I tremble. I only hope that when the enemy reads the list of their names he trembles as I do! Sir William Erskine and General Hay will be a very nice addition to this list! However I pray God and the Horse Guards to deliver me from General Lightburne and Colonel Sanders.

Wellington was also critical of politicians and the press who wanted to cut expenditure on the army:

The country has not a choice between Army and no arms, between peace or war. They must have a large and efficient Army, one capable of meeting the enemy abroad, or they must expect to meet him at home; and then farewell to all considerations of greater or lesser expense, and to the ease, the luxury and

*happiness of England. God forbid that I should ever see the day on which
hostile armies should contend within the United Kingdom.*

By autumn 1813, Wellington's army had won more victories in Spain and had crossed into
France. Here, on the River Nivelle, Marshal Soult was holding the high ground. On 10 November,
Wellington, now a field marshal in recognition of his victory at Vitoria earlier that year, was sitting on
the grass on top of a small mountain surrounded by the commander of the Light Division and the
two brigadiers. As he peered through his telescope, he said quietly:

*These fellows think themselves invulnerable, but I will beat them out, and
with great ease.*

Colborne agreed that the French would be beaten, but queried how easy this would be.
Wellington explained that the French would have no inkling of where he would attack in strength
and would therefore not dare concentrate. Colborne said that he now understood, and got to his feet
with his fellow officers to return to their commands.

'Oh, lie still', said Wellington, and proceeded to explain in detail to the officers around him
exactly how he proposed to attack. This incident afforded a glimpse of how Wellington placed great
trust in those officers on whom he felt he could rely.

Having turfed Soult out of every position he tried to hold, on the Nivelle, the Nive and St Pierre
and the following year at Orthez, Wellington entered Toulouse on 12 April to learn that Napoleon
had abdicated.

*An illustration from a contemporary publication shows the advance of Wellington's troops at
the decisive Battle of Waterloo*

PREPARING FOR THE FINAL CLASH

Wellington had one more battle to fight, at Waterloo, when he engaged the emperor for the first and only time. Napoleon returned from exile on 1 March 1815 and roused France in a final spell in power known as the Hundred Days. Wellington, now a duke, was appointed to command the Allied army consisting of British, King's German Legion, Brunswickers and Netherlands troops based in what is now Belgium (which did not exist as a separate country until 1830). The Prussians under Marshal Gebhard von Blücher were to act in concert with him in the same theatre of operations. When asked by the diarist Thomas Creevey whether he was confident, Wellington replied:

> By God, I think Blücher and I can do the thing. No, I think Blücher and I
> can do the business.

And, pointing at a British infantry soldier sightseeing in the park, he continued:

> There, it all depends on that article there whether we do the business or not.
> Give me enough of it and I am sure.

While publicly maintaining a bullish attitude, Wellington kept any private doubts he may have had to himself. Many of his Peninsula veterans had been shipped off to America in 1814 to take part in a war that had erupted against the United States since 1812. Although it was now over, there had not been time to bring them back. So about half his British troops were untried and unused to his methods. The King's German Legion (KGL), originally recruited in French-occupied Hanover to fight for their king – who also happened to be George III of Great Britain and Ireland – were splendid troops, steady and utterly reliable, but there were not many of them. The Brunswick troops were also dependable. The Netherlanders were an unknown entity. A year before many of them had fought in Napoleon's army; and in the event a sizeable proportion would spend the Battle of Waterloo cooking in the Forest of Soignes in rear of the battlefield. They were no doubt hedging their bets, and should Napoleon prevail, were well placed to emerge and join him on his march to Brussels. Wellington planned to ensure that when his army deployed, it would be done in such a way that the unreliable Netherlands regiments were mixed in with British, Brunswickers or KGL.

On the evening of 15 June, Wellington attended the duchess of Richmond's ball in Brussels. Earlier he had received intelligence that Napoleon had crossed the frontier into Belgium that morning, but thought he might be making for Mons. Meanwhile he delayed deploying his whole army until he was sure where the main thrust would come; holding most of it at a high state of readiness. At the ball, the prince of Orange, one of Wellington's corps commanders, brought news that Napoleon was heading straight up the Brussels road. Wellington surmised, correctly, that Napoleon intended to strike the Prussians east of the road, while holding him off, after which the French commander would then attack him with his whole army. Indeed, that very evening, the forward troops of Wellington's army had clashed with leading elements of two French corps commanded by Marshal Ney at Quatre Bras, a mere 22 miles (35 km) south of Brussels. Wellington asked his host for a map, and he and the duke of Richmond took it to the duke's dressing room. Wellington declared:

> *Napoleon has humbugged me by God, he has gained 24 hours march on me.*

The duke of Richmond asked him what he intended to do. Pointing at Waterloo, Wellington replied:

> *I have ordered the army to concentrate at Quatre Bras, but we shall not stop*
> *him there, so I must fight him here.*

The distinguished military historian Richard Holmes has expressed doubts over whether Wellington had already ordered the army to concentrate at Quatre Bras, and suggests that no doubt he rather wished he had. What Ney had run into were Netherlanders that the prince of Orange had ordered there contrary to Wellington's orders. His prediction that he must fight at Waterloo is highly likely, since he had closely reconnoitred Mont St Jean and the adjacent area soon after arriving in Belgium.

Having ordered his army to march that very night for Quatre Bras, Wellington rode out of Brussels the next morning, overtaking his long columns of infantry, squadrons of cavalry and guns as they marched and rode south. He arrived at about 10 a.m. That afternoon Napoleon attacked the Prussians at Ligny, east of Quatre Bras, and pushed them back. Napoleon hoped he had inflicted such a severe drubbing on Blücher that he would retire back over the Rhine. He did not.

Meanwhile, the battle raging at Quatre Bras grew hotter and hotter as each side fed troops into the inferno. Wellington was soon on the spot, often in the thick of the fighting. At one stage he had to ride for his life pursued by French cavalry; he headed for a square of the 92nd Highlanders, and shouting 'lie down 92nd' he jumped his horse Copenhagen over the Highlanders into the middle of the square. The pursuing cavalrymen were met by a lethal blast of musket fire, which emptied many saddles.

At another of the frequent crisis points, Wellington had to restrain the 92nd from attacking the French infantry too early, shouting at their colonel, the Peninsula veteran, Cameron of Classiefern,

> *Take your time Cameron, you'll get your fill of it before night … Now,*
> *92nd, you must charge those two columns of infantry.*

The charge saw off the French, but Cameron was killed.

When the Prussians withdrew, Wellington knew that he too must pull back to Waterloo:

> *Old Blücher has had a damned good licking and back to Wavre, 18 miles. As*
> *he has gone back we must go too. I suppose in England they will say that we*
> *have been licked. I can't help it, but as they have gone back we must go too.*

A CLOSE-RUN THING

Wellington stayed until the next morning and then, covered by cavalry and in pouring rain, marched his exhausted battalions back up the Brussels road. He deployed on the ridge south of Mont St Jean. Napoleon sent a corps to watch Blücher and keep him away from Wellington, and deployed on the ridge south of the Allied army. Blücher assured Wellington that he would do his utmost to join him the next day from Wavre, 12 miles (19 km) from where Wellington was making a stand.

Wellington pulled most of his infantry back on the reverse slope as was his custom. He garrisoned two farms, Hougoumont Château and La Haye Sainte, forward of his main position to break up attacks and provide defended localities that he hoped would buy time for him. Asked if he really expected to hold Hougoumont with the 1500 men he had sent there, Wellington replied:

> Ah, but you don't know Macdonell. I've thrown Macdonell into it.

Lieutenant Colonel James Macdonell of the Coldstream Guards had the light companies of the foot guards battalions and some KGL riflemen under his command at Hougoumont. La Haye Sainte was held by men of 2nd Light Battalion KGL with some British riflemen of the 1st/95th (The Rifle Brigade) in a sand pit across the road.

Wellington's second-in-command and cavalry commander, Lord Uxbridge, made an attempt to find out what the plan was, reasonable enough in case he might have to take over in the event of the duke being killed or wounded. Wellington disapproved of him as he had eloped with his sister-in-law, Lady Charlotte Wellesley, and subsequently married her; scandalous conduct by the standards of the time. Wellington had not asked for Uxbridge as second-in-command, and in any case was not in the habit of sharing his plans with anyone unless they enjoyed his full trust; which his brother-in-law did not. Wellington asked, rhetorically:

> Who will attack first tomorrow, I or Bonaparte?

> Bonaparte, Uxbridge tentatively replied.

> Well, Bonaparte has not given me any idea of his projects: and as my plans
> depend on his, how do you expect me to tell you what mine are?

Sensing that perhaps he had been a trifle too brusque, the duke then added:

> There is one thing certain, Uxbridge, that is, that whatever happens, you and
> I will do our duty.

As Richard Holmes has pointed out, Wellington was at fault in not telling Uxbridge his plans. Uxbridge was no fool, besides being an experienced and competent soldier. Wellington had ridden over the ground extensively, and had his plan perfectly clear in his head. He could have explained the reason why, for example, he had held a reserve back at Tubize (15,000 men who in the event never fired a shot, but were so placed to guard against a French attempt at enveloping Wellington's right). He could have underlined the vital role of Hougoumont.

The Battle of Waterloo, on 18 June 1815, started with a French attack on Hougoumont, and attacks on the château lasted all day. Hougoumont was held, although at times the situation was desperate. Wellington kept a close eye on the château throughout the battle. When he saw fire break out there he sent a message to Macdonell, written on goatskin, of which he kept a pad handy:

> I see that the fire has communicated itself from the hay stack to the roof of the
> Château. You must however still keep your men in those parts to which the
> fire does not reach. Take care that no Men are lost by the falling in of the
> Roof or floors. After they will have fallen in, occupy the Ruined Walls inside
> of the Gardens, particularly if it should be possible for the Enemy to pass
> through the Embers to the Inside of the House.

Written on horseback, under fire, this is a model of clarity. Every one of Wellington's aides was killed or wounded at his side during the battle. He seemed to be everywhere, now inside an infantry square during French cavalry charges, now riding up to the crisis point of the battle.

Seeing a danger to the ground to the northeast of Hougoumont, he quickly moved up a brigade to secure it. When Major General Halkett sent a message asking that his brigade be relieved because it had lost two-thirds of its men, Wellington replied:

> Tell him, what he asks is impossible; he and I, and every Englishman on the
> field, must die on the spot we now occupy.

All the time he was plugging gaps, shoring up weak spots, Wellington kept turning his telescope to his left for sign of the Prussians. They had been delayed by mud on the roads, and troops sent by Napoleon, but Blücher encouraged his men with shouts of: 'Forward, boys. I have given my word to Wellington and you would not have me break it'.

At about 7 p.m., the Prussians were close and Wellington sent his Prussian liaison officer Major General Baron Friedrich von Müffling across to establish the link-up with the leading Prussian corps, von Ziethen's. At this time, Fitzroy-Somerset, the last of Wellington's aides was hit in the arm by a musket ball; he walked to the field hospital where it was amputated. A little later a grapeshot whizzed over Wellington's horse, hitting Uxbridge in the knee, who exclaimed:

> By God sir, I've lost my leg.

> By God sir, so you have, Wellington replied.

But before this Napoleon sent in seven battalions of his guard to administer what he hoped would be the coup de grâce to Wellington before Blücher was on the scene in strength. As they tramped up the slope towards where Maitland's guards brigade were lying down behind the ridge, Wellington, as ever in the right place right behind Maitland, shouted:

Now Maitland! Now is your time! Up Guards! Make ready! Fire!

A smashing blast of fire swept the leading ranks of the Imperial Guard, as two other British brigades and Colborne's light infantry, swung in on each flank, and poured musketry fire into the Frenchmen. Not even the Imperial Guard could stand this sort of punishment. They broke and fled.

Wellington, begged by one of his remaining staff to take care, replied: 'So I will, directly I see those fellows driven off', waving to indicate a general advance of his army, and shouting: 'Go on Colborne! Go on. They won't stand. Don't give them time to rally.' As the British soldiers cheered, he admonished them: 'No cheering, my lads, but forward to complete your victory'.

Despite warnings that he was approaching ground swept by fire, Wellington replied: 'Never mind. Let them fire away. The battle's gained; my life's of no consequence now.' He rode forward to meet Blücher by La Belle Alliance, Napoleon's headquarters throughout the battle. Blücher agreed that the Prussians would continue with the pursuit, and Wellington rode back to his headquarters.

When he was shown the casualty list, including one of his aides dead, and another about to die, he brushed tears away, saying:

Well, thank God, I don't know what it is to lose a battle; but certainly nothing can be more painful than to gain one with the loss of so many of one's friends.

He wrote to his brother Richard:

It was the most desperate business I was ever in. I never took so much trouble about any battle, and I was never so near being beat. Our loss is immense, particularly in that best of all instruments, British Infantry. I never saw the infantry behave so well.

MARSHAL ANDRÉ MASSÉNA

'Comrades, in front of you are 4000 young men belonging to the richest families in Vienna, they have come with post horses as far as Bassano; I recommend them to you.'

GENERAL OF DIVISION ANDRÉ MASSÉNA AT THE BATTLE OF RIVOLI, 1797

Along with several of Napoleon's marshals, Masséna (1758–1817) started his army career as a private soldier, eventually propelled into the limelight by the French Revolution. Before joining the army he had made two voyages in a merchant vessel from Nice, his birthplace. Not liking life at sea, Masséna enlisted in the Royal Italian Regiment at the age of 17. After 14 years service he achieved the rank of adjutant, in the French army a warrant officer, and left the army in frustration at his inability to gain further promotion to commissioned officer rank.

Having rejoined the army on the outbreak of the revolution in 1789, Masséna soon shot up the promotion ladder, becoming a general commanding a division at the age of 35. He made his name as a commander during the Italian campaign of 1796–7 against the Austrians. At the time, Austria – rich and powerful, and with a large army – was the principal land opponent of the French Republic. The plan behind the French campaign was to traverse the whole of northern Italy, enter Austria through the Tyrol, and having linked up with the Army of the Rhine, dictate peace terms to the Austrians. The first step was to drive the Austrians out of Italy, and the task was given to the young General Napoleon Bonaparte.

Early on Masséna caught Napoleon's eye, and he said to him: 'Your corps [meaning his division] is stronger than that of any other general – you yourself are equivalent to six thousand men.'

After a number of battles in which the Austrians were worsted by Napoleon, he encountered the Austrian army under Field Marshal Count Alvinzi at Rivoli on 14 January 1797. The battlefield lies between Lake Garda and the River Adige, and the dominant feature is Monte Baldo. To begin with the battle did not go well for the French, and Napoleon called for his reserve, Masséna's division, to restore the situation. Masséna rode ahead of his division to carry out a reconnaissance, nearly getting

As well as playing a major role in Napoleon's defeat of the Austrians at Rivoli, Masséna routed the Russians at Zurich in 1799, as shown in this painting by François Bouchot (1837)

captured in the process. The Austrians shouted 'Prisoner! Prisoner!' but Masséna calmly turned his horse about, and rode off whistling to rejoin his men. By now it seemed that the Austrians had Napoleon penned in on the flat land round Rivoli, and held all the high ground. But once again, the French ability to be 'quicker on the draw' tactically speaking saved them.

Masséna's division responded to his jibe about the 4000 young men with a roar of laughter, and shouting 'En avant!' charged forward, smashing their way through the Austrians holding part of the key ground. This attack, followed up by aggressive assaults by the rest of Napoleon's army, secured victory for the French.

NAPOLEON BONAPARTE

'Soldiers, here is the battle you have so much wanted! Henceforward victory depends on you; we need it.'

NAPOLEON BONAPARTE (1769–1821)
BEFORE THE BATTLE OF BORODINO, 7 SEPTEMBER 1812

Napoleon was born on 15 August 1769 on the island of Corsica, part of France since the previous year. After attending the royal military school at Brienne, and the École Militaire in Paris, he was commissioned into the artillery aged 16. Had he not enthusiastically supported the French Revolution in 1789, Napoleon might well have lived and died a nonentity. His performance at the siege of Toulon, held by the British, Spanish and French royalists, gave him the opportunity to demonstrate his skill as an artilleryman, and he was promoted to brigadier general. After earning the thanks of the ruling Directorate by dispersing a counter-revolutionary mob in Paris with what he called a 'whiff of grapeshot', he commanded the Army of the Interior, before being given command of the Army of Italy. His career began to gather momentum between 1796 and 1797 thanks to him winning a succession of battles at Lodi, Castiglione, Arcola and Rivoli. By early 1797 he controlled northern Italy on behalf of the French Republic.

In 1798 he made the momentous decision to invade Egypt, announcing to his army:

> Soldiers! You are about to undertake a conquest whose effect on the world's civilization and trade are incalculable. You will inflict upon England a blow which is certain to wound her in her most sensitive spot, while waiting for the day when you can deal her a death blow.

Napoleon cast himself in the role of a liberator freeing the Egyptians from the Mamelukes, a Caucasian warrior caste who ruled the country. They nominally owed allegiance to the Ottoman empire, but in fact lived off the Egyptian population. Napoleon issued a proclamation, which coming from a republican atheist had a surprising beginning: 'In the name of God, the clement and the merciful. There is no divinity save Allah; He has no son and shares his power with no one'.

The proclamation continued with a lengthy agenda outlining Napoleon's promises to the Egyptians, concluding with:

> Happy, thrice happy are those Egyptians who side with us. They shall prosper in fortune and rank. Happy are those who stay in their dwellings without taking sides with either of the parties now at war. When they know us better, they will hasten to join us in all sincerity.
>
> But woe, woe to those who side with the Mamelukes and help them to make war on us. There shall be no salvation for them, and their memory will be wiped out.

On 21 July 1798 Napoleon's disciplined squares massacred the Mamelukes at the Battle of the Pyramids. The Mamelukes fought with their customary bravery, but were essentially 12th-century

Napoleon on the Field of Eylau *by the French painter Antoine-Jean Gros. This bloody battle in February 1807 was one of a series of victories by Napoleon that forced Russia to sue for peace*

soldiers engaging a late 18th-century army. However, ten days later Nelson destroyed the French fleet at the Battle of the Nile (August 1798) and Napoleon's army was stranded. A year later Napoleon returned to France to seize power, abandoning his army. His victories at Marengo and Hohenlinden were followed by the brief Peace of Amiens, which ended in 1803. In an effort to emulate Charlemagne, Napoleon had himself crowned emperor in 1804. The following year saw his greatest victories, at Ulm in October and Austerlitz in December. The day before the Battle of Austerlitz, against a combined Russian and Austrian army, he issued an order:

> *The positions which we occupy are formidable, and while the Russians march upon our batteries I shall attack their flanks.*
>
> *Soldiers! I shall in person direct all your battalions; I shall keep out of range if, with your accustomed bravery, you carry disorder and confusion into the ranks of the enemy; but if the victory is for a moment uncertain, you shall see your Emperor expose himself in the front rank.*
>
> *Note that no man shall leave the ranks under the pretext of carrying off the wounded. Let every man be filled with the thought that it is vitally necessary to conquer these paid lackeys of England who so strongly hate our nation.*

After his favourite campaign meal of potatoes fried with onions, Napoleon went round the troops' bivouacs. Instantly the soldiers recognized him and stood cheering him, finally escorting him back to his bivouac with blazing torches of straw on poles. The battle the next day was Napoleon's masterpiece. Between them the Russians and Austrians lost some 15,000 killed, 12,000 taken prisoner and180 guns. The French suffered 1300 dead, 7000 wounded and about 600 prisoners. The Austrians sued for peace, and the Russians retreated back to Poland.

Having defeated the Prussians at Jena and Auerstadt in 1806, the Russians at Eylau and Friedland (1807), he shattered the Austrians at Wagram (1809).

DEFEATS IN IBERIA AND RUSSIA

In 1807, Napoleon made the first of his great strategic mistakes, invading Spain and Portugal. Having taken part in the initial campaign, he left Spain and never returned. The war in the Iberian Peninsula lasted for another seven years and resulted in the defeat of his armies at the hands of the British under Wellington and his Spanish and Portuguese allies. The resulting drain on France's resources was immense, eventually contributing to Napoleon's defeat.

His second major strategic mistake was to invade Russia. Before the Grand Army of 450,000 men and 1146 guns crossed the River Niemen, Russia's western boundary, on 24 June 1812, Napoleon addressed his men. After listing the reasons why he was declaring war on Russia, including the tsar's failure to join in the blockade of British goods imposed by Napoleon on the countries of Europe under his rule (the 'Continental System'), he concluded:

> *Let us advance then, let us cross the Niemen and carry the war into her*
> *territory! The second Polish war will be as glorious for French arms as the*
> *first; but this time, the peace we shall conclude will carry with it its own*
> *guarantee; it will put an end to the fatal influence which Russia for the last*
> *fifty years has exercised over the affairs of Europe.*

Napoleon pinned his hopes on winning a decisive battle on the border, and finishing the war in three weeks. His reference to the 'Polish war' was cynically aimed at Polish nationalists to secure their support for his campaign by dangling the prospect of Polish independence following the defeat of Russia. He had no intention of restoring a Polish state despite the charms of his Polish mistress Marie Walewska.

On three occasions, at Minsk, Vitebsk and Smolensk, the Russians, by judiciously withdrawing, frustrated Napoleon's plan for an all-out battle to bring the war to a successful conclusion. Napoleon might have wintered at Smolensk, indeed most of his commanders tried to persuade him to do so. But he pressed on towards Moscow, now 200 miles (320 km) away, believing that the Russians would be bound to fight to defend the city.

He found the Russians under General Kutusov drawn up at Borodino, 70 miles (113 km) from Moscow, on the Smolensk–Moscow road. At 2 a.m. on the morning of 7 September Napoleon issued his pre-battle order of the day:

> *Soldiers! Here is the battle you have so much wanted! Henceforward victory*
> *depends on you; we need it. It will give us abundance; good winter quarters*
> *and an early return to the homeland! Conduct yourselves as at Austerlitz, at*
> *Friedland, at Vitebsk, at Smolensk, so that remotest posterity will cite with*
> *pride your conduct on this day.*

Adding, with a measure of speechwriter's licence:

> *Let them say of you: He was present at this great battle under the walls*
> *of Moscow!*

Napoleon's aim was all-out victory, Kutusov's was to preserve his army. Napoleon's unimaginative, frontal piecemeal attacks cost the Grand Army between a quarter and a third of its strength. Although by late afternoon Napoleon had pushed the Russians out of their defensive redoubts, they formed up in unbroken ranks in rear clearly determined to continue fighting. Napoleon, jibbing at committing his Guard and risking losing his sole reserve, ordered his army to bivouac for the night. The next morning Kutusov pulled back towards Moscow; Napoleon claimed victory.

The Grand Army entered Moscow on 14 September. They were forced out on 19 October following the burning of the city on the tsar's orders. A mere 20,000 men staggered out of Russia on 13 December, by which time Napoleon had deserted them, heading for Paris.

Despite the disaster in Russia, Napoleon was still capable of pulling off victories against the alliance arrayed against him. But eventually overwhelmed by the combination of Prussia, Russia, Austria and Great Britain, he abdicated on 20 April 1814, and was exiled to the island of Elba. On 1 March 1815 he returned to France and mustered an army, only to be finally defeated at Waterloo by the combined efforts of the Prussian and Anglo-Dutch armies on 18 June 1815. His order of the day to his soldiers on 14 June, before the Battle of Ligny against the Prussians, which preceded the engagement at Waterloo, was pure Napoleon:

> *Soldiers! You were one against three at Jena against these same arrogant*
> *Prussians; at Montmirail, you were one against six. Madmen! A moment's*
> *prosperity has blinded them. If they enter France they will find their graves.*
> *Soldiers we have forced marches to make, battles to fight, dangers to*
> *encounter, but with constancy the victory will be ours; the rights, the honour,*
> *of our country will be reconquered. For every Frenchman who has courage*
> *the moment has come to conquer or die.*

Napoleon ended his days in exile on the island of St Helena in the middle of the Atlantic Ocean, dying on 5 May 1821.

ADMIRAL HORATIO NELSON

'England expects that every man will do his duty.'

HORATIO NELSON (1758–1805) BEFORE THE BATTLE OF TRAFALGAR, 1805

Just before midday on 21 October 1805, Vice Admiral Lord Nelson's fleet, led by his flagship, HMS *Victory*, slowly approached the combined French and Spanish fleets off Cape Trafalgar. Nelson, in his own words, 'decided to amuse the fleet with a signal'. He turned to his flag lieutenant, John Pasco, saying that he wanted to make the signal 'Nelson confides that every man will do his duty'. But he ordered Pasco to be quick 'for I have one more signal to make which is for close action'.

Pasco explained that as there were no groups of signal flags for 'Nelson', or 'confides', these words would have to be spelt out with a flag for each letter. There were, however, flag groups for 'England' and 'expects'. Nelson replied:

That will do, Pasco, make it directly.

The 32 flags making this signal were hoisted. Every word except 'duty', which had to be spelt out, had a three-flag group in the book. Nelson's second-in-command, Rear Admiral Collingwood in the *Royal Sovereign*, at first expressed irritation at seeing the hoist of signal flags run up from *Victory*'s deck:

I wish Nelson would stop signalling: we know well enough what to do.

But, when the signal was translated, he said, 'Good man'.

This was the first occasion that a signal of this length had been made to a fleet. It was made possible by the marine vocabulary devised and privately published by Captain Home Popham in 1800 as a complement to the official signal book issued to all ships. The marine vocabulary was not in general issue in the Royal Navy by 1805, but a month previously Nelson had called at the Admiralty to obtain several copies, which he distributed through his fleet.

Nelson then ordered Pasco to hoist numbers 8 and 63 from the Signal Book, meaning 'Prepare to anchor at the close of day', followed by number 16: 'Engage the enemy more closely'.

No further signal was made by the *Victory* until the battle was won. As Collingwood had said, everybody knew exactly what to do.

GENERAL ULYSSES S. GRANT

'Find out where your enemy is. Get at him as soon as you can. Strike at him as hard as you can and as soon as you can, and keep moving on.'

ULYSSES S. GRANT AT THE START OF THE TENNESSEE RIVER CAMPAIGN, 1862

In an era when the art of public speaking was much practised and prized, Ulysses S. Grant (1822–85) was not much given to making speeches or striving for effect. To be theatrical was utterly against his nature. Yet, at Fort Donelson on the Cumberland river in Tennessee, in February 1862, while still a brigadier general, Grant first came to the notice of the American public; not only for what he did, but also for what he said. Having captured Fort Henry on the Tennessee river on 6 February, Grant had moved swiftly to invest the Confederates at Fort Donelson under Major General Simon Bolivar Buckner. He and Grant were old friends dating back to their time at West Point; Buckner had once bailed Grant out when he was in debt.

Surrounded by Union troops, and deserted by his two superiors, Buckner asked for a truce, hoping to be granted generous terms by an old comrade. Grant responded:

> No terms except an unconditional and immediate surrender can be accepted.
> I propose to move immediately upon your works.

Buckner had no choice but to surrender. Coming at a time when the ten-month-old American Civil War was still painfully gathering momentum, the news of the surrender was greeted with euphoria in the North. Church bells were rung. The *New York Times* predicted that the fall of Fort Donelson so soon after the capitulation of Fort Henry heralded an early end to the war. 'The monster [the South] is already clutched and in his death struggle', announced the paper pompously.

After the disgrace of the First Battle of Bull Run (Manassas), the North needed a hero. Now they had one, with the happy coincidence that his initials – U. S. for Ulysses Simpson – also stood for 'Unconditional Surrender'.

Two months later at Shiloh on the Tennessee river, Grant, now a major general, fought a pivotal battle in his development as a commander. In the intervening weeks, he had been through difficult

times. Major General Halleck, the overall Union commander in the Western theatre of operations, and a pedantic old woman, sacked Grant for drunkenness, merely on hearsay; in the meanwhile claiming the victory at Donelson for himself. In late March Grant's fortunes changed, being reinstated to take command of the 42,000 strong Union Army of the Tennessee in place of Major General Smith who died of tetanus. Grant found his army encamped, without any attempt at a tactical deployment, on the Confederate side of the river, for no other reason than that the flat ground made for a good camping site. Neither he nor Brigadier General Sherman in overall command of the Union troops pending Grant's arrival, expected an attack. Furthermore, the Union Army was about to be joined by 20,000 men under Major General Don Carlos Buell. All seemed quiet.

Taking advantage of the poor tactical deployment of the Union Army, the Confederate commander General A. S. Johnston attacked on 6 April 1862, driving the unprepared Northerners back towards Pittsburgh Landing where they had come ashore. By nightfall, Johnston was dead, and the Union Army holding on by the skin of its teeth around Pittsburgh Landing. But Buell had arrived with reinforcements.

The Confederates were confident that the morrow would see the Union troops pushed back into the river. Grant's army had just been driven back 2 miles (3 km), one division had surrendered *en masse*, another shattered and its commander killed. His other three divisions were badly shaken and reduced to half strength. Grant who had distinguished himself all day, calmly directing operations from his horse, including siting the artillery which brought the Confederate attack to a halt, thought otherwise. When Sherman said to him privately that they had taken a beating that day, Grant replied:

> *Lick 'em tomorrow though.*

Asked by his staff if the prospect did not look 'gloomy', Grant was more forthcoming (for him, that is):

> *Not at all. They can't force our lines around those batteries tonight. It is too late. Delay counts everything with us. Tomorrow we shall attack them with fresh troops and drive them, of course.*

He was as good as his word. At dawn the Union Army attacked, driving the Confederates back to Shiloh Church where General Beauregard, now in command, ordered retreat. 'Bloody' Shiloh was the first great battle in the Western theatre and a considerable shock to the men on both sides. The total casualties on both sides were almost exactly the same as the American Revolution, the War of 1812 and the Mexican War added together. It was a portent for the future.

Grant was criticized by Halleck for not following up the Confederates, while at the same time Halleck sent a message saying, 'Your army is not now in a condition to resist attack'. Grant, far too busy working out what he would do to the enemy to be worried about what the enemy might do to him, ignored Halleck's clucking.

SUPREME UNION COMMANDER

After Shiloh, Grant fought and won a series of battles as he tightened his grip on the Confederate stronghold of Vicksburg on the Mississippi river. After a brilliant campaign in co-operation with the US Navy, he took the town in July 1863, cutting the Confederacy in half. By the end of the year he had won at Chattanooga and Lookout Mountain, paving the way for his subordinate, Sherman, to advance on and capture Atlanta. Grant's success was rewarded by promotion to lieutenant general, the first in American history, and appointment to command all the Union armies. Grant's enemies complained to President Lincoln that he drank, to which the latter replied: 'I need this man, he fights'.

Although Grant was responsible for the activities of all the Union armies in the war, he did not stay in Washington, but accompanied Meade and the Army of the Potomac with the aim of defeating Lee and the Army of Northern Virginia. Until now, Northern generals had been obsessed with capturing Richmond, the capital of the Confederacy. Grant realized that, to use a modern military expression, Lee's army was the 'centre of gravity' of the Confederacy in the Eastern theatre of operations, not Richmond. He issued orders accordingly:

> I shall not give my attention so much as to Richmond as to Lee's army, and I want all commanders to feel that hostile armies, and not cities, are to be their objectives.

Before this he had instructed Meade:

> Sherman [in the West] will move at the same time as you do, or two or three days in advance, Jo Johnston's Army being his objective point and the heart of Georgia his ultimate aim. Lee's army will be your objective point. Wherever Lee goes, there you will go also.

To Sherman, who had taken over from Grant in the West, and with whom he had campaigned and knew what was in his mind, he said:

> I do not propose to lay down for you a plan of campaign but simply to lay down the work that is desirable to have done and leave you free to execute it in your own way. Submit to me however as early as you can your plan of operation.

Grant showed his tenacity once the Army of the Potomac engaged Lee. In May 1864, Lee actually outfought Grant at the Battles of the Wilderness, Spotsylvania and Cold Harbour, but whereas other generals would have withdrawn to recuperate, Grant pressed on:

> I propose to fight it out on this line if it takes all summer.

It took all summer and well into the spring of the following year, but Lee could not sustain his casualties, and was forced to react to Grant's relentless pressure. The outcome was Lee's surrender at the Battle of Appomattox on 9 April 1865.

Hearing Union batteries firing salutes at the news of the surrender, Grant sent to have them stopped; to him it was unfitting: 'The rebels are our countrymen again'.

LIEUTENANT GENERAL NATHAN BEDFORD FORREST

'I did not come here for the purpose of surrendering my command.'

NATHAN BEDFORD FORREST AT FORT DONELSON, 16 FEBRUARY 1861

On 16 February 1861, Nathan Bedford Forrest (1821–77), commanding a Confederate cavalry regiment, was part of the garrison of Fort Donelson on the Cumberland river, Tennessee besieged by the Union Major General Grant. Brigadier General Buckner, left in command of the fort after his superiors Generals Floyd and Pillow had escaped, saw no alternative to surrender. Forrest thought otherwise. Saying 'I did not come here for the purpose of surrendering my command', he gathered together his regiment and some infantry who were swung up behind the troopers. In the darkness he rode out of Fort Donelson over swampy ground, where at times the water came up to his soldiers' saddle blankets, and which he reckoned would not be well covered by Union troops. He was right. 'Not a gun fired at us, not an enemy seen or heard.' After the escape he addressed his regiment:

Men, if you do as I say, I will always lead you to victory.

He was unable to keep his promise on only two occasions. The first was when he was defeated at Parker's Crossroads in December 1862, but escaped with his command. The second was on 20 April 1865, in the closing days of the war, when he failed to stop a Union raid on Selma, Alabama. He surrendered only when the war was over.

At the outbreak of the American Civil War, Nathan Bedford Forrest was almost 40 years old, a millionaire who had risen from poverty to make a fortune dealing in slaves, cotton, property and livestock. He had only attended school for six months. He enlisted as a private soldier in the Confederate Army, before raising a cavalry regiment at his own expense, and commanding it as a lieutenant colonel. It was this regiment that he led out of Fort Donelson.

Forrest came to notice in his first battle north of Bowling Green, Kentucky. Confronted by a superior force he stood in his stirrups, and swinging his sabre, roared 'Charge! Charge!' He personally accounted for three Union officers, killing two and wounding one. Forrest was the only

Confederate cavalryman who really worried Grant. His actions during the Atlanta campaign of 1864 caused Sherman to exclaim: 'That devil Forrest must be hunted down and killed if it costs ten thousand lives and bankrupts the Federal treasury. There will never be peace in Tennessee until Forrest is dead.'

In Corinth, Mississippi, in June 1962, while recovering after having a ball removed from near his spine without anaesthetic, Forrest issued a notice:

> *I will receive 200 able-bodied men if they will present themselves at my headquarters by the first of June with a good horse and gun. I wish none but those who desire to be actively engaged. My headquarters for the present is at Corinth, Miss. Come on boys if you want a heap of fun and to kill some Yankees.*

In December 1862 Union forces nearly collared Forrest at Parker's Crossroads. He found his road blocked by Dunham's Union cavalry brigade, and was driving them back when he was hit from the rear by Fuller's brigade. Forrest shouted:

> *Charge both ways!*

His brigade evaded capture by crossing the Tennessee river, but had to leave behind the 300 prisoners, 6 guns and 300 horses he had captured.

In April–May 1863, Forrest was engaged in a running fight with Union raiders under Colonel Streight through northwestern Alabama. The pursuit, starting on 29 April, continued by day and night. Forrest ordered:

> *Shoot at everything blue and keep up the scare.*

and on another occasion:

> *Devil them all night.*

Eventually, although outnumbered two to one by Streight, Forrest persuaded him to surrender at Cedar Bluff on 3 May.

At West Point, Mississippi, on 21 February 1864, Forrest, now commanding a cavalry division including a large number of ill-trained reinforcements, was pursuing retreating Union troops under Major General William S. Smith. Attacking them when they made a stand, he saw one of his own troopers, a raw recruit, fleeing from the engagement. Forrest dismounted, and grabbing a piece of brushwood, flung him down by the roadside and thrashed him, before jerking him upright and pushing him back into the fight:

> *Now, God damn you, go back to the front and fight. You might as well be killed there as here. For if you ever run away again you'll not get off so easy.*

The story quickly spread through the division, but also through both armies. It was eventually picked up by the northern magazine *Harper's Weekly*, which depicted 'Forrest Breaking in a Conscript'.

Two days later, the Union troops took up a strongly defended position approachable only by a narrow causeway. Forrest sent a regiment round to strike the enemy in the rear, while he ordered a frontal assault. Realizing this was a daunting task for green troops, he led the assault personally, roaring:

Come on boys!

His men recalled years later: 'his immediate presence seemed to inspire everyone with his terrible energy, more like that of a piece of powerful steam machinery than of a human being'.

Led by Forrest, they drove the Union troops from the ridge, continuing the pursuit until nightfall, when Forrest halted them. Smith kept marching hoping to outdistance Forrest. But Forrest's troopers up before dawn, soon caught the weary Union soldiers. Smith made the mistake of dropping off part of his division in the hope of delaying Forrest while the rest kept marching. After a running fight through the town of Pontotoc, the Confederates ran into one of Smith's stop lines and were brought to a halt by Federal fire. Forrest came forward and on being told by his leading brigade commander that the Federals were about to charge, said: 'Then we will charge them'. The Confederates routed the Union troops, who as they fled forced a Federal battery off the road, shouting: 'We'll all be killed'.

The pursuit continued to Ivey's Hill some way off, where another stop line had deployed. This time the Union troops directed a withering blast of fire at Forrest's two brigades advancing across open ground. Both brigade commanders were hit, one in the hand, and the other, Jeffrey Forrest, the youngest of the general's five brothers, through the throat. General Forrest reached him immediately after he slid from his horse, and found him dead. Sixteen years Nathan's junior, his mother had died giving birth to him, and Nathan had raised him like a son. After bending over him for a minute, Forrest rose and ordered his bugler to sound the charge. Forrest led his men into a savage gutter fight. Within an hour, he had two horses killed under him, and had dispatched three enemy soldiers with his pistol and sword.

Smith pulled back again, blowing bridges behind him, and this time the 50-mile (80-km) long pursuit ended. A Union colonel remarked: 'the expedition filled every man connected with it with a burning shame'. Forrest's young recruits were filled with pride at their achievement, and their heightened morale enabled him to win against even greater odds and achieve much in the months to come in West Tennessee. Here he raided for three months before pulling back into Mississippi.

At Brice's Crossroads, Mississippi, on 10 June 1864, Union forces, outnumbering him two to one, closed in on Forrest, and he decided to hit them before they could concentrate. The weather promised to be scorching hot. He told his troops:

Their cavalry will move out ahead of their infantry and should reach the crossroads three hours in advance. We can whip their cavalry in that time. As soon as the fight opens they will send back to have the infantry hurried in. It is

going to be hot as hell, and coming on the run for five or six miles, their
infantry will be so tired out we will ride right over them.

Forrest inflicted a crushing defeat on the three brigades sent to defeat him, fighting the battle by 'ear', finally taking the Union infantry on the flank, with Forrest shouting another of his favourite cries:

Hit 'em on the end.

And as the retreat of the Union soldiers turned into a rout:

Keep the skeer [scare] on them.

A month later, Major General Andrew Jackson Smith, at the head of two divisions, was sent to deal with Forrest and encountered him at Tupelo, Mississippi. Smith took up a strong position, which delighted Forrest, who announced:

One thing is certain the enemy cannot remain long where he is. He must
come out, and when he does, all I ask or wish is to be turned loose with my
command. I shall be on all sides of him, attacking day and night. He shall not
cook a meal or a have a night's sleep, and I will wear his army to a frazzle
before he gets out of the country.

The Confederate attacks on Smith's position were going nowhere with heavy losses, when Smith decided that as he was running short of ammunition, he would pull back. It was not the first time in history, nor the last, that a superior force would retreat, harassed on its march by half its number.

GRACIOUS IN DEFEAT

The end of the war found Forrest at Gainesville, Alabama on 8 May 1865. He had just suffered defeat at the hands of Major General James Harrison Wilson at Selma. He was in a foul mood, his arm in a sling with his fourth wound of the war, suffered in a fight on horseback with a young Union captain. The young officer had hacked at Forrest's upraised arm, before the general managed to draw his revolver and kill him. Forrest commented:

If that boy had known enough to give me the point and not the edge, I should
not be here to tell about it.

The young Union officer was the 30th man personally killed by Forrest in the course of the Civil War. In the process he had had 29 horses shot from under him:

I was a horse ahead, at the close.

Now this man, the only one on either side to rise from private to lieutenant general, contemplated heading for Mexico, rather than laying down his arms. Riding with his adjutant that evening, the young man reminded the general of the duty they owed to their country, particularly Forrest who could set an example by leading his men into peace.

The next day, Forrest addressed his men, they furled their battle flags, and led by him, gave their parole to fight no more against the Union:

Soldiers

By an agreement made between Lieutenant General Taylor, commanding the Department of Alabama, Mississippi, and East Louisiana, and Major General Canby, commanding US forces, the troops of this department have been surrendered. I do not think it proper or necessary at this time to refer to the causes which have reduced us to this extremity, nor is it now a matter of material consequence as to how such results were brought about. That we are beaten is a self-evident fact, and any further resistance on our part would be justly regarded as the height of folly and rashness. Reason dictates and humanity demands that no more blood be shed. Fully realizing and feeling that such is the case, it is your duty and mine to lay down our arms, submit to the 'powers that be', and aid in restoring peace and establishing law and order throughout the land. The terms upon which you were surrendered are favourable, and should be met on our part by a faithful compliance with all the stipulations and conditions therein expressed.

Civil war, such as you have just passed through, naturally engenders feelings of animosity, hatred, and revenge. It is our duty to divest ourselves of all such feelings, and, so far as it is in our power to do so, to cultivate feelings towards those with whom we have so long contested and heretofore so widely but honestly differed. Neighbourhood feuds, personal animosities, and private differences should be blotted out, and when you return home a manly, straightforward course of conduct will secure the respect even of your enemies. Whatever your responsibilities may be to government, to society, or to individuals, meet them like men. The attempt made to establish a separate and independent confederation has failed, but the consciousness of having done your duty faithfully and to the end will in some measure repay for the hardships you have undergone.

I have never on the field of battle sent you where I was unwilling to go myself, nor would I now advise you to a course which I felt myself unwilling to pursue. You have been good soldiers, you can be good citizens. Obey the laws, preserve your honour, and the government to which you have surrendered can afford to be and will be magnanimous.

N. B. Forrest
Lieutenant General

One of the most famous raiders in history, Forrest was rated by General Joseph E. Johnston as the American Civil War's greatest soldier.

ADMIRAL DAVID FARRAGUT

'Damn the torpedoes! Full speed ahead!'

REAR ADMIRAL DAVID FARRAGUT AT MOBILE BAY, 5 AUGUST 1864

David Farragut (1801–70) was nine years old when he first went to sea as a midshipman in the US Navy in 1810. At 12 years of age he was the prize master of a captured ship during the war of 1812 with Britain. Although born in Tennessee and settled in Norfolk, Virginia, when Virginia seceded from the Union, he went north, taking his Virginia-born wife with him.

In December 1861, Farragut, now a commodore aged 60, was given command of the naval force in a joint expedition to capture New Orleans; Major General Benjamin Butler commanded the 15,000 strong army component. The city, which lay 90 miles (145 km) upriver from the mouth of the River Mississippi, was of great commercial and strategic importance as the gateway to the Mississippi Valley. Its capture would be a severe blow to the Confederacy. To maintain secrecy, a new US Navy blockading squadron was deployed in the western Gulf of Mexico. This was linked with deliberately planted rumours that General Butler was headed for Pensacola, Mobile or Galveston.

CAPTURING NEW ORLEANS

New Orleans was defended by militia, dispersed in small forts covering the numerous water approaches to the city. Some 75 miles (120 km) downriver stood two brick forts: Fort Jackson on the west bank and St Philip on the east bank, manned by a total of 500 men and containing some 75 to 80 guns. Just downriver from the forts a boom consisting of hulks and chain barred the way. The ram *Manassas*, the *Louisiana* (without an engine) and the uncompleted *Mississippi* with an assortment of other vessels, including fire barges, comprised the Confederate river defence force.

Farragut had 24 wooden warships giving him a total of 200 guns, and 19 schooners each armed with a 13-inch mortar. The mortars started bombarding on 18 April 1862, hoping to silence the forts before the wooden ships started to steam up river. Although a huge number of mortar bombs were fired (in one day alone some 2997 at Fort Jackson), after a week it became clear to Farragut that they were doing little damage, so he decided to take his ships up river without waiting for the forts to be reduced. It was a brave decision: all naval officers were taught that one gun ashore in hitting power and accuracy was the equivalent of four afloat. Forts could mount bigger guns than ships, provided a steady gun platform, and were almost impossible to set on fire. Attacking forts with wooden ships was not a recommended practice. Farragut decided to make the attack at night hoping that in the confusion of a night battle he would be able to get his ships past the forts and through the boom. He issued an order to be read out to all ships' companies:

> *I wish you to understand that the day is at hand when you will be called upon*
> *to meet the enemy in the worst form of our profession. Hot and cold shot will,*
> *no doubt, be freely dealt to us, and there must be stout hearts and quick*
> *hands to extinguish the one and stop holes in the other.*

Farragut ordered chains to be arrayed on the sides of his wooden ships to protect engines and magazines. Rope ladders were hung at several points to allow carpenters to get quickly to plug holes in the ships' sides. Mud was smeared on the ships' sides to provide a rudimentary form of camouflage. Sand was strewn around each gun to provide a grip when the decks became slippery with blood.

In his flagship, the *Hartford*, Farragut led the second of his three divisions of warships. He wanted to be in the leading ship, but was dissuaded by his captains. He climbed high on the mizzen rigging, standing with his feet on the ratlines and with his back to the shrouds. While trying to dodge a fire barge, the *Hartford*'s helmsman ran her into shallow water right under the guns of Fort St Philip. Farragut jumped down to the quarterdeck just at the mizzen rigging was sliced away by a bursting shell, and his ship ran aground. The gunners in the nearest casemate in the fort, possibly thinking a landing party would burst forth from the *Hartford*, did not wait to be proved wrong and deserted their guns. Meanwhile the fire barge was pushed by a tug against the *Hartford*'s quarter. Flames curled up and caught the rigging. Most of *Hartford*'s gunners on that side recoiled from the mass of flame shooting out from the burning pine and pitch in the fire barge.

Farragut's clerk seized a 20-pound shell, with the aim of rolling it into the fire barge where it would explode. Farragut, seeing him kneeling on the deck unscrewing the fuse cap, mistook his purpose, and shouted:

> *Come, sir, this is no time for prayer!*

And to the gunners:

> *Don't hold back from that fire, boys. There's a hotter fire than that waiting*
> *for men who don't do their duty. Give that rascally little tug a shot.*

Calmed by Farragut's example, the gun crews returned to their guns and sank the tug. The clerk unscrewed the fuses of three shells and dropped them into the fire barge, which exploded and sank. By going full astern, the *Hartford* clawed her way off the mud bank and resumed her course up river.

By now the crews of all but three of the Confederate vessels had headed their craft for the bank in panic, abandoned them and fled into the swamps. Of the three ships whose skippers had elected to fight it out, one, a revenue cutter, was reduced to matchwood by the fire of three Union ships. The ram, the *Manassas*, careered downriver out of control, not helped by the fact that the leadsman accidentally hit the helmsman on the head while taking a sounding, knocking him overboard. The gunners of both forts opened fire on her, mistaking her for a Union ship. Her engines were smashed by shot penetrating her sides, and she lurched off into a mud bank. Her crew scrambled ashore and were pursued by shot from Union gunboats.

The unarmoured Confederate paddlewheel steamer, the *Governor Moore*, did the most damage. She gallantly attacked the fastest ship in the Union squadron, the 1300-ton screw steamer the *Varuna*. Although outgunned, she managed to sink the *Varuna*, causing huge numbers of casualties, but at the expense of over half her own crew. Intent on taking on the whole Union squadron, the *Governor Moore*'s skipper headed downriver, until the first lieutenant at the helm, shouting that they had insufficient men left, put the helm over and made for the bank. Five Union ships opened up on her, and she exploded as she beached. Fifty-seven of her ship's company of 93 were killed and 17 wounded.

At dawn all of Farragut's warships except the *Varuna* and three gunboats had passed the forts safely. The Confederate fleet was completely destroyed. The city of New Orleans capitulated as Farragut's ships approached with loaded guns pointing straight at the hysterical crowd packing the quayside. The garrisons of Forts Jackson and St Philip surrendered the following day.

Farragut continued upriver and eventually took Baton Rouge and Natchez. Vicksburg, protected by the guns on high bluffs overlooking the Mississippi, was going to take more than a squadron of warships to crack and did not fall for another year. But for opening the river to the Union as far as Vicksburg, Farragut was promoted to rear admiral.

He continued operating on the Mississippi until mid-1863, taking part in numerous engagements, culminating in the capture of Port Hudson on 9 July, the last remaining Confederate stronghold on the Mississippi after the fall of Vicksburg five days earlier.

THE BATTLE OF MOBILE BAY

By 1864 Mobile, Alabama, was the last major port on the Gulf of Mexico still in Confederate hands. Along with Wilmington, North Carolina, it was a haven for blockade-runners taking much-needed supplies to the South. Farragut had wanted to take the port immediately after New Orleans before the defences could be strengthened, but had been ordered to remain on the Mississippi until the river was denied to the Confederacy from source to mouth. Once this mission was over, the *Hartford* and other ships of his squadron needed docking at Brooklyn Navy Yard before being deployed again.

Farragut, with 14 wooden ships, was off Mobile by early January 1864. There intelligence confirmed his worst fears; not only had the city's defences been greatly strengthened, but the rebels had built a monster ironclad, the CSS *Tennessee*, more formidable than any warship since the CSS *Virginia* (formerly the USS *Merrimack*). At over 60 metres (200 ft) and with a 15-metre (50-ft) beam, the *Tennessee* was clad in 15 centimetres (6 ins) of armour over 60 centimetres (2 ft) of oak and pine, and mounted six 6.4 and 7-inch rifled guns (two each side and one each firing forward and astern). She had just two flaws. Her maximum speed was six knots, and the steering chains from her wheelhouse to her rudder ran over her armoured deck, and so were vulnerable to enemy fire.

Farragut was well aware of the damage that an ironclad could do to wooden ships, having studied reports of the the *Virginia*'s actions in Hampton Roads off Virginia until the revolutionary turret ironclad USS *Monitor* had arrived on the scene. He also had personal experience of the danger posed by an ironclad, when at Vicksburg the *Arkansas* had damaged and sunk a number of his ships. He decided to wait until he had ironclads of his own, four of which had been promised by June 1864.

Of the two entrances to Mobile Bay, only one was navigable by Farragut's heavier vessels. This passage, between Dauphin Island and Mobile Point, was heavily defended by forts, obstructed by rows of piles driven into the sea-bed. A line of mines, then called 'torpedoes', had been laid just below the surface off Mobile Point. The safe passage round the mines was marked by a red buoy for the benefit of blockade runners and Confederate ships, but the channel ran right under the guns of Fort Morgan on Mobile Point. As he waited for reinforcements, Farragut rehearsed his captains in the tactics he meant to employ, and sent in boat crews by night to sink or recover as many mines as possible. Many were found to be defective, their firing mechanisms corroded by salt water.

At last, by 4 August, Farragut had his four ironclads: the *Manhattan* and *Tecumseh*, each with 25 centimetres (10 ins) of armour and twin 15-inch guns in a revolving turret; and the *Chickasaw* and *Winnebago*, twin turrets with a pair of 11-inch guns in each. Farragut planned for them to lead the way followed by his seven heavier wooden ships, each with a gunboat lashed on the port side, away from Fort Morgan, to provide back-up power in the event of engine failure on the big ships. Just before the attack started, Union soldiers would land on Dauphin Island to attack Fort Gaines, on the far side of the channel. Farragut was asked on the evening of 4 August if he would authorize an issue of rum to all hands to prepare them for the fight. He replied:

> No, I have never found that I needed rum to enable me to do my duty. I will order two cups of good coffee to each man at 2 o'clock, and at 8 o'clock I will pipe all hands to breakfast in Mobile Bay.

At 6 a.m. on 5 August the attack started. The leading ironclad, the *Tecumseh*, anxious to engage the *Tennessee*, which had already opened fire, tried to cut across the minefield and hit a mine. She sank in a few minutes, taking all but about 20 of her 114 crew with her. The captain of the *Brooklyn*, the leading wooden ship, shocked by the sight of the sinking *Tecumseh*, chose that moment to hesitate.

Instead of pressing on as ordered, he went astern and bore down on the next in line, the *Hartford*, Farragut's flagship. Farragut, who had climbed the rigging for a better view above the smoke, with a rope round him to stop him crashing to the deck 6 metres (20 ft) below, hailed the *Brooklyn* demanding to know the reason for her manoeuvre. 'Torpedoes ahead', was the reply.

All Farragut's ships were taking heavy fire from the guns on Mobile Point, especially from the water battery sited just above sea level and able to fire point-blank. Wounded in the *Hartford* were falling faster than the surgeons could cope with, dead bodies were laid in a row on deck. *Brooklyn* blocked most of the channel, and the whole plan was coming apart. Farragut hesitated for a moment, then, having ascertained from the pilot in the *Hartford* that there was sufficient water to pass the *Brooklyn* on her port side, shouted that he would take the lead. As Farragut's flagship passed the *Brooklyn*, somebody shouted a warning about torpedoes, to which Farragut barked his famous reply:

Damn the torpedoes! Full speed ahead!

While the *Hartford* steamed full ahead, her crew heard the dreaded sound of mines scraping against her hull. Fortunately for her the mines of that era were detonated by unreliable impact fuses, or equally unpredictable electrical detonation by wires from shore. The other ships of Farragut's squadron followed and also struck mines, but all survived. They were then confronted with the Confederate Admiral Buchanan in the *Tennessee* with three gunboats.

The three Confederate gunboats were quickly seen off and fled; only one survived the subsequent chase by Union gunboats. The *Hartford* dodged round the ungainly *Tennessee*, and continued to head into Mobile Bay. Buchanan gave up trying to catch the *Hartford*, and turned his attention to the ships astern of her, exchanging broadsides as *Tennessee* ran down the line of wooden sloops. Some of the Union ships were damaged by the *Tennessee*'s guns, but pressed on behind Farragut. *Tennessee* headed for protection under the guns of Fort Morgan.

Farragut anchored 4 miles (6 km) inside the bay, and piped all hands to breakfast at 8.35, only 35 minutes later than he had forecast the night before. The enticing aroma of hot coffee, bacon and beans wafted up from the galleys in the Union squadron. But breakfast was rudely interrupted when the *Tennessee* was spotted steaming for Farragut's squadron. She was soon surrounded and fired on from all quarters. Her steering chain was cut so she could not manoeuvre. Eventually, with half her gun port shutters jammed shut by hits, and unable to turn to bring her serviceable guns to bear, she struck her colours. It took a further two weeks to reduce Fort Morgan, the last fort held by the Confederates. Farragut did not try to capture the port of Mobile, 35 miles (56 km) inland. With Mobile Bay held by the Union Navy, the port was closed to blockade runners for the rest of the war.

On 23 December 1864, Farragut was promoted to vice admiral, the rank having been established in the United States Navy the previous day. He was one of the first senior Union men to enter Richmond, the capital of the Confederacy, and the first American ever to hold the rank of admiral, to which he was promoted on 23 July 1866.

GENERAL THOMAS 'STONEWALL' JACKSON

'We will give them the bayonet.'

JACKSON, ON BEING TOLD THAT THE CONFEDERATES WERE BEING BEATEN AT THE FIRST
BATTLE OF BULL RUN (MANASSAS), 21 JULY 1861

Thomas Jonathan Jackson (1824–63) was not given to long speeches, and although what was probably his longest is included here, much of what he said to his troops and to his fellow commanders was terse and to the point. Having graduated without distinction from West Point, the Mexican war of 1846–8 gave him his first chance to shine, and he was promoted from lieutenant to major. He never smoked, gambled or drank. His diet was sparse. In the field he would suck on a lemon, if one was available, and he frequently rode with one arm held above his head to improve his circulation. In 1851 he resigned from the army to teach at the Virginia Military Institute (VMI), where his strange habits earned him the nickname 'Tom Fool Jackson'.

General Robert E. Lee, who perhaps admired Jackson most, described him thus:

> *A man he is of contrast so complete that he appears one day a Presbyterian deacon who delights in theological discussion and the next, a reincarnated Joshua. He lives by the New Testament and fights by the Old. Almost 6 feet in height and weighing about 175 pounds, he has blue eyes, a brown beard and a commonplace, somewhat rusty appearance.*

Jackson commanded a company of VMI cadets at John Brown's hanging in 1859, and on the outbreak of the Civil War in April 1861, he took a battalion of cadets to Richmond to provide drillmasters for the army being formed by the State of Virginia. By the First Battle of Bull Run, or Manassas, in July 1861, he was commanding a brigade. (The Confederates called the battle Manassas after the nearby Manassas Junction on the intersection of the Orange & Alexandria and Manassas Gap Railroads, while the Federals called it Bull Run after the river of that name, which they had to cross to attack the Confederate Army.) He had raised the brigade at Harper's Ferry, and spent a brief period with it in the Shenandoah Valley. At Manassas, he and his unit earned the nickname 'Stonewall'. The Confederates were in disarray and on the point of losing the battle, when

Brigadier General Bee rallying his own brigade, pointed to Jackson's men standing like a 'stone wall'
on Henry Hill, a key feature, and ordered his own men to form up behind them. As the Federals
approached, Jackson told his men to lie down just below the crest and out of sight of the attackers.
Riding to the centre of his brigade line he gave the order for the counterstroke, quoted at the head
of this chapter. His regiments sprang from the ground and dashed forward yelling like fury, and,
after being joined by the remnants of flanking brigades, swept the Federals from the field.

Engraving (c.1870) of Harper's Ferry, West Virginia, famous for the 1859 raid by the abolitionist John Brown on the Federal Armoury. Thomas Jackson raised his brigade here in 1861

Promoted to major general to command in the Shenandoah Valley, he bade farewell to his brigade, although it was destined to form part of his command. He said, in the longest speech he ever made to his troops:

> I am not here to make a speech, but simply to say farewell. I first met you at Harper's Ferry, at the commencement of the War, and I cannot take leave of you without giving expression to my admiration of your conduct from that day to this, whether on the march, in the bivouac, or on the bloody plains of Manassas, where you gained the well-deserved reputation of having decided the fate of battle.
>
> Throughout the broad extent of the country through which you have marched, by your respect for the rights and property of the citizens, you have shown that you are soldiers not only to defend, but able and willing both to defend and protect. You have already won a brilliant reputation throughout the army of the whole Confederacy; and I trust, in future, by your deeds in the field, and by the assistance of the same kind Providence who has hitherto favoured our cause, you will win more victories and add lustre to the reputation you now enjoy. You have already gained a proud position in the future history of this our second War of Independence. I shall look with great anxiety to your future movements, and I trust whenever I shall hear of the First Brigade on the field of battle, it will be of still nobler deeds achieved and higher reputation won.

Jackson paused, before giving way to impulse:

> In the Army of the Shenandoah you were the First Brigade! In the Army of the Potomac you were the First Brigade! In the Second Corps of the army you

108

are the First Brigade! You are the First Brigade in the affections of your
general, and I hope by your future deeds and bearing you will be handed
down to posterity as the First Brigade in this our Second War of
Independence. Farewell!

Jackson galloped from the field with the cheers of his soldiers following him.

MASTERY OF THE SHENANDOAH VALLEY

In the Shenandoah Valley between March and June 1862, Jackson conducted one of the most brilliant military campaigns in history. The valley, sometimes known as the 'breadbasket' of the Confederacy for its productive farms, was even more important strategically, offering a backdoor route into Maryland across the Potomac at Harper's Ferry, and hence the possibility of threatening Washington. Here Jackson with 17,000 troops frustrated the efforts of 60,000 Union soldiers. He fought four pitched battles, six skirmishes and numerous minor actions. Thanks to his fast marching and lightning manoeuvres he managed to bring superior force to bear at every engagement except Cross Keys. He took 3500 prisoners, 10,000 priceless rifled muskets (many Confederate troops were still armed with smoothbores) and nine rifled guns, as well as a large quantity of stores. But more importantly he tied down at least 38,000 Union soldiers destined to join Union General McClellan threatening Richmond, with more planned to follow, but for Jackson keeping them pinned down in the Shenandoah.

During this campaign, the words his soldiers heard from Jackson more often than any other were:

Press on, men; press on.

Like all the best generals, he knew that he must sometimes be ruthless to save his men's lives. When one regimental commander asked for a halt to rest his weary men, Jackson's response was:

Colonel, I yield to no man in sympathy for the gallant men under my
command, but I am obliged to sweat them tonight that I may save their blood
tomorrow.

The next day, in a decisive battle, he routed the Federals at Winchester. Jackson rode among his soldiers waving his cap in the air:

Order forward the whole line! The battle's won! Very good! Now let's holler!

The rebel yell echoed off the houses in the town, as Jackson joined in. An officer remonstrated with him for being so far forward, Jackson shouted at him:

Go back and tell the whole army to press forward to the Potomac.

THE SECOND BULL RUN CAMPAIGN

Having finished his successful diversion in the Shenandoah Valley, Jackson was summoned by Lee to take part in the peninsular campaign against McClellan. Here Jackson, commanding two divisions plus a brigade, was strangely comatose and missed several chances to destroy Union formations. He may have been exhausted by his efforts in the Shenandoah, because on one occasion he went to sleep still chewing a biscuit at a staff conference. Jarred awake by his own head nodding, he said:

> *Now gentlemen, let us at once to bed and rise with the dawn, and see if*
> *tomorrow we cannot do something.*

Sadly nothing came of his efforts the following day. He was on much better form during the Second Manassas/Bull Run campaign, when thanks to Lee's brilliance the Confederates outmanoeuvred the Union Army under General Pope. Jackson had a hard fight at Cedar Mountain, when his troops began to break under a Union attack. He rode in among the retreating Confederate soldiers; drawing his sword, which no one had ever seen him do before in battle, he brandished it above his head roaring:

> *Rally, brave men, and press forward! Your general will lead you; Jackson will*
> *lead you! Follow me!*

The Confederates halted, and with their own officers taking up Jackson's cry, rallied. A few minutes later, Major General A.P. Hill came up with the Confederate Light Division and trounced the Union troops.

After Cedar Mountain, Jackson was sent by Lee in a wide flanking march to cut Pope's communications at Bristoe Station, 50 miles (80 km) in blazing heat, on dirt roads with nothing but green corn and apples to eat on the way.

Jackson's men hit Bristoe Station at sunset, derailed two trains and destroyed the railway bridge, before seizing Manassas Junction, a vast Union stores depot. The Confederates were now in between Pope and home. Pope was aware that Lee had split his army, and despite enjoying greater overall superiority, completely failed to defeat the Confederates in detail. He moved too slowly to catch Jackson at Manassas. Instead of fleeing southeast to escape as Pope thought he would, Jackson moved in the opposite direction, to Groveton to block Pope's route north across the Potomac via the Stone Bridge. Here Jackson packed his troops into woods on a ridge, intending to delay Pope while Lee brought up the rest of the Army of Northern Virginia under Longstreet to smash him.

When the first Federal column approached, Jackson rode off the ridge for a good look; his own men watched in horror, thinking that he would be shot or even captured. Suddenly, he wheeled and galloped back up the slope to where his divisional commanders had sat on their horses watching him. Touching his cap he said:

> *Bring up your men, gentlemen.*

As the divisional commanders and Jackson cantered back to their troops, a great roar went up from the Confederates in the woods on the ridge, like wild animals about to be released on their prey. The fight that followed was one of the toughest of the war, but eventually the Union troops pulled back. Jackson did not pursue.

The next morning Longstreet linked up with Jackson, who had established a very strong defensive position in an unfinished railway cutting. Here through a long day's bitter fighting, he withstood the main weight of the Union attack. Unfortunately Longstreet failed to attack the Union flank as it engaged Jackson and a great opportunity to inflict a crushing defeat on Pope was lost.

The next day Pope, fooled into thinking that Jackson was retreating, attacked to finish him off. But Jackson had merely pulled most of his force back into the woods along Sudley Mountain to his rear, while leaving sufficient men at the railway cutting to delay any attacker until he could move his men back into position. Pope fell for this ruse and attacked again with even larger force than the day before. Jackson rushed his men forward, but with three Union corps (62,000) facing Jackson's three divisions (20,000), Pope nearly broke through. At one point an officer rode up to Jackson, with the news that his brigade commander had been wounded, and that the troops were badly shaken and needed help.

> *What brigade, sir?* Jackson asked.
>
> *The Stonewall Brigade.*
>
> *Go back. Give my compliments to them, and tell the Stonewall Brigade to maintain her reputation.*

They held, just. This time Longstreet did attack, albeit belatedly. Pope was driven back, but a strongly held defensive position at Henry Hill House enabled him to get his army over the Bull Run to Centreville. Jackson followed up over the river at Sudley Springs, and marched in pouring rain to turn Pope's flank. At Chantilly, he met a Union force sent to block him. Here, in a thunderstorm louder than cannon fire and drenching rain, a savage fight ensued. Jackson was in a bad mood because his march had been slowed by the weather One of his colonels sent a messenger asking that his men be withdrawn from the contest because their cartridges were too wet to ignite. Jackson replied:

> *My compliments to the colonel, and tell him the enemy's ammunition is just as wet as his.*

At nightfall the Union forces withdrew. Pope retreated into the defences round Washington where Lee could not follow.

SWANSONG AT CHANCELLORSVILLE

The engagement with which Jackson's name is most closely linked is Chancellorsville, in May 1863, also regarded as Lee's greatest battle. The Union Army (134,000 men), now under command of

'Fighting Joe' Hooker greatly outnumbered Lee's 60,000 who were entrenched above Fredericksburg on the Rappahannock river. Longstreet, with two divisions, was away on a foraging expedition. Hooker designed an excellent plan. He would keep Lee occupied at Fredericksburg with two corps, while he took five corps on a long flank march, cross the Rappahannock well upriver from Fredericksburg at United States Ford, and hit Lee in the rear. By early on 1 May, Hooker was positioned in strength in the vicinity of Chancellorsville well placed to attack Lee's rear.

Lee, however, was not playing Hooker's game. Warned by his cavalry commander, Stuart, Lee left a mere 10,000 men in the Fredericksburg position and took the rest of his army west to deal with the Union forces in his rear. Hooker, put out by this unexpected reaction by Lee stopped his advance on Fredericksburg and hunkered down around Chancellorsville. Stuart meanwhile discovered that Hooker's right flank was 'in the air', and open to being outflanked. On his return from his reconnaissance, Stuart found Lee and Jackson in conference wondering how to get at the Union Army. Having heard Stuart's news, Jackson proposed to Lee that he take his whole corps to attack Hooker's right flank.

The following day, Jackson set out with 31,000 men led by cavalryman, Colonel Fitzhugh Lee, and screened by the thick woods in this section of Virginia, aptly known as 'the Wilderness', Jackson's corps marched along back roads round the Union Army. According to Fitzhugh Lee, Jackson's 'eyes burned with a brilliant glow, his face radiant with the success of his flanking movement'. Meanwhile Jackson was riding with the leading division.

Hooker had been warned that a mass of Confederate troops was moving across his front, but said that this was Lee retreating from Fredericksburg, because that is what he wanted to believe.

Finally, an hour and a half before sundown, Jackson's corps was in position to attack, although the rear formations had still to catch up. Rodes's division would jump off first.

> *Are you ready, General Rodes?* asked Jackson.
>
> *Yes, sir,* replied Rodes.
>
> *You can go forward then,* added Jackson.

Jackson hit the Union right like the crack of doom, and it folded. Jackson went back to send in the follow-up divisions. He spurred on Hill with the words:

> *Press them! Cut them off from the United States Ford, Hill. Press them!*

Hooker was only saved by darkness, and by what we would now call 'friendly fire'. Jackson, riding back with Hill from a reconnaissance in preparation for continuing the attack through the night, was shot at by some of his own pickets. He was badly wounded and evacuated. The Confederate attack ground to a halt that night. Although Stuart, who had taken over when Jackson was wounded, continued attacking the next day, Hooker pulled back into a tight horseshoe round Chancellorsville,

*In a lithograph of the Confederate generals (1867) by John Smith, 'Stonewall' Jackson is seen to the
immediate right of his commanding officer Robert E. Lee (centre)*

with both flanks on the river. The Confederates attacked again and again with frantic bravery, but
could not dislodge the Union force that outnumbered them two to one, and with no open flank.

Finally, Hooker ordered the Union corps facing Fredericksburg to attack Lee's rear, but Lee saw
them off. Eventually Hooker slunk back across the Rappahannock. Horace Greeley, the editor of the
New York Tribune, frothed:

> My God, *it is horrible, horrible. And to think of it – 130,000 magnificent
> soldiers cut to pieces by less than 60,000 half-starved ragamuffins!'*

This great Confederate victory came at a price: Jackson started to recover from an amputation of
his left arm just below the shoulder, but died of pneumonia eight days after being wounded. It was a
grievous loss to the Confederacy. Even before he died, while Lee was trying to drive Hooker into the
Rappahannock without success, he said of Jackson: 'He has lost his left arm, but I have lost my right'.

Jackson's soldiers laughed at his eccentricities, but loved him all the same. Stories told about him
were legion; a favourite was that whereas it took Moses 40 years to lead the children of Israel through
the wilderness, 'Old Jack' would have double-marched them through in three days on half rations.

CAPTAIN JEAN DANJOU

On 30 April 1863, a large Mexican force attacked a convoy of bullion being escorted by the 3rd Company of the 1st Battalion, French Foreign Legion, destined for the French expeditionary force besieging Puebla in Mexico. The company consisted of Captain Jean Danjou (1828–63), normally the battalion quartermaster, two second lieutenants, Maudet and Vilain and 62 legionnaires. Danjou had fought in Algeria, the Crimea and in the Austro-Sardinian War at Magenta and Solferino. He had lost a hand in Algeria and now wore a wooden one.

Danjou fought a skilful withdrawal action, repelling several cavalry charges, finally taking up a defensive position in a hacienda near the village of Camerone. As the legionnaires were making ready behind the 1-metre (3-ft) high walls surrounding the hacienda, the Mexican commander came forward under a flag of truce and pointed out that his 800 cavalry and 1200 infantry greatly outnumbered Danjou's company, and demanded his surrender. Danjou replied:

> *We have munitions. We will not surrender.*

Turning to his men, he swore to fight to the death, and asked them to do the same.

Wave after wave of Mexican attacks rolled in. At midday, Danjou was shot in the chest and died. At about 2 p.m., 2nd Lieutenant Vilain was killed and the hacienda caught fire. The smoke and heat of the fire added to the torment of thirst and hunger endured by the legionnaires who had not eaten since the previous day.

By 5 p.m. only five legionnaires under Maudet were still standing. Before ordering yet another assault, the Mexican commander gave Maudet the chance to surrender. It was refused. The Mexicans poured over the walls, to be confronted by Maudet and five men with fixed bayonets backed against a wall in a corner of the hacienda. At Maudet's command, the legionnaires fired their last round and charged the surrounding Mexicans. Maudet and two legionnaires fell, riddled with bullets. Corporal Maine and two legionnaires were on the point of being shot, when a Mexican officer shouted at them to surrender. They agreed but only if they were allowed to care for their wounded and keep their weapons. The Mexican officer agreed, saying: 'Nothing can be refused to men like you'.

The men of the 3rd Company had kept their promise to Danjou, fighting for 11 hours. Danjou's wooden hand was eventually recovered. It now occupies an honoured place in the training depot of the French Foreign Legion, where the battle is commemorated every year on Camerone Day.

MAJOR GENERAL
GEORGE PICKETT

'Up men and to your posts! Don't forget
today you are from old Virginia!'

<small>MAJOR GENERAL GEORGE PICKETT AT THE BATTLE OF GETTYSBURG, 3 JULY 1863</small>

At 9 o'clock in the morning on the third day of the Battle of Gettysburg, the three brigades of the division led by Major General George Pickett (1825–75), 4600 men and Virginians all, arrived to join the rest of the Confederate Army under General Robert E. Lee. Pickett reported to his corps commander, Lieutenant General James 'Pete' Longstreet of the Confederate I Corps, while

The Battle of Gettysburg in Pennsylvania turned the tide of the American Civil War in favour of the Union. 'Pickett's charge' was a key moment in the engagement

his division shook out behind Seminary Ridge. Longstreet, not noted for a cheerful disposition, was even gloomier than usual. Lee had ordered him to send in three divisions, including Pickett's, to attack the Union positions on Cemetery Hill, over half-a-mile (0.8 km) away over gently sloping open ground. He had told Lee that he needed 30,000 men to have a chance of success, and now he was going to have to attack with well under half that number. Longstreet foresaw bloody failure but, having failed to persuade Lee to change his mind, set to organize the attack in his usual plodding way.

Pickett on the other hand was elated. He had spent the first two days of the battle held in reserve, and trudging up the 25 dusty miles (40 km) of the Chambersburg pike in the July heat. After a disappointing war to date, he saw this attack, which he thought would win the war for the Confederate cause, as his big chance. Not over blessed with brains, Pickett passed out last of his class at West Point. 'The Union got the clever ones', he would jest, 'and look what good it's done them.' A year after graduating, he was the first American to scale the ramparts at the Battle of Chapultepec in 1848, which earned him headlines in the newspapers. Provoking an incident with the British during a joint occupation of Puget Sound in 1860 brought more publicity. But hitherto, his participation in the Civil War, through no fault of his, had been undistinguished.

A MAGNIFICENT BUT FUTILE GESTURE

Pickett was a dandy. His shoulder-length ringlets were perfumed, his long moustache curled up at the ends. His highly polished boots, golden spurs, riding crop and gilt buttons on a beautifully cut uniform led an English observer attached to Lee's Army of Northern Virginia, Lieutenant Colonel Freemantle of the Coldstream Guards, to describe him as: 'a desperate looking character'.

The attack that was about to take place has gone down in history as 'Pickett's charge'. This is a misnomer, but it has stuck, like innumerable other historical errors. Longstreet was in command. Pickett's sole overall responsibility was to form the ten brigades for the attack, of which only three were his, and set them off.

Before the Confederate bombardment on the Union line began, Colonel Alexander, commanding his artillery was astounded to receive a note from Longstreet, which read:

> If the artillery fire does not have the effect to drive off the enemy or greatly demoralize him, so as to make our effort pretty certain, I would prefer that you should not advise Pickett to make the charge. I shall rely a great deal upon your judgement to determine the matter and shall expect you to let General Pickett know when the moment offers.

Reading between the lines of this note, it is clear that Longstreet was trying to pass the buck to Alexander to take the responsibility for stopping the attack; in effect telling Lee that the charge was bound to fail. When Alexander queried the note, Longstreet merely rephrased the order:

> Colonel, the intention is to advance the infantry if the artillery has the desired effect of driving the enemy's [artillery] off, or having other effect such as to warrant us in making the attack. When that moment arrives advise General Pickett, and of course advance such artillery as you can use in aiding the attack.

This still left the loophole: 'if the artillery has the desired effect'; something that in Alexander's view was unlikely to be attained, for in his experience no Union battery had ever been driven from a prepared position by artillery fire. Alexander, however, assumed General Lee would not have ordered the attack without ensuring that it was well supported by other troops, and went to confer with Pickett. He found him full of confidence. He replied to Longstreet's second message: 'When our fire is at its best, I will advise General Pickett to advance'. Shortly after the Confederate bombardment began.

After about an hour of furious fire, which caused many casualties and much damage among Union guns and infantry, the Union artillery counter-fire slackened. It was a ruse. The Union artillery commander, Brigadier General Hunt, reckoning that the Confederates would attack if they thought they had won the artillery fire-fight, ordered his gunners to slacken the rate of fire. At the same time he ordered one battery that had taken heavy punishment to retire. Alexander, seeing this, sent a note to Pickett: 'for God's sake come quick ... or my ammunition will not let me support you properly'.

Having gone forward to check with Longstreet, whom he found perched on a fence, Pickett returned to his troops to order the advance to begin. Pickett addressed his division, but only the portion quoted could be heard above the din. The brigades stepped off. Longstreet preceded them as far as the gun line, where the Confederate fire was slackening. From Alexander he learned that he did not have enough ammunition to support the infantry on its way to the objective. Longstreet burst out: 'Go and stop Pickett right where he is, and replenish your ammunition'.

Alexander replied: 'We can't do that sir, the train [artillery supply wagons] has but little. It would take an hour to distribute it, and meanwhile the enemy would improve [their positions] all the time.'

With deep emotion, Longstreet, slowly muttered: 'I do not want to make this charge. I do not see how it can succeed. I would not make it now but that General Lee has ordered it, and expects it.'

As the Confederate infantry advanced they were flayed by Union shells and when closer by canister, which tore great gaps in their ranks, but they still came on. About 90 metres (100 yds) from the Union positions, the Confederates halted and dressed their lines. A few Confederates penetrated the Union positions behind stone walls, before being repulsed by counter-attacks. Some 4000 were taken prisoner. The survivors trickled back into the Confederate lines.

Lee took full responsibility for the failure of his army to defeat the Union Army, writing to the president of the Confederacy, Jefferson Davis:

> *The conduct of the troops was all that I could desire or expect, and they deserved success so far as it can be deserved by heroic valour and fortitude. More may have been required of them than they were able to perform, but my admiration of their noble qualities and confidence in their ability to cope successfully with the enemy has suffered no abatement from the issue of this protracted and sanguinary conflict.*

Perhaps because he was the only Confederate general officer who took part in the charge that bears his name to survive the Gettysburg campaign, Pickett's leadership has been criticized. (The other general officer survivor of the charge, Major General Pettigrew, was killed on 14 July during the retreat from Gettysburg.) But he took his divisional headquarters to within 180 metres (200 yds) of the Union infantry, and well within range of dozens of guns and several thousand rifles. He was lucky not to be hit. His division tends to get the lion's share of coverage in much of the literature, which may account for jealousy directed at Pickett by commentators from states in the Confederacy other than Virginia, but its performance was as good as any other division, and better than many.

MAJOR GENERAL GEORGE MEADE

'Why you craven fool, until this battle is decided, you do not know, neither do I, if you will have a government to apply to. If I hear any more from you, I will give you a gun and send you to the front line to defend your rights.'

MAJOR GENERAL GEORGE MEADE BEFORE THE BATTLE OF GETTYSBURG, 1–3 JULY 1863

Major General George Meade (1815–72) was given command of the Union Army of the Potomac just two days before the Battle of Gettysburg, 1–3 July 1863. As the battle was about to reach its climax – with the Confederate 'Pickett's Charge' on the Union centre – a civilian approached Meade and complained that his house had been commandeered as a hospital by the Union Army and that as a result his garden was becoming littered with graves and amputated limbs.

Meade, who once described himself as a 'snapping old turtle' (he was actually only 49 but looked considerably older), instantly rounded on the man. The general's robust response to this whining nuisance was not followed by a procession of lawyers with dollar signs in their eyes bearing writs, as would be the case today.

MARSHAL JOSEPH JOFFRE

Joffre (1852–1931) was the son of a Pyrenean barrel-maker. His military career prospered largely because of his sound republican credentials at a time when French politicians were inclined to left-wing views, including deep suspicion of the military, and the army was riven by politics. His greatest asset was an imperturbable nature; he regarded any interruption to his lengthy and substantial meals and long nights asleep as wholly unacceptable, even in the worst national crisis.

As commander-in-chief of the French army before the First World War, he bears a large part of the responsibility for the near-catastrophic Plan Seventeen, which, in the event of war with Germany, called for the main weight of the French army to attack on the right flank, in Alsace and Lorraine. His saving grace was his recognition that the plan was failing, leading him to redeploy to meet the threat posed by the German offensive on the French left. He discerned the moment to strike when the German First Army, on the far right flank of the German offensive, instead of swinging west of Paris, turned and headed east of the city, exposing it to a counter-attack on the River Marne.

Before Joffre began the attack he issued a message to be read to all troops in the French army:

We are about to engage in a battle on which the fate of our country depends and it is important to remind all ranks that the moment has passed for looking to the rear; all our efforts must be directed to attacking and driving back the enemy. Troops that can advance no farther must, at any price, hold on to the ground they have conquered and die on the spot rather than give way. Under the circumstances which face us, no act of weakness can be tolerated.

Although the battle saved France, it was not as conclusive as Joffre had hoped. He failed to inflict a crushing defeat on the German army. Thanks in part to good German generalship, plus lack of co-ordination of the French counter-stroke, the Germans were able to withdraw in good order to the line of the River Aisne. There they resisted all further attempts to push them back any further, digging in on the Aisne until finally dislodged in late 1918.

In 1915 Joffre presided over a series of French offensives, none of which produced any result except massive casualties. He was taken by surprise by the German attack at Verdun in February 1916, and that, linked with failure to achieve any marked success elsewhere on the Western Front in 1916, resulted in him being put out to grass in favour of General Robert Nivelle at the end of the year. As a consolation, he was created a marshal of France, deservedly for his creditable performance in the hour of France's greatest danger in 1914.

GENERAL FERDINAND FOCH

'Hard pressed on my right. My centre is yielding.
Impossible to manoeuvre. Situation excellent.
I am attacking.'

FERDINAND FOCH, 1914

Thus ran the report submitted by General Ferdinand Foch (1851–1929) to General Joffre, the French commander-in-chief, at 8 p.m. on 8 September 1914. He had just been promoted to command the French Ninth Army, and played a major part in stemming the tide of the German advance in the northern sector of the Western Front in 1914.

Before the First World War, Foch was a leading advocate of the 'attack at all costs' school of military thought in France, and along with many other senior commanders bears the blame for the French tactics of 1914 that failed with huge losses. He was, nevertheless, sufficiently successful to survive being sacked, or *dégommé* (literally 'cleaned off', or 'unstuck'), by General Joffre – the fate of many French generals. By mid-1916 Foch was commanding an Army Group, but when Joffre was removed at the end of that year, he too lost his command. He was soon back, replacing General Nivelle as commander-in-chief, after the latter's failed offensive. Foch ended the war as Allied commander-in-chief. Although his role was co-ordination of the Allied armies, not command of them, he was one of the principal architects of victory in autumn 1918.

His statue outside Victoria Station in London is inscribed: 'I am conscious of having served England as I served my own country'.

MARSHAL PHILIPPE PÉTAIN

On 25 February 1916, with the loss of the key Fort Douaumont, the German offensive at Verdun seemed poised to succeed. Mass panic swept through the city, and even the lion-hearted French soldiers looked as if they might break. The day before, sensing that all was not going well, the French high command decided to appoint General Philippe Pétain (1856–1951) to command the Verdun sector. He was nowhere to be found. Finally, his aide-de-camp had a brainwave, went to the Hôtel Terminus of the Gare du Nord in Paris and tracked his boss down, but found not only the general's shoes outside the door for cleaning, but also a lady's. He knocked, Pétain answered and told his aide-de-camp that he would set out the following morning.

Arriving just in time to learn of the fall of Fort Douaumont, Pétain set up his headquarters at Souilly, about 15 miles (24 km) south of Verdun. Here, despite being in the grip of pneumonia, he issued orders that there would be no further retreat, and took control of the battle, stalling the German offensive in that sector of the battlefield, the right bank of the River Meuse.

Six weeks later, fresh German attacks were launched on the left bank of the Meuse, and again it seemed that they would break through. Pétain issued his most famous order of the day:

Courage, on les aura! (*'Courage, we shall have them!'*)

Although the Germans gained some ground, their attacks slowly lost momentum and ground to a halt. Then in July, the British attacked on the Somme, and the Germans, faced with a new threat, closed down their offensive at Verdun.

Pétain was the son of a peasant from the Pas de Calais and in 1914 was a passed-over infantry colonel. Within two years he was to become the saviour of Verdun and France. He spoke plainly to his soldiers, was mindful of their welfare, and they trusted him. The improvements in welfare, leave, and supply he made at Verdun greatly boosted morale. Yet his reputation was permanently destroyed by his role as head of the collaborationist Vichy regime in France during the Second World War.

FIELD MARSHAL
SIR DOUGLAS HAIG

'Every position must be held to the last man.'

ORDER OF THE DAY ISSUED BY FIELD MARSHAL SIR DOUGLAS HAIG, 11 APRIL 1918

O n 21 March 1918, the German army began its great, all-out assault on the Western Front, aimed at defeating the British Expeditionary Force (BEF) before the Americans could build up their combat-effective strength in France. For although America had entered the war in April 1917, such was the state of the country's preparedness for war that it was not until the end of May 1918 that the first major action by the American Expeditionary Force (AEF) took place. In March 1918 there were around 250,000 Americans in France, but only around half were in seven untrained, incomplete divisions, the remainder being on lines of communications and logistic duties. The Germans were determined to exploit this window of opportunity.

On 5 April, after 16 days of ferocious fighting the March attack ended just 9 miles (15 km) short of Amiens.. But there was more to come. What had originally been planned as a supporting attack now became a second offensive north of the original push. The Germans got within 5 miles (8 km) of the key railway junction of Hazebrouck and only 22 miles (35 km) from the coast at Dunkirk. On 11 April the outlook was so grim that Field Marshal Sir Douglas Haig (1861–1928), commander-in-chief of the BEF, issued a special order of the day to be read out to all ranks:

> Three weeks ago today the enemy began his terrific attacks against us on a 50-mile front. His objects are to separate us from the French, to take the Channel Ports and destroy the British Army.
>
> In spite of throwing already 106 Divisions into the battle and enduring the most reckless sacrifice of life, he has as yet made little progress towards his goals.
>
> We owe this to the determined fighting and self-sacrifice of our troops. Words fail me to express the admiration which I feel for the splendid resistance offered by all ranks of our Army under the most trying circumstances.
>
> Many amongst us now are tired. To those I would say that Victory will belong to the side which holds out the longest. The French Army is moving rapidly and in great force to our support.
>
> There is no other course open to us but to fight it out. Every position must be held to the last

man: there must be no retirement. With our backs to the wall and believing in the justice of our cause each one of us might fight on to the end. The safety of our homes and the Freedom of mankind alike depend upon the conduct of each one of us at this critical moment.

In his handwritten draft, Haig had added a further sentence:

Be of good cheer, the British Empire will win in the end.

He subsequently crossed it out, possibly thinking that it detracted from the force of what eventually went out.

The BEF held, and by 29 April the German offensive petered out. The two offensives cost the Allies 351,793 casualties, and the Germans 348,300. But the BEF's resilience was demonstrated by the fact that beginning in August and ending in November, Haig's soldiers fought and won a series of battles, each bigger than any fought by the British in the Second World War, and soundly defeated the German army, taking more prisoners and guns than the French and American armies put together.

CAPTAIN LLOYD WILLIAMS

'Retreat, hell, we just got here.'

CAPTAIN LLOYD WILLIAMS, USMC, 5 JUNE 1918

The final phase of the last offensive by the Germans on the Western Front in the First World War began on 27 May 1918. It sliced through the French army and by 3 June the Germans were on the Marne, as they had been in 1914, and only 56 miles (90 km) from Paris. On 5 June, as the French government was making preparations to flee from Paris, up the Paris–Metz road marched the Marine Brigade, part of the United States 2nd Division to reinforce the French XXI Corps. Mixed in with the crowd of refugees was a flood of disorganized French soldiers. As they passed the Marines, they advised them to fall back. In response, Captain Lloyd Williams (1887–1918) of the 2nd Battalion, 5th Marines is reputed to have uttered the immortal line:

Retreat, hell, we just got here.

Williams's pithy rejoinder quickly spread through the Marine Brigade. When its commander, Brigadier General James Harbord, received a message from General Degoutte, commander of

French XXI Corps, demanding to know why men from his brigade were withdrawing, Harbord immediately verified this information with Major Thomas Holcomb, commanding officer of the 2nd Battalion, 6th Marines, the forward battalion. Holcomb reassured him in no uncertain terms:

> When I do any running it will be in the opposite direction. Nothing doing in
> the fall-back business.

The Marine Brigade command then adapted Williams's phrase to send the following reply to Degoutte:

> Retreat? Hell – we only just got here!

SERGEANT MAJOR DANIEL DALY

In the late afternoon of 6 June 1918, the 3rd Battalion of the 5th Regiment, United States Marine Corps was involved in an attack to take Belleau Wood, which straddled the Paris–Metz road. It was the Marine Brigade's first major battle. As the platoon of Gunnery Sergeant Daniel Daly (1873–1937) advanced across an open field, German machine-gun bullets cracked through the wheat stalks, felling marines: the whole company hesitated, some started to go to ground. Daly swung his rifle with fixed bayonet over his head, yelling:

> Come on you sons of bitches. Do you want to live forever?

The attack swept on and took the edge of the wood. Daly won the Navy Cross, the second most prestigious American medal after the Congressional Medal of Honor. He already had two of those.

His first was for his actions during the defence of the American Legation in Beijing during the Boxer Rebellion. There on 15 July 1900, Private Daly had held an advanced position alone under heavy fire while awaiting reinforcements.

In October 1915, in Haiti, Daly was part of a 40-man reconnaissance patrol. While crossing a river at night it was ambushed by some 400 Cacos guerrillas. The marines had one machine-gun, carried on a mule. The patrol fought their way back to the river bank, but the mule carrying the gun was killed and fell in the river. During the night, as the Cacos attacked again, the patrol commander Major Butler called for someone to recover the gun. Daly volunteered, found the mule and returned with the gun. After daybreak, the column attacked in three directions, one party being commanded by Daly; all three broke through the ring of Cacos. Daly was awarded his second Medal of Honor.

Emperor Haile Selassie

'Everyone will now be mobilized and all boys old enough to carry a spear will be sent to Addis Ababa. Married men will take their wives to carry food and to cook. Those without wives will take a woman without a husband. Women with small babies need not go. The blind, those who cannot walk, or for any reason cannot carry a spear, are exempted. Anyone found at home after receipt of this order will be hanged.'

Mobilization Order by Emperor Haile Selassie 1935

In October 1935, Italian forces from Somaliland and Eritrea invaded Abyssinia (Ethiopia). Abyssinia was ruled by His Imperial Majesty Haile Selassie I (1892–1975), Conquering Lion of the Tribe of Judah, King of Kings of Ethiopia and Elect of God, who taken the throne in 1930.

The Italian dictator Benito Mussolini invaded Abyssinia in order to boost his domestic popularity at a time when Italy was in economic crisis. He sent in almost half a million men and 450 aircraft. At first, despite the overwhelming technical superiority enjoyed by the Italians, the campaign did not go smoothly. Only after the appointment of Marshal Badoglio as commander were the Italians finally able to defeat the Abyssinians at Maych'ew. Although Badoglio had initially opposed the invasion, this did not deter him from taking the title of duke of Addis Ababa on his return to Italy after the campaign.

In fact Abyssinian resistance was never completely crushed. Haile Selassie proclaimed to his people: 'Be cunning, be savage. Do not mass as now, hide, strike suddenly; fight the nomad war.'

In May 1936, Haile Selassie left Abyssinia in a British ship, and in June spoke to the Assembly of the League of Nations in Geneva. On being introduced by the President of the Assembly as His Imperial Majesty, the emperor of Ethiopia, Italian journalists in the galleries jeered, heckled and whistled. It later transpired that they had been issued with whistles by Mussolini's son-in-law Count Ciano. After waiting for the hecklers to be ejected, Haile Selassie began:

> I, Haile Selassie I, Emperor of Ethiopia, am here today to claim that justice, which is due to my people, and the assistance promised to it eight months ago, when fifty nations asserted that aggression had been committed in violation of international treaties.

He pointed out that the same European states that found in Ethiopia's favour at the League of Nations were now refusing it credit and war supplies while aiding Italy, which was using chemical weapons against military and civilian targets. The League of Nations did nothing, thereby giving encouragement to Hitler and Mussolini to embark on fresh acts of aggression. Haile Selassie went into exile in England.

The invasion of Abyssinia proved a strategic blunder. When Italy entered the Second World War on 10 June 1940, its occupation forces in Abyssinia pushed out to seize outposts in Anglo-Egyptian Sudan, the British colony of Kenya and occupied British Somaliland. Although the Italians greatly outnumbered British forces in the region, they were cut off from reinforcement and supply, and soon adopted a defensive frame of mind. In Abyssinia they found themselves facing not only the British, but also Abyssinian rebels, or 'Patriots' as they were called.

A conference in Khartoum in October 1940, attended by Haile Selassie, General Wavell (British C-in-C Middle East), and other senior British commanders, adopted a strategy for expelling the Italians from East Africa and Egypt. This included aid to Haile Selassie to free his country. The Patriots,

trained by the British Special Operations Executive (SOE), would secure an area to which the emperor could return. Major Orde Wingate was appointed as adviser to help train the Patriots.

The Italians were defeated in a series of operations outside Abyssinia, including the Western Desert, Eritrea and Somaliland, which led to the isolation of their forces in Abyssinia. In January 1941, the British began their campaign to drive the Italians out of the country. Wingate and the Patriots, whom he called Gideon Force, played a key role, securing a stronghold for Haile Selassie at Gojjam. Not content with this, Wingate – through a combination of guerrilla tactics and bluff – persuaded the Italians to surrender a large force at Debra Markos, and the emperor re-entered his capital on 5 May 1941. Another 8000-plus Italian troops capitulated at Addis Derra on 20 May. Meanwhile the main British force and the Patriots closed in on the final Italian stronghold in the mountains at Amba Alagi, finally securing its surrender on 16 May. After six months of mopping-up operations, Abyssinia was finally free of the invaders by November.

WINSTON CHURCHILL

'Let us to the task.'

WINSTON CHURCHILL
AS FIRST LORD OF THE ADMIRALTY, 27 JANUARY 1940

On the outbreak of the Second World War, Winston Churchill (1874–1965) was appointed First Lord of the Admiralty, a post he had also held at the start of the First World War. He had been out of office for more than ten years, but was well aware of the inadequate state of Britain's defences, and had spoken often and at length on the subject. Now, back in office, he was even better placed to learn about the slow pace of pre-war rearmament: from insufficient destroyers to the lack of defences of the principal naval base at Scapa in the Orkneys.

On 27 January 1940, after Germany had overrun Poland, but before the invasion of France and the Low Countries, Churchill addressed a meeting at the Free Trade Hall in Manchester. His speech was a masterly overview of the situation: the reasons for rationing; the fact that the burden of the war was, for the moment, being borne by the Royal Navy; and in particular the need for munitions and equipment for the army, which had been badly neglected in the belated efforts to rearm in the late 1930s, while not forgetting the needs of the Navy and Royal Air Force. He ended:

> Come then: let us to the task, to the battle, to the toil – each to our part, each to our station. Fill the armies, rule the air, pour out the munitions, strangle the U-boats, sweep the mines, plough the land, build the ships, guard the streets, succour the wounded, uplift the downcast, and honour the brave. Let us go forward together in all parts of the Empire, in all parts of the Island. There is not a week, nor a day, nor an hour to lose.

THE RIGHT MAN IN A CRISIS

In early May pressure in Parliament and in certain sections of the press was increasingly exerted on the Conservative prime minister, Neville Chamberlain, to hand over the post to Winston Churchill. On 9 May, Chamberlain told Churchill that he would recommend to the king that he, Churchill, should be appointed prime minister. Early on 10 May 1940, German forces attacked Holland, Belgium and France. Chamberlain's reaction was to remain in post on the grounds that now was not

the time to switch leaders. However, he was persuaded that this was unacceptable both to a substantial part of the Conservative Parliamentary Party and to the whole Labour Party; the latter having been invited to join in a National Government, which was seen as a necessary step in uniting the country in the present crisis. On the evening of 10 May, Winston Churchill became prime minister.

On 13 May, Churchill asked the House of Commons to express its confidence in the new administration. It was a pivotal occasion. Churchill was by no means popular with all Conservatives. The Labour Party had yet to prove that it could adapt successfully to working with its political opponents. The news from France and Flanders was becoming more depressing each day. People were thoroughly confused and becoming increasingly apprehensive. Churchill rose and said:

I beg to move, that this House welcomes the formation of a Government representing the united and inflexible resolve of the nation to prosecute the war with Germany to a victorious conclusion.

On Friday evening last I received His Majesty's Commission to form a new Administration. It was the evident wish and will of Parliament and the nation that this should be conceived on the broadest possible basis and that it should include all parties, both those who supported the late Government and also the parties of the Opposition. I have completed the most important part of this task. A War Cabinet has been formed of five Members, representing, with the Opposition Liberals, the unity of the nation. The three party Leaders have agreed to serve, either in the War Cabinet or in high executive office. The Three Fighting Services have been filled. It was necessary that this should be done in a single day, on account of the extreme urgency and rigour of events. A number of other positions, key positions, were filled yesterday and I am submitting a further list to His Majesty to-night. I hope to complete the appointment of the principal Ministers tomorrow. The appointment of the other Ministers usually takes a little longer, but I trust that, when Parliament meets again, this part of my task will be completed, and that the administration will be complete in all respects.

I considered it in the public interest to suggest that the House should be summoned to meet today. Mr Speaker agreed, and took the necessary steps, in accordance with the powers conferred upon him by the Resolution of the House. At the end of the proceedings today, the Adjournment of the House will be proposed until Tuesday 21st May, with, of course, provision for earlier meeting, if need be. The business to be considered during that week will be notified to Members at the earliest opportunity. I now invite the House, by the Motion which stands in my name, to record its approval of the steps taken and to declare its confidence in the new Government.

To form an Administration of this scale and complexity is a serious undertaking in itself, but it must be remembered that we are in the preliminary stage of one of the greatest battles in history, that we are in action in many other points in Norway and in Holland, that we have to be prepared in the Mediterranean, that the air battle is continuous and that many preparations, such as have been indicated by my honourable Friend below the Gangway, have to be made here at home. In this crisis I hope I may be pardoned if I do not address the House at any length today. I hope that any of my friends and colleagues, or former colleagues, who are affected by the political reconstruction, will make allowance, all allowance, for any lack of ceremony with which it has been necessary to act. I would say to the House, as I said to those who have joined this Government: 'I have nothing to offer but blood, toil, tears and sweat.'

We have before us an ordeal of the most grievous kind. We have before us many, many long months of struggle and of suffering. You ask what is our policy? I can say: It is to wage war, by sea, by land and air, with all our might and with all the strength that God can give us; to wage war against a monstrous tyranny, never surpassed in the dark, lamentable, catalogue of human crime. That is our policy. You ask what is our aim? I can answer in one word: It is victory at all costs, victory in spite of all terror, victory, however long and hard the road may be; for without victory, there is no survival. Let that be realised; no survival for the British Empire, no survival for all that the British Empire has stood for, no survival for the urge and impulse of the ages, that mankind will move forward towards its goal. But I take up my task with buoyancy and hope. I feel sure that our cause will not be suffered to fail among men. At this time I feel entitled to claim the aid of all and I say, 'Come then, let us go forward together and with all our united strength'.

When he finished, there was a momentary stunned silence, followed by a standing ovation from all sides of the House. Churchill walked out of the Chamber past the Speaker's Chair almost in tears.

Outside he met Desmond Morton, who had provided him with information from secret sources about Hitler's rearmament from 1933 onwards, and now one of his assistants. Churchill said to Morton: 'That got the sods, didn't it?'

Churchill's first speech as prime minister was perhaps one of the most important in history. It told the world that Britain would fight to the death under a leader who expressed the will of the nation clearly, starkly and truthfully.

THE MIRACLE OF DUNKIRK

On 4 June 1940, Churchill again addressed the House of Commons. The evacuation of the bulk of the British Expeditionary Force (BEF) through Dunkirk had just been completed; although there were still substantial British forces south of the Somme fighting alongside the French.

The Allied strategy began to go wrong in France and Flanders the day the German offensive began on 10 May. The Belgians, having retained a stance of strict neutrality up to that point, appealed for help. Anticipating this last-minute change of heart, the Allies had already drawn up contingency plans. The whole of the BEF and two French armies, the latter consisting of 30 divisions including the whole of the French reserve, rushed into Belgium, leaving the defensive positions they had spent the winter constructing. This was exactly what Hitler wanted. While one army group of 29 divisions kept the Allies occupied in Belgium, another army group of 45 divisions, including three Panzer corps, struck through the thinly defended Ardennes and crossed the River Meuse between Sedan and Dinant. This army group sliced through to the French coast north of the River Somme, curving north to take Boulogne and Calais, cutting the Allied northern armies (including the BEF), off from those in the south. As a result, the BEF was cut off from its main supply ports, which extended from St Nazaire round to Dieppe (Dunkirk was not a main supply port; all the BEF's ammunition and other crucial war fighting stocks were located further south). With every division committed, the French had insufficient troops to create a reserve to mount a counter-attack to hack through the tail of the German armoured spearheads, which would have brought them to a halt; a prospect that worried the German high command greatly. Churchill, visiting the French commander-in-chief, General Maurice Gamelin, asked where his reserve was, to be told 'there isn't one'. So although counter-stroke schemes to attack the German armoured 'corridor' were discussed in the French high command, French incompetence actually made them unachievable.

With the French and Belgian armies retreating on its flanks, cut off from its supplies and threatened on both flanks, the BEF had no alternative but to retreat to Dunkirk and evacuation. The evacuation was successful thanks to three factors. First, the BEF carried out a masterly fighting retreat. Only well-trained and disciplined troops could have achieved what they did. Many armies have found retreat in the face of a more powerful and determined enemy more than they can handle, and have either disintegrated before surrendering, or been cut to pieces with huge loss. The former was the fate of both the Belgians and the French in this campaign. The manner in which the BEF fought earned the respect of their adversaries: the Germans assessed the British soldier as a 'fighter of high value' in their report on the campaign.

Second, the Royal Air Force, although much maligned at the time by the BEF, prevented the *Luftwaffe* from achieving air supremacy, and hence a free run over the beaches and Dunkirk harbour without interference. The *Luftwaffe* wreaked havoc enough as it was.

Third, above all, the success of the evacuation was only possible thanks to sea power; to the skill and total dominance of the Royal Navy, not to any mystical intervention.

Churchill, having touched on many aspects of the evacuation, including the part played by each of the three fighting services, turned to the points he wished to get across: to correct the perception, at least among the civil population, that the Dunkirk operation was a kind of victory, or at least a miracle; and to brace the House and the Nation, for the exertions demanded in the future:

> *Nevertheless, our thankfulness at the escape of our Army and so many men, whose loved ones have passed through an agonising week, must not blind us to the fact that what has happened in France and Belgium is a colossal military disaster. The French Army has been weakened, the Belgian Army has been lost, a large part of those fortified lines upon which so much faith had been reposed is gone, many valuable mining districts and factories have passed into the enemy's possession, the whole of the Channel ports are in his hands, with all the tragic consequences that follow from that, and we must expect another blow to be struck almost immediately at us or at France. We are told that Herr Hitler has a plan for invading the British Isles. This has often been thought of before. When Napoleon lay at Boulogne for a year with his flat-bottomed boats and his Grand Army, he was told by someone. 'There are bitter weeds in England.' There are certainly a great many more of them since the British Expeditionary Force returned.*
>
> *The whole question of home defence against invasion is, of course, powerfully affected by the fact that we have for the time being in this Island incomparably more powerful military forces than we have ever had at any moment in this war or the last. But this will not continue. We shall not be content with a defensive war. We have our duty to our Ally. We have to reconstitute and build up the British Expeditionary Force once again under its gallant Commander-in-Chief, Lord Gort. All this is in train; but in the interval we must put our defences in this Island into such a high state of organization that the fewest possible numbers will be required to give effective security and that the largest possible potential of offensive may be realized. On this we are now engaged.*

NO SURRENDER TO TYRANNY

At this point, Churchill suggested that these defence arrangements should be discussed in secret session 'without the restraint imposed by the fact that they will be read the next day by the enemy'. After dealing with the subject of restraints on enemy aliens and the activities of Fifth Columnists, he continued:

Turning once again, and this time more generally, to the question of invasion, I would observe that there had never been a period in all these long centuries of which we boast when an absolute guarantee against invasion, still less against serious raids, could have been given to our people. In the days of Napoleon the same wind which could have carried his transports across the Channel might have driven away the blockading fleet. There was always a chance, and it is a chance that has excited and befooled the imagination of many Continental tyrants. Many are the tales that are told. We are assured that novel methods will be adopted, and when we see the originality of malice, the ingenuity of aggression, which our enemy displays, we certainly prepare ourselves for every kind of novel stratagem and every kind of brutal and treacherous manoeuvre. I think no idea so outlandish that it should not be considered and viewed with a searching, but at the same time, I hope, with a steady eye. We must never forget the solid assurances of sea power and those which belong to air power if it can be locally exercised.

I have, myself, full confidence that if all do their duty, if nothing is neglected, and if the best arrangements are made, as they are being made, we shall prove ourselves once again able to defend our Island home, to ride out the storm of war, and to outlive the menace of tyranny, if necessary for years, if necessary alone. At any rate, that is what we are trying to do. This is the resolve of His Majesty's Government, every man of them. That is the will of Parliament and the nation. The British Empire and the French Republic, linked together in their cause and in their need, will defend to the death their native soil, aiding each other like good comrades to the utmost of their strength. Even though large tracts of Europe and many old and famous States have fallen or may fall into the grip of the Gestapo and all the odious apparatus of Nazi rule, we shall not flag or fail. We shall go on to the end, we shall fight in France, we shall fight on the seas and oceans, we shall fight with growing confidence in the air, we shall defend our Island, whatever the cost may be, we shall fight on the beaches, we shall fight on the landing grounds, we shall fight in the fields and in the streets, we shall fight in the hills; we shall never surrender, and even if, which I do not for a moment believe, this Island, or a large part of it were subjugated and starving, then our Empire beyond the seas, armed and guarded by the British Fleet, would carry on the struggle, until, in God's good time, the New World, with all its power and might, steps forward to the rescue and liberation of the old.

When he delivered this speech, Churchill did not regard the evacuation from Dunkirk as marking the end of British involvement in France. As he spoke, there were still several thousand British troops in France south of the Somme. Churchill planned to reinforce them, in effect creating a second BEF, not under Lord Gort, but Lieutenant General Sir Alan Brooke, formerly the commander of the BEF's II Corps. Brooke was sent back to France via Cherbourg, but soon assessed the situation as hopeless, and with Churchill's permission ordered the evacuation of all remaining British troops in France.

Churchill must also have been well aware of the fact that although there were indeed substantial 'military forces' in Britain, they were hardly powerful since most of their equipment had been lost at

Dunkirk, and there was in fact enough to equip only one division. Knowing this, it is all the more remarkable that he could be so 'upbeat'.

On 17 June, Churchill broadcast from London, the collapse that Brooke had forecast came about when Marshal Pétain sued for an armistice:

> The news from France is very bad and I grieve for the gallant French people who have fallen into this terrible misfortune. Nothing will alter our feelings towards them or our faith that the genius of France will rise again. What has happened in France makes no difference to our actions and purpose. We have become the sole champions now in arms to defend the world cause. We shall do our best to be worthy of this high honour. We shall defend our Island home, and with the British Empire we shall fight on unconquerable until the curse of Hitler is lifted from the brows of mankind. We are sure that in the end all will come right.

Churchill's allusion to 'the world cause', was especially aimed at the United States, and the underlying message was: 'join us now in fighting Hitler, because if we don't defeat him, you will have to fight him in the end. It would be better for you to face this challenge while we are still around to assist'.

'THEIR FINEST HOUR'

On 18 June 1940, Churchill delivered what is arguably his best-known speech, first to the House of Commons, and then broadcast by the BBC. He wanted the world to know that Britain had no intention of following France's example of capitulation, despite Italy's entry into the war:

> I spoke the other day of the colossal military disaster, which occurred when the French High Command failed to withdraw the northern Armies from Belgium at the moment when they knew the French front was decisively broken at Sedan and on the Meuse. This delay entailed the loss of fifteen or sixteen French divisions and threw out of action for the critical period the whole of the British Expeditionary Force. Our Army and 120,000 French troops were indeed rescued by the British Navy from Dunkirk but only with the loss of their cannon, vehicles and modern equipment. This loss inevitably took some weeks to repair, and in the first two of those weeks the battle in France had been lost. When we consider the heroic resistance made by the French Army against heavy odds in this battle, the enormous losses inflicted upon the enemy and the evident exhaustion of the enemy, it may well be the thought that these 25 divisions of the best-trained and best-equipped troops might have turned the scale. However, General Weygand had to fight without them. Only three British divisions or their equivalent were able to stand in the line with their French comrades. They have suffered severely, but they have fought well. We sent every man we could to France as fast as we could re-equip and transport their formations.

I am not reciting these facts for the purpose of recrimination. That I judge to be utterly futile and even harmful. We cannot afford it. I recite them in order to explain why it was we did not have, as we could have had, between twelve and fourteen British divisions fighting in the line in this great battle instead of only three. Now I put all this aside. I put it on the shelf, from which all historians, when they have the time, will select their documents to tell their stories. We have to think of the future and not of the past. This also applies in a small way to our own affairs at home. There are many who would hold an inquest in the House of Commons on the conduct of the Government – and of Parliaments, for they are in it, too – during the years which led up to this catastrophe. They seek to indict those who were responsible for the guidance of our affairs. Let each man search his conscience and search his speeches. I frequently search mine.

Of this I am quite sure, that if we open a quarrel between the past and the present, we shall find that we have lost the future. Therefore, I cannot accept the drawing of any distinctions between Members of the present Government. It was formed at a moment of crisis in order to unite all the Parties and all sections of opinion. It has received the almost unanimous support of both Houses of Parliament. Its Members are going to stand together, and, subject to the authority of the House of Commons, we are going to govern the country and fight the war. It is absolutely necessary at a time like this that every Minister who tries each day to do his duty shall be respected: and their subordinates must know that their chiefs are not threatened men, men who are here today and gone tomorrow, but that their directions must be punctually and faithfully obeyed. Without this concentrated power we cannot face what lies before us. I should not think it would be very advantageous for the House to prolong this Debate this afternoon under conditions of public stress. Many facts are not clear that will be clear in a short time. We are to have a secret Session on Thursday, and I should think that would be a better opportunity for the many earnest expressions of opinion which Members will desire to make and for the House to discuss vital matters without everything read the next morning by our dangerous foes.

The disastrous military events which have happened during the past fortnight have not come to me with any sense of surprise. Indeed I indicated to the House that the worst possibilities were open; and I made it perfectly clear then that whatever happened in France would make no difference to the resolve of Britain and the British Empire to fight on, 'if necessary for years, if necessary alone'. During the last few days we have successfully brought off the great majority of the troops we had on the line of communication in France; and seven-eighths of the troops we sent out to France since the beginning of the war – that is to say, about 350,000 out of 400,000 men – are safely back in this country. Others are still fighting with the French, and fighting with considerable success in their local encounters with the enemy. We have also brought back a great mass of stores, rifles and munitions of all kinds which have been accumulated in France during the last nine months.

We have, therefore, in this Island today a very large and powerful military force. This force comprises all our best-trained and our finest troops, including scores of thousands of those who have already measured their quality against the Germans and found themselves at no disadvantage. We have under arms at the present time in this Island over a million and a quarter men. Behind these we have the Local Defence Volunteers, numbering over half a million, only a portion of whom, however, are yet armed with rifles or other firearms. We have incorporated into our Defence Forces every man for whom we have a weapon. We expect very large additions to our weapons in the near future, and in preparation for this we intend forthwith to call up, drill and train further large numbers. Those who are not called up, or else are employed during the vast business of munitions production in all its branches – their ramifications are innumerable – will serve their country best by remaining at their ordinary work until they receive their summons. We have also over here Dominion armies. The Canadians had actually landed in France, but have now been safely withdrawn, much disappointed, but in perfect order, with all their artillery and equipment. And these very high-class forces from the Dominions will now take part in the defence of the Mother Country.

Lest the account which I have given of these large forces should raise the question: Why did they not take part in the great battle of France? I must make it clear that; apart from the divisions training and organizing at home, only 12 divisions were equipped to fight upon a scale which justified their being sent abroad. And this was fully up to the number which the French had been led to expect would be available in France at the ninth month of the war. The rest of our forces at home have a fighting value for home defence which will, of course, steadily increase every week that passes. Thus, the invasion of Great Britain would at this time require the transportation across the sea of hostile armies on a very large scale, and after they had been so transported they would have to be continually maintained with all the masses of munitions and supplies that are required for continuous battle – as continuous battle it will surely be.

Here is where we come to the Navy – and after all we have a Navy. Some people seem to forget we have a Navy. We must remind them. For the last thirty years I have been concerned in discussions about the possibilities of oversea invasion, and I took the responsibility on behalf of the Admiralty, at the beginning of the last war, of allowing all regular troops to be sent out of the country. That was very serious step to take, because our territorials had only just been called up and were quite untrained. Therefore, this Island was for several months particularly denuded of fighting troops. The Admiralty had confidence at that time in their ability to prevent a mass invasion even though at that time the Germans had a magnificent battle fleet in the proportion of 10 to 16, even though they were capable of fighting a general engagement every day and any day, whereas now they have only a couple of heavy ships worth speaking of – the Scharnhorst and the Gneisenau. We are also told that the Italian Navy is to come out and gain sea superiority in these waters. If they seriously intend it, I shall only say that we shall be delighted to offer Signor Mussolini a free and safeguarded passage through the Strait of Gibraltar in order that he may play the part to which he aspires. There is a general curiosity in the British Fleet to find out whether the Italians are up to the level they were in the last war or whether they have fallen off at all.

Therefore it seems to me that as far as a sea-borne invasion on a great scale is concerned, we are far more capable of meeting it today than we were at many periods in the last war and during the early months of this war, before our other troops were trained, and while the BEF had proceeded abroad. Now, the Navy have never pretended to be able to prevent raids by bodies of 5,000 or 10,000 men flung suddenly across and thrown ashore at several points on the coast some dark night or foggy morning. The efficacy of sea power, especially under modern conditions, depends upon the invading force being of large size. It has to be of large size, in view of our military strength, to be of any use. If it is of large size, then the Navy have something they can find and meet and, as it were, bite on. Now, we must remember that even five divisions, however lightly equipped, would require 200 to 250 ships and with modern air reconnaissance and photography it would not be easy to collect such an armada, marshal it, and conduct it across the sea without any powerful naval forces to escort it, and there would be very great possibilities, to put it mildly, that this armada would be intercepted long before it reached the coast, and all the men drowned in the sea or, at worst blown to pieces with their equipment while they were trying to land. We also have a great system of minefields, recently strongly reinforced, through which we alone know the channels. If the enemy tries to sweep passages through these minefields, it will be the task of the Navy to destroy the mine-sweepers and any other forces employed to protect them. There should be no difficulty in this, owing to our great superiority at sea.

Those are the regular, well-tested, well-proved arguments on which we have relied during many years in peace and war. But the question is whether there are any new methods by which those solid assurances can be circumvented. Odd as it may seem, some attention has been given to this by the Admiralty, whose prime duty and responsibility is to destroy any large sea-borne expedition before it reaches, or at the moment when it reaches these shores. It would not be a good thing for me to go into details of this. It might suggest ideas to other people which they have not thought of, and they would not be likely to give us any of their ideas in exchange. All I will say is that untiring vigilance and mind-searching must be devoted to the subject, because the enemy is crafty and cunning and full of novel treacheries and stratagems. The House may be assured that the utmost ingenuity is being displayed and imagination is being evoked from large numbers of competent officers, well-trained in tactics and thoroughly up to date, to measure and counterwork novel possibilities. Untiring vigilance and untiring searching of the mind is being, and must be, devoted to the subject, because, remember, the enemy is crafty and there is no dirty trick he will not do.

Some people will ask why, then, was it that the British Navy was not able to prevent the movement of a large army from Germany into Norway across the Skagerrak? But the conditions in the Channel and in the North Sea are in no way like those that prevail in the Skagerrak. In the Skagerrak, because of the distance, we could give no air support to our surface ships, and consequently, lying as we did close to the enemy's main air power, we were compelled to use only our submarines. We could not enforce the defensive blockade or interruption which is possible from surface vessels. Our submarines took a heavy toll but could not, by themselves, prevent an invasion of Norway. In the Channel and in the North Sea, on the other hand, our superior naval surface forces, aided by our submarines, will operate with close and effective air assistance.

This brings me naturally, to the great question of invasion from the air, and of the impending struggle between the British and German Air Forces. It seems quite clear that no invasion on a scale beyond the capacity of our land forces to crush speedily is likely to take place from the air until our Air Force has been definitely overpowered. In the meantime there may be raids by parachute troops and attempted descents of airborne soldiers. We should be able to give those gentry a warm reception both in the air and on the ground, if they reach it in any condition to continue the dispute. But the great question is: Can we break Hitler's air weapon? Now, of course, it is a very great pity that we have not got an Air Force at least equal to that of the most powerful enemy within striking distance of these shores. But we have a very powerful Air Force which has proved itself far superior in quality, both in men and in many types of machine, to what we have met so far in the numerous and fierce air battles which have been fought with the Germans. In France, where we were at a considerable disadvantage and lost many machines on the ground when they were standing round the aerodromes, we were accustomed to inflict in the air losses of as much as two and two-and-a-half to one. In the fighting over Dunkirk, which was a sort of no-man's land, we undoubtedly beat the German Air Force, and gained mastery of the local air, inflicting here a loss of three or four to one day after day. Anyone who looked at the photographs which were published a week or so ago of the re-embarkation, showing the masses of troops assembled on the beach and forming an ideal target for hours at a time, must realize that this re-embarkation would not have been possible unless the enemy had resigned all hope of recovering air superiority at that time and at that place.

In the defence of this Island the advantages to the defenders will be much greater than they were in the fighting around Dunkirk. We hope to improve on the rate of three or four to one which was realized at Dunkirk; and in addition all our injured machines and their crews which get down safely – and surprisingly, a very great many injured machines and men do get down safely in modern air fighting – all of these will fall, in an attack upon these Islands, on friendly soil and live to fight another day; whereas all the injured enemy machines and their complements will be total losses as far as the war is concerned.

During the great battle in France, we gave very powerful and continuous aid to the French Army, both by fighters and bombers; but in spite of every kind of pressure we would never allow the entire metropolitan fighter strength of the Air Force to be consumed. This decision was painful, but it was also right, because the fortunes of the battle in France could not have been decisively affected even if we had thrown in our entire fighter force. That battle was lost by the unfortunate strategical opening by the extraordinary and unforeseen power of the armoured columns, and by the great preponderance of the German Army in numbers. Our fighter Air Force might easily have been exhausted as a mere accident in that great struggle, and then we should have found ourselves at the present time in a very serious plight. But as it is, I am happy to inform the House that our fighter strength is stronger at the present time relatively to the Germans who have suffered terrible losses, than it has ever been; and consequently we believe ourselves possessed of the capacity to continue the war in the air under better conditions than we have ever experienced before. I look forward confidently to the exploits of our fighter pilots – these splendid men, this brilliant youth – who will have the glory of saving their native land, their island home, and all they love, from the most deadly of all attacks.

There remains, of course, the danger of bombing attacks, which will certainly be made very soon upon us by the bomber forces of the enemy. It is true that the German bomber force is superior in numbers to ours; but we have a very large bomber force also, which we shall use to strike at military targets in Germany without intermission. I do not at all underrate the severity of the ordeal which lies before us; but I believe that our countrymen will show themselves capable of standing up to it, like the brave men of Barcelona, and will be able to stand up to it, and carry on in spite of it, at least as well as any other people in the world. Much will depend upon this; every man and every woman will have the chance to show the finest qualities of their race, and render the highest service to their cause. For all of us, at this time, whatever out sphere, our station, our occupation or our duties, it will be a help to remember the famous lines:

'He nothing common did or mean,
Upon that memorable scene.'

I have thought it right upon this occasion to give the House and the country some indication of the solid, practical grounds upon which we base our inflexible resolve to continue the war. There are a good many people who say, 'Never mind. Win or lose, sink or swim, better die than submit to tyranny – and such a tyranny.' And I do not dissociate myself from them. But I can assure them that our professional advisers of all three Services unitedly advise that we should carry on the war, and that there are good and reasonable hopes of final victory. We have fully informed and consulted all the self-governing Dominions, these great communities far beyond the oceans who have been built up on our laws and on our civilization, and who are absolutely free to choose their course, but are absolutely devoted to the ancient Motherland, and who feel themselves inspired by the same emotions which lead me to stake our all upon duty and honour. We have fully consulted them, and I have received from their Prime Minister, Mr Mackenzie King of Canada, Mr Menzies of Australia, Mr Fraser of New Zealand, and General Smuts of South Africa – that wonderful man with his immense profound mind, and his eye watching from a distance the whole panorama of European affairs – I have received from all these eminent men, who all have Governments behind them elected on wide franchises, who are all there because they represent the will of their people, messages couched in the most moving terms in which they endorse our decision to fight on, and declare themselves ready to share our fortunes and to persevere to the end. That is what we are going to do.

We may now ask ourselves: In what way has our position worsened since the beginning of the war? It has worsened by the fact that the Germans have conquered a large part of the coast line of

Western Europe, and many small countries have been overrun by them. This aggravates the possibilities of air attack and adds to our naval preoccupations. It in no way diminishes, but on the contrary definitely increases, the power of our long-distance blockade. Similarly, the entrance of Italy into the war increases the power of our long-distance blockade. We have stopped the worst leak by that. We do not know whether military resistance will come to an end in France or not, but should it do so, then of course the Germans will be able to concentrate their forces, both military and industrial, upon us. But for the reasons I have given to the House these will not be found so easy to apply. If invasion has become more imminent, as no doubt it has, we, being relieved from the task of maintaining a large army in France, have far larger and more efficient forces to meet it. If Hitler can bring under his despotic control the industries of the countries he has conquered, this will add greatly to his already vast armament output. On the other hand, this will not happen immediately, and we are now assured of immense, continuous and increasing support in supplies and munitions of all kinds from the United States: and especially of aeroplanes and pilots from the Dominions and across the oceans coming from regions which are beyond the reach of enemy bombers. I do not see how any of these factors can operate to our detriment on balance before the winter comes: and the winter will impose a strain on the Nazi regime, with almost all Europe writhing and starving under its cruel heel, which, for all their ruthlessness, will run them very hard. We must not forget that from the moment when we declared war on the 3rd September it was always possible for Germany to turn all her Air Force upon this country, together with any other devices of invasion she might conceive, and that France could have done little or nothing to prevent her doing so.

Winston Churchill visiting the city of Manchester after a German bombing raid. Churchill's unwavering resolve and rousing oratory boosted Allied morale throughout the war

We have, therefore, lived under this danger in a slightly modified form, during all these months. In the meanwhile, however, we have enormously improved our methods of defence, and we have learned what we had no right to assume at the beginning, namely, that the individual aircraft and the individual British pilot have a sure and definite superiority. Therefore, in casting up this dread balance-sheet and contemplating our dangers with a disillusioned eye, I see great reason for intense vigilance and exertion, but none whatever for panic or despair.

During the first four years of the last war the Allies experienced nothing but disaster and disappointment. That was our constant fear: one blow after another, terrible losses, frightful dangers. Everything miscarried. And yet at the end of those four years the morale of the Allies was higher than that of the Germans, who had moved from one aggressive triumph to another, and who stood everywhere triumphant invaders, of the lands into which they had broken. During that war we repeatedly asked ourselves the question: How are we going to win? and no one was ever able to answer it with much precision, until at the end, quite suddenly, quite unexpectedly, our terrible foe collapsed before us, and we were so glutted with victory that in our folly we threw it away.

We do not know yet what will happen in France or whether the French resistance will be prolonged, both in France and in the French Empire overseas. The French Government will be throwing away great opportunities and casting adrift their future if they do not continue the war in accordance with their Treaty obligations, from which we have not felt able to release them. The House will have read the historic declaration in which, at the desire of many Frenchmen – and of our own hearts – we have proclaimed our willingness at the darkest hour in French history to conclude a union of common citizenship in this struggle. However matters may go in France or with the French Government, or other French Governments, we in this Island and in the British Empire will never lose our sense of comradeship with the French people. If we are now called upon to endure what they have been suffering, we shall emulate their courage, and if final victory rewards our toils they shall share the gains, aye, and freedom shall be restored to all. We abate nothing of our just demands, not one jot or tittle do we recede. Czechs, Poles, Norwegians, Dutch, Belgians have joined their causes to our own. All these shall be restored.

What General Weygand called the Battle of France is over. I expect that the Battle of Britain is about to begin. Upon this battle depends the survival of Christian civilization. Upon it depends our own British life, and the long continuity of our institutions and Empire. The whole fury and might of the enemy must very soon be turned on us. Hitler knows that he will have to break us in this Island or lose the war. If we can stand up to him, all Europe may be free and the life of the world may move forward into broad, sunlit uplands. But if we fail the whole world, including the United Slates, including all that we have known and cared for, will sink into the abyss of a new Dark Age made more sinister, and perhaps more protracted, by the lights of perverted science. Let us therefore brace ourselves to our duties and so bear ourselves that if the British Empire and its Commonwealth last for a thousand years, men will still say, 'This was their finest hour'.

ADMIRAL SIR ANDREW CUNNINGHAM

At the height of the battle to evacuate British forces from Crete in April 1941, it began to seem that the *Luftwaffe* might sink every Royal Navy warship taking part. The commander-in-chief of the Mediterranean Fleet, Admiral Sir Andrew Cunningham (1883–1963), was being pressed by his staff to abandon the evacuation. He gave his robust response in the signal:

> *It takes the Navy three years to build a ship. It would take three hundred years to build a new reputation. The evacuation will continue.*

And so it did, but at a terrible cost. Cunningham began the operation with 4 battleships, 1 carrier, 11 cruisers, a minelayer and 32 destroyers. Two battleships and the carrier were badly damaged; 3 cruisers were sunk and 5 severely damaged; 6 destroyers were sunk and seven seriously damaged. But he had assured the Admiralty that: 'he was ready and willing to continue the evacuation as long as a ship remained to do so, realising that it was against all tradition to leave troops deliberately in enemy hands'.

Some days before, it became apparent that the Germans were attempting to reinforce their airborne troops on Crete by sea. The *Luftwaffe* fiercely attacked any ships trying to interfere, sinking and badly damaging some of them. Cunningham signalled:

> *Stick it out. Navy must not let Army down. No enemy forces must reach Crete by sea.*

And indeed, no German forces did reach the island by this route.

By the time Cunningham came to command the British fleet in the Mediterranean, he had served ashore in the Second Boer War, and commanded a destroyer in the First World War. He was tough, ruthless and unforgiving of inefficiency. When his destroyer, HMS *Scorpion*, was hit and set ablaze, and a stoker petty officer came to tell him the mess deck was on fire, he merely said: 'Then put it out'.

He was given to colourful language. At the Battle of Matapan, seeing an Italian cruiser hit by two broadsides, he leant over the side of the bridge to say: 'Good! Give the next bugger some of the same'.

One officer said of him:

> *Like the giant panda he had endearing qualities, but he could bite if you got too close.*

Cunningham was one of the great British fighting admirals of the Second World War.

ADOLF HITLER

Before and during the Second World War, Adolf Hitler (1889–1945) often alluded to his service as a private and later as a corporal in the First World War. He did so to reproach his generals with lack of similar frontline service, in the knowledge that they dared not respond. But, more importantly, he also wanted those with personal experience or at least memories of that war, every German over 40 years old, including widows, relatives of the dead and wounded and of course old soldiers, to see him as one of them. His message was also intended for the soldiers fighting in his war. Nowhere is this more clearly conveyed than in the speech he delivered on taking personal command of the army on 22 December 1941, at the end of the first six months of his campaign in Russia:

Soldiers – the battle for the liberty of our people and for the security of its future existence is now approaching its culminating and turning point. I know war from the mighty conflict in the West from 1914 to 1918. I experienced personally the horrors of almost all the battles as an ordinary soldier. I was wounded twice and threatened with blindness.

It is the army which bears the weight of the struggle. In these circumstances I have therefore decided in my capacity as Supreme Commander of the German Armed Forces, to assume personally the leadership of the army.

Thus nothing that torments you, weighs upon you, and oppresses you is unknown to me. I alone, after four years of war, never for a moment doubted the resurrection of my people. With my fanatical will, I, a simple German soldier, succeeded after more than 15 years of labour, in uniting once more the whole German nation and in freeing it from the death sentence of Versailles.

My soldiers, you will therefore believe that my heart belongs solely to you, that my will and my work serve unflinchingly the greatness of my people, that my mind and resolution are directed only towards the destruction of the enemy – that is towards the victorious conclusion of this war.

What I can do for you, my soldiers, by way of care and leadership, will be done. What you can do for me and what you will do, I know you will do with loyalty and obedience until the Reich and our German people are finally saved.

A TISSUE OF LIES

The speech begins and ends with a falsehood: the liberty of the German people, both collectively and individually, was not at stake; that is, until Hitler became head of state and subsequently committed the country to war. He bore sole responsibility for the suppression of freedom within Germany and in the territories he annexed. The unfairness of the Treaty of Versailles was a familiar Hitler stance, the inference being that first, Germany was unjustly accused of having instigated the First World War, and second, in consequence had been victimized by the peace treaty that followed. To the first one might respond that Germany was unquestionably the guilty party in precipitating the First World War, and to the second, that she was let off far more lightly than her opponents would have been had the boot ended up on the other foot. What mattered was that the vast majority of his soldiers accepted what he said without question. The German soldiers of the Second World War gave Hitler unswerving loyalty, and few surrendered until continuing to fight was physically impossible. Indeed, from 1944, many fought on long after it must have been clear that there was little hope of victory.

The day before he committed suicide along with his former mistress, by then wife, Eva Braun, Adolf Hitler dictated his 'political testament'. This was aimed at defending his work and career. It is reproduced in full airing his crackpot theories about history, and bellyaching that fate had once more cheated Germany of victory and conquest. If one was searching for one statement that encapsulates the ideas that motivated this ghastly man, it is this:

> More than thirty years have now passed since I in 1914 made my modest contribution as a volunteer in the first World War that was forced upon the Reich.
>
> In these three decades I have been actuated solely by love and loyalty to my people in all my thoughts, acts, and life. They gave me the strength to make the most difficult decisions which have ever confronted mortal man. I have spent my time, my working strength, and my health in these three decades.
>
> It is untrue that I or anyone else in Germany wanted the war in 1939. It was desired and instigated exclusively by those international statesmen who were either of Jewish descent or worked for Jewish interests. I have made too many offers for the control and limitations of armaments, which posterity will not for all time be able to disregard for the responsibility for the outbreak of this war to be laid on me [sic]. I have further never wished that after the first fatal world war a second against England, or even against America, should break out. Centuries will pass away, but out of the ruins of our towns and monuments the hatred against those finally responsible whom we have to thank for everything, International Jewry and its helpers, will grow.

We then get lies shifting the blame for the outbreak of war over Poland to the British, followed by shifting the blame for the millions of deaths suffered in the war onto the Jews:

> Three days before the outbreak of the German–Polish war I again proposed to the British ambassador in Berlin a solution to the German–Polish problem – similar to that in the case of the Saar district, under international control. This offer also cannot be denied. It was only rejected because the leading circles in English politics wanted the war, partly on account of the business hoped for and partly under influence of propaganda organized by International Jewry.
>
> I have also made it quite plain that, if the nations of Europe are again to be regarded as mere shares to be bought and sold by these international conspirators in money and finance, then that race, Jewry, which is the real criminal of this murderous struggle, will be saddled with the responsibility. I further left no one in doubt that this time not only would millions of children of Europe's Aryan people die of hunger, not only would millions of grown men suffer death, and not only hundreds of thousands of women and children be burnt and bombed to death in the towns, without the real criminal having to atone for this guilt, even if by more humane means.
>
> After six years of war, which in spite of all setbacks, will go down one day in history as the most glorious and valiant demonstration of a nation's life purpose, I cannot forsake the city which is the capital of this Reich. As the forces are too small to make any further stand against the enemy attack at this place and our resistance is gradually being weakened by men who are as deluded as they are lacking in initiative, I should like, by remaining in this town, to share my fate with those, the millions

of others, who have also taken upon themselves to do so. Moreover I do not wish to fall into the hands of an enemy who requires a new spectacle organized by the Jews for the amusement of their hysterical masses.

I have decided therefore to remain in Berlin and there of my own free will to choose death at the moment when I believe the position of the Führer and Chancellor itself can no longer be held.

I die with a happy heart, aware of the immeasurable deeds and achievements of our soldiers at the front, our women at home, the achievements of our farmers and workers and the work, unique in history, of our youth who bear my name.

The German people are then exhorted to continue the struggle, followed by a dig at the army, which unlike the air force and navy, he believed had let him down.

That from the bottom of my heart I express my thanks to you all, is just as self-evident as my wish that you should, because of that, on no account give up the struggle, but rather continue it against the enemies of the Fatherland, no matter where, true to the creed of a great Clausewitz. From the sacrifice of our soldiers and from my own unity with them unto death, will in any case spring up in the history of Germany, the seed of a radiant renaissance of the National Socialist movement and thus of the realization of a true community of nations.

Many of the most courageous men and women have decided to unite their lives with mine until the very last. I have begged and finally ordered them not to do this, but to take part in the further battle of the Nation.

I beg the heads of the Armies, the Navy and the Air Force to strengthen by all possible means the spirit of resistance of our soldiers in the National Socialist sense, with special reference to the fact that also I myself, as founder and creator of this movement, have preferred death to cowardly abdication or even capitulation.

May it, at some future time, become part of the code of honour of the German officer – as is already the case in our Navy – that the surrender of a district or of a town is impossible, and that above all the leaders here must march ahead as shining examples, faithfully fulfilling their duty unto death.

Hitler then turned to the task of disposing of possible successors, and in a calculated insult to the army and air force, appointed Karl Dönitz, the head of the navy, to follow in his footsteps.

Before my death I expel the former Reichsmarschall Hermann Göring from the party and deprive him of all rights which he may enjoy by virtue of the decree of June 29th, 1941; and also by virtue of my statement in the Reichstag on September 1st, 1939, I appoint in his place Grossadmiral Dönitz President of the Reich and supreme Commander of the Armed Forces.

Before my death I expel the former Reichsführer-SS and Minister of the Interior, Heinrich Himmler, from the party and from all offices of State. In his stead I appoint Gauleiter Karl Hanke as

Hitler, seen here addressing a Nazi Party rally, used his rambling and emotive speeches to stir up Germans' resentment against the Versailles Peace Treaty and to foment hatred of the Jews

Reichsführer-SS and Chief of the German Police, and Gauleiter Paul Giesler as Reich Minister of the Interior.

Göring and Himmler, quite apart from their disloyalty to my person, have done immeasurable harm to the country and the whole nation by secret negotiations with the enemy, which they have conducted without my knowledge and against my wishes, and by illegally attempting to seize power in the State for themselves.

Although a number of men, such as Martin Bormann, Dr Goebbels, etc., together with their wives, have joined me of their own free will and did not wish to leave the capital of the Reich under any circumstances, but were willing to perish with me here, I must nevertheless ask them to obey my request, and in this case set the interests of the nation above their own feelings. By their work and loyalty as comrades they will be just as close to me after death, as I hope that my spirit will linger among them and always go with them. Let them be hard but never unjust, but above all let them never allow fear to influence their actions, and set the honour of the nation above everything in the world. Finally, let them be conscious of the fact that our task, that of continuing the building of a National Socialist State, represents the work of the coming centuries, which places every single person under an obligation always to serve the common interest and to subordinate his own advantage to this end. I demand of all Germans, all National Socialists, men, women and all the men of the Armed Forces, that they be faithful and obedient unto death to the new government and its President.

Above all I charge the leaders of the nation and those under them to scrupulous observance of the laws of race and to merciless opposition to the universal poisoner of all peoples, International Jewry.

Given in Berlin, this 29th day of April 1945, 4:00 A.M.
Adolf Hitler
[Witnesses] Dr Joseph Goebbels
Wilhelm Burgdorf (Wehrmacht Adjutant at Hitler's headquarters)
Martin Bormann (Hitler's private secretary)
Hans Krebs (chief of staff)

Hitler had one further message, in which he wished to convey his view that despite his brilliant leadership, the generals had failed him, and were responsible for losing the war:

The people and the armed forces have given their all in this long hard struggle. The sacrifice has been enormous. But my trust has been misused by many people. Disloyalty and betrayal have undermined resistance throughout the war.

It was not therefore granted to me to lead the people to victory. The Army General Staff cannot be compared to the General Staff in the First World War. Its achievements were far behind those of the fighting front.

The efforts and sacrifices of the German people in this war have been so great that I cannot believe that they have been in vain. The aim must still be to win territory in the East for the German people.

The following day, despite the rhetoric about his heart belonging to his soldiers, he deserted them by committing suicide, instead of going to join them in their last battle. Just as he had abandoned them nearly three years earlier, when by chance his train stopped opposite a troop train loaded with wounded soldiers from the Eastern front. Hitler ordered the blinds drawn in the dining car where he was enjoying lunch among china, crystal and silver.

ADMIRAL WILLIAM HALSEY

'The Third Fleet's sunken and damaged ships have been salvaged and are retiring at high speed towards the enemy.'

ADMIRAL WILLIAM 'BULL' HALSEY IN A MESSAGE TO FLEET ADMIRAL CHESTER NIMITZ, 14 OCTOBER 1944

In October 1944, the United States Third Fleet consisting of 17 aircraft carriers, accompanied by battleships and escorts, and commanded by Admiral William Halsey (1882–1959), mounted a raid on the Japanese-held island of Taiwan and the Ryukyu Islands. The Japanese claimed to have inflicted huge losses on the Americans with *kamikaze* suicide aircraft. In fact American losses were small – hence Halsey's quip above.

Halsey was a tough, fighting admiral, whose pithy remarks greatly cheered his men, especially when times were hard. When the Japanese attacked Pearl Harbor on 7 December 1941, Halsey was away with his US Pacific Fleet carriers on manoeuvres. Coming back into harbour, he was overheard to say: 'by the time we have finished with them, Japanese will be spoken only in hell'. Halsey's memorable line went round the carriers, and the rest of the battered Pacific Fleet, in a few hours.

During the first six months of the war in the Pacific, his Carrier Task Force 16 raided Japanese-held islands. On the bulkhead of his quarters, in whichever ship he flew his flag, he stuck a notice reading: 'Kill Japs, Kill Japs, Kill More Japs'. On 18 April 1942, Halsey's carriers launched the raid on Japan, in which Colonel James Doolittle, United States Army Air Force, led a sortie of 16 B-25 Mitchell bombers to bomb Tokyo, Kobe, Nagoya, Yokosuka and Yokohama.

After this, Halsey changed his notice to read, 'Hit hard, hit fast, hit often', a precept he was to put into effect on several occasions directing the American offensive in the Solomons in 1943 and 1944. He commanded the Third Fleet during the largest naval battle in the history of the world at Leyte Gulf. Here his impulsive nature led him to fall for a Japanese deception ploy, and he led his carriers away to attack a decoy 'carrier fleet', leaving the US beachhead with just the small carriers and battleships of the under-strength US Seventh Fleet to guard the landing force. Fortunately this was just enough to avert disaster, and Halsey remained in command.

The Japanese surrender was signed on board Halsey's flagship, the battleship USS *Missouri* in Tokyo Bay on 2 September 1945.

Lieutenant Colonel 'Chesty' Puller

'Be a model of valour by example and precept.'

Lieutenant Colonel Lewis B 'Chesty' Puller, 1942

Thus did the commander of the 1st Battalion, 7th US Marines address his officers and non-commissioned officers before their landing as part of the 1st Marine Division on Guadalcanal in the Solomon Islands on 7 August 1942. Puller (1898–1971) had seen action before in Nicaragua, earning two Navy Crosses.

Puller's battalion made a name for itself on Guadalcanal in bitter fighting when at times the outcome swung in the balance. Having hit the Japanese hard on Mount Austen, Puller's battalion was involved in an attack across a river near the coast with two other battalions. It went badly. Part of Puller's battalion detached on an outflanking move by sea found itself cut off from the beach by strong Japanese forces. The senior officer was killed, the radios failed and ammunition ran low. Learning of the situation, Puller boarded a destroyer and, with some landing craft, mounted a rescue operation. Afterwards he addressed his officers:

> Gentlemen at least we've all been blooded now. I don't want you to be mooning over the losses and feeling sorry for yourselves or taking all the blame on your shoulders. We've all got to leave this world some day; we're all in the same pickle. And there are worse things than dying for your country. Some things about our action in the last four days I want you to remember forever. There are some we would like to forget – but they'll be in your mind's eye as long as you live. I hope we've all learned something. Now take care of your men and make yourselves ready. We haven't seen anything yet.
>
> One other thing. Back there on the hillside at Mount Austen, I had trouble getting company officers up. I hope you saw what it cost us in casualties. Never do I want to see that again in my command. I want to see my officers leading. I want you to know that you're leaders, and not simply commanders. You cannot operate a military force in the field under these conditions with commanders alone. Civilians wouldn't know what I was

talking about, but you've found out now that it's true. There are many
qualities in one man, but one that is absolutely necessary is stark courage.
Give that idea to your men in your own way.

Puller's next operation on Guadalcanal was a stunning success. About a month later in the face of a determined Japanese attack, Puller's unit found itself facing two complete Japanese regiments aimed at pushing him off a key ridge. At a critical stage in the battle, Puller got a message from one company commander that his ammunition was almost expended. His response was:

You've got bayonets, haven't you?

The Japanese attack failed in the face of Puller's rocklike defence.

Puller served with the 1st Marine Division for the rest of the Pacific campaign. The Korean War found him commanding the 1st Marine Regiment in the 1st Marine Division as part of the United Nations (mainly American) forces engaged against the invading North Koreans. After the epic Inchon landings that reversed the course of the war in Korea, the 1st Marine Division was sent to the Chosin Reservoir near the border with China on the east side of Korea. The massive Chinese invasion of Korea took most of the United Nations forces by surprise, and sent them retreating helter-skelter southwards. The 1st Marine Division, although cut off, performed differently. Ordered by the US Army corps commander to retreat to the coast, abandoning equipment and supplies, the divisional commander, Major General Smith announced that his division would fight its way out taking everything with it. He maintained: 'we are not retreating, we are attacking in a new direction'.

On being told that the Chinese had cut his main supply route, Puller's sanguine response was:

That simplifies our problem of finding these people and killing them.

Likewise, on being told to clear the main supply route up to where a large part of the division was cut off, he announced:

Boys, we've been seeking the enemy and now we have found them. They are
in front of us, behind us, and on both our flanks.

Eventually the 1st Marine Division fought its way to the coast in one of the epic withdrawals of history. Puller came out with more transport than his regiment had at the beginning of the campaign having picked up abandoned army trucks on the way. The performance of this unit, led by officers like Puller, was one of the few bright spots in the disastrous retreat following the Chinese offensive.

GENERAL DOUGLAS MACARTHUR

'I shall return.'

GENERAL DOUGLAS MACARTHUR ON RETREATING FROM THE PHILIPPINES, MARCH 1942

Just a few hours after the devastating raid on Pearl Harbor on 7 December 1941, Japanese forces attacked United States airbases in Manila in the Philippines , destroying most of the aircraft on the ground. Japanese landings in the islands followed soon after. The commander of all US forces in East Asia was General Douglas MacArthur (1880–1964). After three months of fighting his troops were forced back on to the Baatan Peninsula, and the island of Corregidor. On orders from President Roosevelt, MacArthur and a small staff were evacuated to Australia in a motor-torpedo boat on 11 March 1942. On arrival in Australia, he made the promise quoted above. He was awarded the Congressional Medal of Honor.

Admiral Chester Nimitz, commander-in-chief of the US Navy Pacific Fleet and MacArthur divided responsibility for conducting the war against the Japanese in the Pacific between them. MacArthur commanded the South Pacific Area (the southwest Pacific territories of New Guinea and the Philippines and adjoining islands), with Nimitz commanding the Pacific Ocean area north of that. MacArthur's strategy for retaking the Pacific territories was to seize the smaller, more weakly defended islands as bases, and leave the strongly defended ones to wither on the vine. As the US Navy increasingly commanded the sea after the Battle of Midway in June 1942, the Japanese garrisons on these islands could do little to interfere except by air.

Starting in late 1942, and continuing on into 1943 he secured northern New Guinea and the Solomon Islands. Despite MacArthur's policy of trying to avoid attacking the stronger Japanese positions, Buna on the north coast of New Guinea proved a hard nut to crack. American and Australian forces were attacking from the south, overland. On 29 November 1942, MacArthur put Lieutenant General Robert Eichelberger in charge of the operation, telling him:

> Bob, I am putting you in command at Buna. Relieve Harding, and all officers who won't fight. If necessary put sergeants in charge of battalions and corporals in charge of companies – anyone who will fight. Time is of the essence. I want you to take Buna, or not come back alive.

One place MacArthur did not bypass, despite pressure to do so by President Roosevelt, was the Philippines. On 20 October 1944, MacArthur waded ashore at Leyte, fulfilling his promise of two years earlier. The campaign to liberate the whole of the Philippine archipelago took until July the following year. By then MacArthur had been promoted to the new rank of general of the army, the American equivalent to field marshal. On 2 March, 1945, he was present just after the recapture of Corregidor, and said to the commanding officer of the American regimental combat team:

> I see that the old flagpole still stands. Have your troops hoist the colours to its peak, and let no enemy ever haul them down.

After being made supreme commander of all Allied forces in the Pacific, MacArthur took Iwo Jima in March 1945, followed by Okinawa in June. In September 1945 he took the surrender of Japan aboard the USS *Missouri* in Tokyo Bay. As chief of the occupation forces in Japan he oversaw the introduction of democratic government in that country.

CONFLICT IN KOREA

Following the outbreak of the Korean War in June 1950, MacArthur (by then aged 70) took command of all United Nations (UN) units (mainly American and South Korean) there on 8 July. The North Korean invaders pushed back the UN forces into a perimeter around the port of Pusan in the far south of the country. Some commentators predicted that this was the end, and evacuation was the only solution. MacArthur thought otherwise, and suggested an amphibious hook at Inchon, the port of the South Korean capital, Seoul, which then lay 150 miles (240 km) behind enemy lines.

The staffs both in Washington and in the Pacific were dead set against the idea. The US Navy said it was impossible: the tidal range was too great, sea walls made the landing difficult and the area was mined. It is worth bearing in mind that in 1950, only five years after the end of the Second World War, there were plenty of senior officers with a wealth of experience in amphibious operations from the Pacific to Normandy, they understood the perils, and they did not like what they saw at Inchon. MacArthur thought otherwise, saying to a doubting staff officer:

> It will be like an electric fan. You go to the wall and pull the plug out, and the fan will stop. When we get ashore at Inchon, the North Koreans will have no choice but to pull out, or surrender.

On 23 August 1950, a final meeting took place at MacArthur's headquarters in Japan. A string of senior officers, including the chief of naval operations from Washington, told him his plan was impossible. The last to speak was Rear Admiral Doyle. MacArthur rose, puffing on his corncob pipe and spoke quietly, for 45 minutes:

> Admiral, in all my years of military service that is the finest briefing I have ever received. Commander, you have taught me all I ever dreamed of knowing about tides. Do you know in World War I they got our divisions to Europe through submarine-infested seas? I have a deep admiration for the Navy. From the humiliation of Baatan the Navy brought us back. I never thought I would see the day that the Navy would be unable to support the army in its operations ...
>
> It is plainly apparent that here in Asia is where the Communist conspirators have elected to make their play for global conquest. The test is not in Berlin or Vienna, in London, Paris or Washington. It is here and now – it is along the Naktong River in South Korea [the Pusan perimeter] ...

MacArthur then reminded them that General Wolfe's plan to capture Quebec from the French in 1759 had been opposed by his staff. He continued:

> The very arguments you have made as to the impracticabilities involved will tend to ensure for me the elements of surprise. For the enemy commander will reason that no one would be so brash as to make such an attempt. . .

I can almost hear the ticking of the second hand of destiny. We must act now or we will die … We shall land at Inchon, and I shall crush them.

Having made clear by his final remark that he intended to be present for the landings, MacArthur returned to his chair. The chief of naval operations, head of the US Navy, stood up with tears in his eyes and pledged: 'General, the Navy will get you to Inchon'.

The landings were an outstanding success. The North Koreans fell back in disarray, and the force in Pusan broke out. MacArthur followed the retreating North Koreans right up to the border with China. The war looked as good as won, when the Chinese intervened, pushing the UN forces back down the peninsula. MacArthur was finally relieved of command by the US president for demanding that nuclear weapons be used against the Chinese. He returned to a hero's welcome in New York.

RETURN TO WEST POINT

On 12 May 1962, two years before he died, Douglas MacArthur returned to West Point to address the cadets. He had graduated top of his class there in 1903. After service in the Philippines he fought in France in the First World War, first as chief of staff of the 42nd Division, and then as its commander at the age of 37. General Pershing, the US commander-in-chief, called him the 'greatest leader of troops we have'. On one occasion, MacArthur was talking to the then-Major Patton, when enemy shells started falling close by. Both stood looking at each other, neither wanting to be the first to suggest that they take cover. Then Patton flinched, and a fleeting grimace of annoyance with himself passed over his face. MacArthur merely said: 'Don't worry Major, you never hear the one that gets you'.

MacArthur returned from France as the youngest ever general in the US regular army, to become the youngest ever superintendent of West Point, and eventually army chief of staff. Now he was back at West Point, gaunt from a recent bout of flu. He addressed the assembled Corps of Cadets:

General Westmoreland, General Groves, distinguished guests, and gentlemen of the Corps. As I was leaving the hotel this morning, a doorman asked me, 'Where are you bound for, General?' and when I replied, 'West Point,' he remarked, 'Beautiful place, have you ever been there before?'

No human being could fail to be deeply moved by such a tribute as this, coming from a profession I have served so long and a people I have loved so well. It fills me with an emotion I cannot express. But this award is not intended primarily for a personality, but to symbolize a great moral code – the code of conduct and chivalry of those who guard this beloved land of culture and ancient descent. That is the meaning of this medallion. For all eyes and for all time, it is an expression of the ethics of the American soldier. That I should be integrated in this way with so noble an ideal arouses a sense of pride and yet of humility which will be with me always.

'Duty', 'Honour', 'Country' – those three hallowed words reverently dictate what you want to be, what you can be, what you will be. They are your rallying point to build courage when courage

seems to fail, to regain faith when there seems to be little cause for faith, to create hope when hope becomes forlorn. Unhappily, I possess neither that eloquence of diction, that poetry of imagination, nor that brilliance of metaphor to tell you all that they mean.

The unbelievers will say they are but words, but a slogan, but a flamboyant phrase. Every pedant, every demagogue, every cynic, every hypocrite, every troublemaker, and, I am sorry to say, some others of an entirely different character, will try to downgrade them even to the extent of mockery and ridicule.

But these are some of the things they do. They build your basic character. They mould you for your future roles as the custodians of the nation's defence. They make you strong enough to know when you are weak, and brave enough to face yourself when you are afraid.

They teach you to be proud and unbending in honest failure, but humble and gentle in success; not to substitute words for action; not to seek the path of comfort, but to face the stress and spur of difficulty and challenge; to learn to stand up in the storm, but to have compassion on those who fall; to master yourself before you seek to master others; to have a heart that is clean, a goal that is high; to learn to laugh, yet never forget how to weep; to reach into the future, yet never neglect the past; to be serious, yet never take yourself too seriously; to be modest so that you will remember the

Wading through the water from a landing craft on 20 October 1944, Douglas MacArthur (centre, in sunglasses) fulfils his pledge to return to the Philippines

simplicity of true greatness; the open mind of true wisdom, the meekness of true strength.

They give you a temperate will, a quality of imagination, a vigour of the emotions, a freshness of the deep springs of life, a temperamental predominance of courage over timidity, an appetite for adventure over love of ease. They create in your heart the sense of wonder, the unfailing hope of what next, and the joy and inspiration of life. They teach you in this way to be an officer and a gentleman.

And what sort of soldiers are those you are to lead? Are they reliable? Are they brave? Are they capable of victory?

Their story is known to all of you. It is the story of the American man at arms. My estimate of him was formed on the battlefields many, many years ago, and has never changed. I regarded him then, as I regard him now, as one of the world's noblest figures; not only as one of the finest military characters, but also as one of the most stainless.

His name and fame are the birthright of every American citizen. In his youth and strength, his love and loyalty, he gave all that mortality can give. He needs no eulogy from me, or from any other man. He has written his own history and written it in red on his enemy's breast.

But when I think of his patience under adversity, of his courage under fire, and of his modesty in victory, I am filled with an emotion of admiration I cannot put into words. He belongs to history as furnishing one of the greatest examples of successful patriotism. He belongs to posterity as the instructor of future generations in the principles of liberty and freedom. He belongs to the present, to us, by his virtues and by his achievements.

In twenty campaigns, on a hundred battlefields, around a thousand campfires, I have witnessed that enduring fortitude, that patriotic self-abnegation, and that invincible determination which have carved his statue in the hearts of his people.

From one end of the world to the other, he has drained deep the chalice of courage. As I listened to those songs of the glee club, in memory's eye I could see those staggering columns of the First World War, bending under soggy packs on many a weary march, from dripping dusk to drizzling dawn, slogging ankle deep through mire of shell-pocked roads; to form grimly for the attack, blue-lipped, covered with sludge and mud, chilled by the wind and rain, driving home to their objective, and for many, to the judgment seat of God.

I do not know the dignity of their birth, but I do know the glory of their death. They died unquestioning, uncomplaining, with faith in their hearts, and on their lips the hope that we would go on to victory. Always for them: Duty, Honour, Country. Always their blood, and sweat, and tears, as they saw the way and the light.

And twenty years after, on the other side of the globe, against the filth of dirty foxholes, the stench of ghostly trenches, the slime of dripping dugouts, those boiling suns of the relentless heat, those torrential rains of devastating storms, the loneliness and utter desolation of jungle trails, the bitterness of long separation of those they loved and cherished, the deadly pestilence of tropic disease, the horror of stricken areas of war.

Their resolute and determined defence, their swift and sure attack, their indomitable purpose, their complete and decisive victory – always victory, always through the bloody haze of their last reverberating shot, the vision of gaunt, ghastly men, reverently following your password of Duty, Honour, Country.

The code which those words perpetuate embraces the highest moral laws and will stand the test of any ethics or philosophies ever promulgated for the uplift of mankind. Its requirements are for the things that are right, and its restraints are from the things that are wrong. The soldier, above all other men, is required to practise the greatest act of religious training – sacrifice. In battle and in the face of danger and death, he discloses those divine attributes which his Maker gave when he created man in his own image. No physical courage and no brute instinct can take the place of the Divine help which alone can sustain him. However horrible the incidents of war may be, the soldier who is called upon to offer and to give his life for his country, is the noblest development of mankind.

You now face a new world, a world of change. The thrust into outer space of the satellite, spheres and missiles marked the beginning of another epoch in the long story of mankind – the chapter of the space age. In the five or more billions of years the scientists tell us it has taken to form the earth, in the three or more billion years of development of the human race, there has never been a greater, a more abrupt or staggering evolution. We deal now not with things of this world alone, but with the illimitable distances and as yet unfathomed mysteries of the universe. We are reaching out for a new and boundless frontier. We speak in strange terms: of harnessing the cosmic energy; of making winds and tides work for us; of creating unheard of synthetic materials to supplement or even replace our old standard basics; of purifying sea water for our drink; of mining ocean floors for new fields of wealth and food; of disease preventatives to expand life into the hundred of years; of controlling the weather for a more equitable distribution of heat and cold, of rain and shine; of space ships to the moon; of the primary target in war, no longer limited to the armed forces of an enemy, but instead to include his civil populations; of ultimate conflict between a united human race and the sinister forces of some other planetary galaxy; of such dreams and fantasies as to make life the most exciting of all time.

And through all this welter of change and development your mission remains fixed, determined, inviolable. It is to win our wars. Everything else in your professional career is but corollary to this vital dedication. All other public purpose, all other public projects, all other public needs, great or small, will find others for their accomplishments; but you are the ones who are trained to fight.

Yours is the profession of arms, the will to win, the sure knowledge that in war there is no substitute for victory, that if you lose, the Nation will be destroyed, that the very obsession of your public service must be Duty, Honour, Country.

Others will debate the controversial issues, national and international, which divide men's minds. But serene, calm, aloof, you stand as the Nation's war guardians, as its lifeguards from the raging tides of international conflict, as its gladiators in the arena of battle. For a century and a half you have defended, guarded and protected its hallowed traditions of liberty and freedom, of right and justice.

Let civilian voices argue the merits or demerits of our processes of government. Whether our strength is being sapped by deficit financing indulged in too long, by federal paternalism grown too mighty, by power groups grown too arrogant, by politics grown too corrupt, by crime grown too rampant, by morals grown too low, by taxes grown too high, by extremists grown too violent; whether our personal liberties are as firm and complete as they should be.

These great national problems are not for your professional participation or military solution. Your guidepost stands out like a tenfold beacon in the night: Duty, Honour, Country.

You are the leaven which binds together the entire fabric of our national system of defence. From your ranks come the great captains who hold the Nation's destiny in their hands the moment the war tocsin sounds.

The long grey line has never failed us. Were you to do so, a million ghosts in olive drab, in brown khaki, in blue and grey, would rise from their white crosses, thundering those magic words: Duty, Honour, Country.

This does not mean that you are warmongers. On the contrary, the soldier above all other people prays for peace, for he must suffer and bear the deepest wounds and scars of war. But always in our ears ring the ominous words of Plato, that wisest of all philosophers: 'Only the dead have seen the end of war.'

The shadows are lengthening for me. The twilight is here. My days of old have vanished – tone and tints. They have gone glimmering through the dreams of things that were. Their memory is one of wondrous beauty, watered by tears and coaxed and caressed by the smiles of yesterday. I listen then, but with thirsty ear, for the witching melody of faint bugles blowing reveille, of far drums beating the long roll.

In my dreams I hear again the crash of guns, the rattle of musketry, the strange, mournful mutter of the battlefield. But in the evening of my memory I come back to West Point. Always there echoes and re-echoes: Duty, Honour, Country.

Today marks my final roll call with you. But I want you to know that when I cross the river, my last conscious thoughts will be of the Corps, and the Corps, and the Corps.

I bid you farewell.

Field Marshal Bernard Montgomery

'*1. The enemy is now attempting to break through our positions in order to reach Cairo, Suez and Alexandria, and drive us from Egypt.*

2. The Eighth Army bars the way. It carries great responsibility and the whole future of the war will depend on how we carry out our task.

3. We will fight the enemy where we now stand; there will be no withdrawal and no surrender.

Every officer and man must continue to do his duty as long as he has breath in his body.

If each one of us does his duty, we cannot fail; the opportunity will then occur to take the offensive ourselves and to destroy once and for all the enemy forces now in Egypt.

4. Into battle then, and with stout hearts and with the determination to do our duty.

And may God give us the victory.'

Bernard Montgomery (then Lieutenant General) Special Message to Officers and Men of the Eighth Army 23 August 1942, before the Battle of Alam Halfa

Bernard Law Montgomery (1887–1976) was born in London on 17 November 1887. After nearly being expelled from Sandhurst for setting light to a fellow cadet's shirt tails, he was commissioned into the Royal Warwickshire Regiment in 1908. Wounded in the First World War leading his platoon at the First Battle of Ypres, he was awarded the Distinguished Service Order. Duty on the staff followed, and then promotion to lieutenant colonel.

In the interwar years, Montgomery made a name for himself as a superb trainer of troops, and following the outbreak of the Second World War in 1939 he was sent to France as commander of the 3rd Infantry Division in the British Expeditionary Force. His cool handling of his division in the retreat to Dunkirk so impressed his corps commander, Lieutenant General Brooke, that he became a firm supporter of Montgomery for the rest of the Second World War. In August 1942, he was sent to take over the Eighth Army in the Western Desert, which had been driven back to Alamein by Field Marshal Rommel. On arrival on 13 August, Montgomery found an atmosphere of uncertainty, with the Army fearful of being pushed back yet again. He immediately gave orders that there would be no

further withdrawals, and that very day addressed his staff in what has been described as one of the most important military speeches in British history, rebuilding the morale of a broken army:

1. I want first of all to introduce myself to you. You do not know me. I do not know you. But we have got to work together; therefore we must understand each other and we must have confidence in each other. I have only been here a few hours. But from what I have seen and heard since I arrived I am prepared to say, here and now, that I have confidence in you. We will then work together as a team; and together we will gain the confidence of this great Army and go forward to victory in Africa.

2. I believe that one of the first duties of a commander is to create what I call 'atmosphere', and in that atmosphere his staff, subordinate commanders, and troops will live and work and fight.

I do not like the general atmosphere I find here. It is an atmosphere of doubt, of looking back to select the next place to which to withdraw, of loss of confidence in our ability to defeat Rommel, of desperate defence measures by reserves in preparing positions in Cairo and the Delta.

All that must cease.

Let us have a new atmosphere.

3. The defence of Egypt lies here at Alamein and on the Ruweisat Ridge. What is the use of digging trenches in the Delta? It is quite useless; if we lose this position we lose Egypt; all the fighting troops now in the Delta must come here at once, and will. Here we will stand and fight; there will be no further withdrawal. I have ordered that all plans and instructions dealing with further withdrawal be burnt, and at once. We will stand and fight here.

If we can't stay here alive, then let us stay here dead.

4. I want to impress on everyone that the bad times are over. Fresh Divisions from the UK are now arriving in Egypt, together with ample reinforcements for our present Divisions. We have 300 to 400 Sherman new tanks and these are actually being unloaded at Suez now. Our mandate from the Prime Minister is to destroy the Axis forces in North Africa; I have seen it, written on half a sheet of notepaper. And it will be done. If anyone here thinks it can't be done, let him go at once; I don't want any doubters in this party. It can be done, and it will be done; beyond any possibility of doubt.

5. Now I understand that Rommel is expected to attack at any moment. Excellent. Let him attack.

I would sooner it didn't come for a week, just give me time to sort things out. If we have two weeks to prepare we will be sitting pretty; Rommel can attack as soon as he likes, after that, and I hope he does.

6. Meanwhile, we ourselves will start to plan a great offensive; it will be the beginning of a campaign that will hit Rommel and his Army for six right out of Africa.

But first we must create a reserve Corps, mobile and strong in armour, which we will train out of the line. Rommel has always had such a force in his Africa Corps, which is never used to hold the line but which is always in reserve, available for striking blows. Therein has been his great strength. We will create such a corps ourselves, a British Panzer Corps; it will consist of two armoured Divisions and one motorised Division; I gave orders yesterday for it to begin to form, back in the Delta.

I have no intention of launching our great attack until we are completely ready; there will be pressure from many quarters to attack soon; I will not attack until we are ready, and you can rest assured on that point.

Meanwhile, if Rommel attacks while we are preparing, let him do so with pleasure; we will merely continue with our own preparations and we will attack when we are ready and not before.

7. I want to tell you that I always work on the Chief-of-Staff system. I have nominated Brigadier de Guingand as Chief-of-Staff Eighth Army. I will issue orders through him. Whatever he says will be taken as coming from me and will be acted on at once. I understand there has been a great deal of 'belly-aching' out here. By 'belly-aching' I mean inventing poor reasons for not doing what one has been told to do.

This is all to stop at once. I will tolerate no belly-aching.

If anyone objects to doing what he is told, then he can get right out of it, and at once. I want that made clear right down through the Eighth Army.

8. I have little more to say just at present. And some of you may think it is quite enough and may wonder if I am mad.

I assure you I am quite sane.

I understand there are people who often think I am slightly mad; so often that I now regard it as rather a compliment.

All I have to say to that is that if I am slightly mad, there are a large number of people I could name who are raving lunatics!

What I have done is to get over to you the 'atmosphere' in which we will now work and fight; you must see that atmosphere permeates right down through the Eighth Army to the most junior private soldier. All the soldiers must know what is wanted; when they see it coming to pass there will be a surge of confidence throughout the Army.

I ask you to give me your confidence and to have faith that what I have said will come to pass. There is much work to be done.

The orders I have given about no further withdrawal will mean a complete change in the layout of our dispositions; also that we must begin to prepare for our great offensive.

The first thing we must do is to move our HQ to a decent place where we can live in reasonable comfort and where the Army Staff can all be together and side by side with the HQ of the Desert Air Force. This is a frightful place here, depressing, unhealthy and a rendezvous for every fly in Africa; we shall do no good work here. Let us get over there by the sea where it is fresh and healthy. If officers are to do good work they must have decent messes, and be comfortable. So off we go on the new line.

The Chief-of-Staff will be issuing orders on many points very shortly, and I am always available to be consulted by the senior officer of the staff. The great point to remember is we are going to finish with this chap Rommel once and for all. It will be quite easy. There is no doubt about it.

He is definitely a nuisance. Therefore we will hit him a crack and finish him.

Even the most cynical staff officers were electrified. The official photographer, Captain Keating, who had seen much action and been wounded five times so far in the Second World War, was sure that 'this was the man who had victory'.

VICTORY IN NORTH AFRICA

Having seen off Rommel's attack at the ensuing Battle of Alam Halfa, Montgomery turned his attention to the Battle of Alamein. On the morning of 23 October 1942, his personal message was read out to all the soldiers:

1. When I assumed command of Eighth Army I said that the mandate was to destroy Rommel and his Army, and that it would be done as soon as we were ready.

2. We are ready now.

The battle which is now about to begin will be one of the decisive battles of history. It will be the turning point of the war. The eyes of the whole world will be on us, watching anxiously which way the battle will swing.

We can give them their answer at once. It will swing our way.

3. We have first-class equipment; good tanks; good anti-tank guns; plenty of artillery and plenty of ammunition; and we are backed by the finest air striking force in the world.

All that is necessary is that each one of us, every officer and man, should enter this battle with the determination to see it through – to fight and to kill – and finally, to win.

'Monty' reading the lesson at an open-air church service in September 1944, shortly before his promotion to field marshal

If we all do this there can be only one result – together we will hit the enemy for 'six' right out of North Africa.

4. The sooner we win this battle, which will be the turning point of this war, the sooner we shall all get back home to our families.

5. Therefore, let every officer and man enter the battle with a stout heart, and with the determination to do his duty so long as he has breath in his body.

AND LET NO MAN SURRENDER AS LONG AS HE IS UNWOUNDED AND CAN FIGHT.

Let us all pray the 'The Lord mighty in battle' will give us the victory.

With these words, the Eighth Army was launched into battle, and victory.

Having pushed Rommel all the way back to Tunisia, Montgomery's Eighth Army linked up with British First Army and the Americans who had landed in Morocco and Algeria. The Germans surrendered at Tunis on 12 May 1943. Montgomery played a leading role in the Allied invasion of Sicily and Italy, eventually handing over command of the Eighth Army on the River Sangro at the end of December 1943, on being ordered to take command of the 21st Army Group for the invasion of Normandy in 1944.

THE NORMANDY LANDINGS

Thanks to Montgomery's drive and initiative, the somewhat unrealistic Allied plan for the invasion was radically amended. His personal message to all troops was read out to the soldiers once they had embarked in the ships for Normandy or, in the case of airborne troops, in sealed camps by their take-off airfields:

The time has come to deal the enemy a terrific blow in Western Europe.

The blow will be struck by the combined sea, land and air forces of the Allies – together constituting one great Allied team under the supreme command of General Eisenhower.
On the eve of this great adventure I send my best wishes to every soldier in the Allied team.

To us is given the honour of striking a blow for freedom which will live in history; and in the better days that lie ahead men will speak with pride of our doings.

Let us pray that 'The Lord Mighty in Battle' will go forth with our armies, and that His special providence will aid us in the struggle.

I want every soldier to know that I have complete confidence in the successful outcome of the operations that we are now to begin. With stout hearts and enthusiasm for the contest, let us go forward to victory. And as we enter battle, let us recall the words of a famous soldier spoken many years ago:

'He either fears his fate too much,

Or his deserts are too small,

Who dare not put it to the touch

To win or lose it all.'

Good luck to each one of you. And good hunting on the mainland.

The landings on 6 June 1944 went well, despite encountering serious problems, especially on Omaha Beach. But the Battle of Normandy fought in accordance with Montgomery's master plan was a stunning victory. By March 1945, Montgomery's 21st Army Group was preparing to cross the Rhine. In the intervening months since the end of the Battle of Normandy all had not gone smoothly with the Allied plans, largely thanks to General Eisenhower's lack of grip, and his failure to establish a sound strategy for the land campaign in Northwest Europe. Setbacks included the failed operation to establish a foothold across the Rhine at Arnhem, blame for which can be laid at Montgomery's door; and the German offensive in the Ardennes. The initial defeats suffered by the Allies in the Ardennes owed much to the American General Bradley's inadequate deployment of formations under his command, spreading assets too thinly in response to Eisenhower's strategy of attacking everywhere.

But, now, on 23 March 1945, Field Marshal Montgomery, promoted in August the previous year, issued another of his orders of the day, to be read out to all troops:

1. On the 7th February I told you we were going into the ring for the final and last round; there would be no limit; we would continue fighting until our opponent was knocked out. The last round is going very well on both sides of the ring – and overhead.

2. In the West, the enemy has lost the Rhineland; and with it the flower of at least four armies – the Parachute Army, Fifth Panzer Army, Fifteenth Army, and Seventh Army; the First Army, farther to the South, is now being added to the list. In the Rhineland battles, the enemy has lost about 150,000 prisoners, and there are many more to come; his total casualties amount to about 250,000 since 8th February.

3. In the East, the enemy has lost all Pomerania east of the Oder, an area as large as the Rhineland, and three more German armies have been routed. The Russian armies are within about 35 miles of Berlin.

4. Overhead, the Allied Air Forces are pounding Germany day and night. It will be interesting to see how much longer the Germans can stand it.

5. The enemy has in fact been driven into a corner, and he cannot escape.

Events are moving rapidly.

The complete and decisive defeat of the Germans is certain; there is no possibility of doubt on this matter.

6. 21 ARMY WILL NOW CROSS THE RHINE

The enemy possibly thinks he is safe behind the great river obstacle. We all agree that it is a great obstacle; but we will show the enemy that he is far from safe behind it. This great Allied fighting machine, composed of integrated land and air forces, will deal with the problem in no uncertain manner.

7. And having crossed the Rhine, we will crack about on the plains of Northern Germany, chasing the enemy from pillar to post. The swifter and more energetic our action, the sooner the war will be over, and that is what we all desire; to get on with the job and finish off the German war as soon as possible.

8. Over the Rhine, then, let us go. And good hunting to you all on the other side.

9. May 'The Lord mighty in battle' give us the victory in this our latest undertaking; as He has done in all our battles since we landed in Normandy on D-Day.

Having crossed the Rhine, 21st Army Group, on the left of the Allied armies, eventually reached the Baltic on 7 May. The war in Europe was at an end.

MONTY – A NATURAL LEADER OF MEN

Montgomery understood soldiers. He had spent a lifetime with them, and realized that the younger ones especially needed reassurance. Nowhere was this more evident than in his speeches to troops as he toured the UK before the Normandy landings. Most of those to whom he spoke had never been in a battle, and many expected to die in the forthcoming campaign. His talks were a mixture of information and encouragement; the constant theme that he and his soldiers would see the thing through together:

> *Finish the thing off. You and I are together … with God's help we will see the job through to the end.*

To infantrymen he would say:

> *You. What's your most valuable possession?*
> *Answer: My rifle, Sir.*
> *No it isn't; it's your life, and I am going to save it for you. Now listen to me …*

Followed by an explanation how he would never make the infantry attack without full artillery and air support.

His speeches were peppered with references to God, and delivered in his high-pitched voice. But they were without bombast and utterly sincere. Soldiers have an inherent ability to detect the merest whiff of 'bullshit' in addresses by senior officers; a quality notably absent in what Montgomery said. Instead thousands of young men were uplifted and comforted by his transparent sincerity.

MAJOR GENERAL ORDE WINGATE

'No patrol is to report the jungle impenetrable, until it has penetrated it.'

ORDER ISSUED BY MAJOR GENERAL ORDE WINGATE, 1943

The uncompromising language used by Orde Wingate (1903–44) to those he commanded was greatly admired by some, while others (admittedly a minority) thought he was mad. Wingate was a regular British artillery officer, who first came to notice just before the Second World War in what was then Palestine. There he commanded a special force of Jewish paramilitaries, which achieved a measure of success against Arab terrorists who were attacking Jewish settlements and oil pipelines. General Sir Archibald Wavell, the British commander-in-chief in the Middle East at the time and until mid-1941, subsequently tasked Wingate with commanding Abyssinian guerrillas in the successful campaign to eject the Italians from what is now Ethiopia. In 1942, Wavell, now commander-in-chief in India, sent for Wingate to organize long-range penetration patrols against the Japanese who had invaded Burma that January. In the interval Wingate had nearly been court-martialled twice and attempted suicide once.

Wingate has often been likened to T. E. Lawrence ('of Arabia'). Yet in many ways he was more like General Charles Gordon, who was killed in Khartoum in January 1885 after being besieged by Sudanese Mahdists. Both were deeply religious to the point of fanaticism, believing they were chosen by God, and therefore any attempt to frustrate them in their purpose was tantamount to blasphemy. The British representative in Cairo once said of Gordon: 'It is not easy to deal with a man who in moments of difficulty takes his instructions from Isaiah'. He could just as well have been speaking of Wingate, who was brought up in a missionary family affiliated with the Plymouth Brethren.

OPERATIONS WITH THE CHINDITS

Eventually Wavell tasked Wingate with raising a special brigade for long-range penetration operations behind Japanese lines in Burma. He led this formation, the 77th Brigade, on the first of his two expeditions into Burma. He chose as his formation sign the *Chinthe*, the mythical lion that guards Burmese temples. It came to be mispronounced as 'Chindit' by his brigade and the name stuck.

Orde Wingate (right), commander of the Chindits, at his headquarters at Assam, on the border between India and Burma, in 1943

Wingate usually addressed his soldiers in a quiet but convincing manner, at odds with his unkempt appearance and battered sun helmet. His speeches pulled no punches:

> *You are going to be trained to infiltrate the Japanese lines in Burma. You will be the first troops to fight back since the debacle of the loss of Burma. You will be in for a very hard time training for this operation, but you will show the Japanese that you are better soldiers than them.*

He managed to convince most of the soldiers, especially the young and impressionable that they would be able to do just what he prophesied. Before setting out from Imphal to march to the River Chindwin and into Burma, Wingate sent out an order of the day:

> *Knowing the vanities of man's efforts and the conclusion of his purpose, let us pray that God may accept our services and direct our endeavours, so that when we shall have done all we shall see the fruits of our labours and be satisfied.*

In fact the achievements of the Chindits in the first expedition were negligible in strictly military terms. Of some 3000 men who marched into Burma in February, 2182 had returned four months later. Of nearly 1000 missing, about 450 were battle casualties. Few of those who did return, debilitated by malnourishment and disease, were fit for further operations. At first Wingate was far from satisfied, indeed rather depressed, expecting to be court-martialled for failure. He should have remembered one of his favourite precepts: 'Everything is propaganda'.

General Slim, then commanding XV Corps and later the Fourteenth Army, certainly quickly realized that here was an unrivalled opportunity to restore morale among British and Indian soldiers who had come to regard the Japanese as invincible. Stories of the Chindits were quickly circulated to the press, emphasizing that they had beaten the Japanese at their own game. The propaganda elements in the operation were milked for all they were worth; there was little else.

PIONEER OF 'SPECIAL OPS'

However, Wingate was able to persuade a number of influential people, not least Winston Churchill, that long-range penetration operations could play an important part in the Allied reconquest of Burma. His Chindit force was greatly expanded to around six times the original force. For a while it included an American regiment, equivalent to a British brigade, called Merrill's Marauders. However, the senior American in the Burma theatre of operations, General Stilwell, soon demanded that they be placed under his command. Wingate's response to the American officer who gave him the news, and confirmed that Wingate's British superiors had assented, was characteristically blunt:

> You can tell General Stilwell he can stick his Americans up his arse.

Eventually, all but one of Wingate's brigades, Fergusson's 16th, were flown into Burma from Assam by gliders towed by DC-3 Dakota aircraft. The 16th Brigade had to march. Wingate addressed the units of this brigade before they set off:

> You are about to start on the toughest march that has ever been attempted.
> For the first month you will travel through the rain belt, where it rains almost
> every day of the year. You will cross the Naga Hills, some of which are over
> 8,000 feet high. After you have crossed the Chindwin, the hills will get
> smaller, the rainfall will be less, but the jungle will go on and on. You won't
> all come back; but if this going seems tough just remember that after it is all
> over you will have forgotten the hardships and will remember only the
> achievements. It is not natural for Europeans to march in this climate and
> then sleep on the ground in damp blankets, so take care of your bodies first,
> and then your weapons. Nature will be your biggest enemy. Don't strain
> yourself, if you can't go any further pass the word to your officer and he will
> halt. Good luck and God go with you.

The first battalion to reach the Chindwin was the 2nd Leicesters, whose badge was a tiger, and who were known as 'the tigers'. Wingate sent a signal saying:

> Well done Leicesters. Hannibal eclipsed.

The 2nd Leicesters were an old-fashioned British infantry battalion that had fought in the desert, and were élitist, self-regarding and confident. They were not particularly honoured by being Chindits, and indeed if they had been asked to express their feelings on the matter, might have answered that the Chindits were honoured by the inclusion of the Leicesters in the force. Their commanding officer, Lieutenant Colonel Wilkinson, dismissed the signal by saying that all such references were over his head.

After the next three brigades were flown in, Wingate sent another signal to all the force:

> *Our task is fulfilled. We have inflicted a complete surprise upon the enemy. All our columns are inside the enemy's guts. Let us thank God for the great success.*

The commanding officer of the 2nd Leicesters merely recorded: 'Long message from Force [HQ], impossible to decipher, but something in it about guts and God'.

This was not the first time that Wingate had struck a false note when addressing older, more experienced soldiers. Before his second expedition, while visiting the 111th Brigade, he spoke to the 1st Battalion the Cameronians, a very tough, hard-bitten unit that had already fought and defeated the Japanese. The author John Masters, who was the chief of staff of this brigade, and later commanded it, recalled that Wingate fixed the nearest man of the 700-strong battalion with his eye and rasped: 'You're going to die'. He then turned his gaze on another rifleman, 'Many of you are going to die, or suffer wounds, or near-starvation. All of you will meet hardship worse than anything you have imagined.'

Certainly, this was better than implying that the whole campaign would be a walk-over. But the terms in which the message was delivered antagonized the men. John Masters saw that from the commanding officer downwards there was an almost visible rising of regimental ésprit de corps against Wingate. The battalion decided that he was trying to frighten them into bravery. They all resented it, and switched off, so the rest of Wingate's message was lost.

A few days after sending the 'guts and God' signal, Wingate was killed in an air crash. It is difficult to get a dispassionate judgement on him, especially from anyone with whom he came in contact. He was usually either hated or worshipped. He had great vision, was a good planner and an outstanding self-publicist. He was not a particularly good commander of large numbers of men in the field. His only effort at fighting a brigade-size battle was a failure. In the opinion of Slim, arguably as least as good a general as Montgomery – if not better – the effect of the Chindits on the course of the war in Burma was highly overrated at the time. As time goes by, there seems no reason to revise this view.

LIEUTENANT GENERAL NOBUO TANAKA

'Now is the time to capture Imphal. Our death-defying infantry group expects certain victory when it penetrates the main fortress of the enemy.'

LIEUTENANT GENERAL NOBUO TANAKA, JAPANESE 33RD DIVISION, 1944

In early 1944, the Japanese, who had driven the British out of Burma two years before, decided to take the British supply bases in Assam. This would frustrate any British attempts to stage a comeback in Burma, and might even provide a jumping-off point for a Japanese invasion of India. The British commander of the Fourteenth Army, Lieutenant General William Slim ordered that the bases were to be held at all costs. And so began the battle for Imphal, which lasted for four months.

The Japanese general tasked with this mission, Renya Mutaguchi, who commanded the Fifteenth Army, gambled on capturing the bases quickly. But the huge supply dumps at Imphal were doggedly defended by British, Indian and Gurkha troops; air supply also enabled them to hold out against the encircling Japanese. By early May, after the battle had been raging for about a month, it was clear to General Mutaguchi that hopes of taking Imphal were a delusion. Nevertheless he tried again.

It was at this stage that Lieutenant General Tanaka (1885–1945), who had taken over command of the 33rd Division, the White Tigers, confided to his diary that his division faced annihilation. Despite this, he issued an order of the day, of which the opening part is quoted above. It continued:

> The coming battle is the turning point. It will denote the success or failure of the Greater Asia War. You men have got to be fully in the picture as to what the present position is; regarding death as something lighter than a feather, you must tackle the task of capturing Imphal.
>
> For that reason it must be expected that the division will be almost annihilated. I have confidence in your firm courage and devotion and believe you will do your duty, but should any delinquencies occur you have got to understand that I shall take the necessary action.

In the front line rewards and punishments must be given on the spot
without delay. A man who does well should have his name sent in at once.
On the other hand, a man guilty of any misconduct should be punished at
once in accordance with the military code.

Further, in order to keep the honour of his unit bright, a commander may
have to use his sword as a weapon of punishment, exceedingly shameful
though it is to have to shed the blood of one's own soldiers on the battlefield.

Fresh troops have now arrived and the time is at hand – the arrow is about
to leave the bow.

The infantry group is in high spirits: afire with valour and dominated by
one thought and one only – the duty laid on them to annihilate the enemy.

On this battle rests the fate of the Empire. All officers and men fight
courageously!

One British officer who served in Burma took the view that such an uncompromising order would have alienated any Western army. But General Slim conceded: 'there can be no question of the supreme courage and hardihood of the Japanese soldiers who made the attempts [to capture Imphal]. I know of no army that could have equalled them'.

The Japanese attacks ended in utter failure, but not without savage fighting. On 7 July, Mutaguchi was ordered to withdraw from the Imphal front. By now his soldiers were in a desperate state, reduced to half a pint of gruel per day, mixed with grass and bean paste. But the Japanese kept on fighting, as they pulled back into Burma. They paid a high price for Mutaguchi's logistic gamble. Of some 85,000 who marched on Assam, half died in battle, and a further 20,000 of malaria, dysentery and starvation on the retreat out of Assam to the Chindwin river marking the border with Burma. Only around 100 prisoners were taken; the most senior officer taken alive was a captain.

An intelligence report on Japanese morale by the Indian 17th Division (the Black Cats), the great rivals of the Japanese 33rd, stated:

It would be false optimism to imagine that Japanese morale was appreciably
lowered by their early reverses in this campaign [Imphal]. *Some thought the*
presence of 16 prisoners of war significant after all the months that the
Division had spent trying to capture a single Japanese. It was not particularly
significant because:
(a) 90% of those taken were wounded when captured
(b) 4100 were killed before 16 prisoners of war were taken.

No one can accuse the Japanese soldiers of not trying to carry out the orders of their commanders unto death if necessary.

GENERAL GEORGE S. PATTON

‘Wars may be fought with weapons, but they are won by men. It is the spirit of the men who follow and of the man who leads that gains victory.’

GENERAL GEORGE S. PATTON ON THE EVE OF D-DAY, 5 JUNE 1944

George S. Patton made what were probably his most memorable speeches as commander of the United States Third Army. His pre-battle speech before taking his army to Normandy was usually delivered to a division at a time, with troops assembled round a platform and if possible up the side of a hill. Most of the men had never been in battle before and wondered what it would be like. He would address this subject, not shy away from it. Patton's reputation had preceded him, but most had never seen him in person. His speeches were outrageously profane and by modern standards completely politically incorrect. But they chimed in with the views of many of the American soldiers of the time; not least their image of themselves. He would usually begin:

Men, this stuff we hear about America wanting to stay out of the war – not wanting to fight – is a lot of bullshit. Americans love to fight – traditionally! All real Americans love the sting and clash of battle. When you were kids, you all admired the champion marble player, the fastest runner, the big league ball players, the toughest boxers. Americans love a winner and will not tolerate a loser. Americans play to win all the time. I wouldn't give a hoot in hell for a man who lost and laughs. That's why Americans have never lost and will never lose a war, for the very thought of losing is hateful to an American.

You are not all going to die. Only two percent of you here today would die in a major battle. Death must not be feared. Every man is frightened at first in battle. If he says he isn't, he's a goddamn liar. Some men are cowards, yes, but they fight just the same, or get the hell shamed out of them watching men fight who are just as scared. Some of them get over their fright in a minute under fire, some take an hour, and for some it takes days. But the real man never lets fear of death overpower his honour, his sense of duty to his country, and his innate manhood. All through your army career you men have bitched about what you call, 'this chicken-shit drilling.' That is all for a purpose – TO INSURE INSTANT OBEDIENCE TO ORDERS AND TO CREATE

ALERTNESS. I don't give a damn for a man who is not always on his toes. You men are veterans, or you would not be here. You are ready! A man, to continue breathing, must be alert at all times. If not someone, sometime, some German sonofabitch, will sneak up behind him and beat him to death with a sockful of shit.

There are four hundred neatly marked graves somewhere in Sicily all because ONE MAN went to sleep on his job. But they are German graves, because we caught the bastards asleep before they did. We have the best food, the finest equipment, the best spirit and the best men in the world. Why by God I actually pity the sons of bitches we are going up against. The individual heroic stuff is a lot of crap. The bilious bastard who wrote that kind of stuff for the Saturday Evening Post didn't know any more about real battle than he did about fucking.

My men don't surrender. I don't want to hear of any soldier under my command being captured unless he is hit. Even if you are hit, you can still fight. That's not just bullshit either. The kind of a *man I want under me is like the Lieutenant who, with a Luger against his chest, swept aside the gun with his hand, jerked his helmet off with the other and busted hell out of the Boche with the helmet. Then he picked up the gun and killed another German. All the time this man had a bullet through his lung. That's a man for you!*

All the real heroes are not storybook combat fighters either. Every single man in the Army plays a vital part. Every little job is essential to the whole scheme. What if every truck-driver suddenly decided that he didn't like the whine of those shells and turned yellow and jumped headlong into a ditch? He could say to himself, 'They won't miss me – just one guy in thousands.' What if every man said that? Where in the hell would we be now? No, thank God, Americans don't say that. Every man does his job. Every man serves the whole. Every department, every unit, is important to the vast scheme of things. The Ordnance is needed to supply the guns, the Quartermaster is needed to bring up the food and clothes for us – for where we are going there isn't a hell of a lot to steal! Every last damn man in the mess hall, even the one who heats the water to keep us from getting diarrhoea, has a job to do. Even the Chaplain is important, for if we get killed and he is not there to bury us we would all go to hell. Each man must not only think of himself, but think of his buddy fighting alongside him. We don't want yellow cowards in the Army. They should be killed off like flies. If not, they will go back home after the war, goddamn cowards, and breed more cowards. The brave men will breed more brave men. One of the bravest men I saw in the African campaign was the fellow I saw on a telegraph pole in the midst of furious fire ... I stopped and asked him what the hell he was doing up there at that time. He answered, 'Fixing the wire, sir.' 'Isn't it a little unhealthy up there right now?' I asked. 'Yes, sir, but this goddamn wire has got to be fixed.' There was a real soldier ... [and] you should have seen those trucks on the road to Gabes. The drivers were magnificent. All day they crawled along those sonofabitchin' roads, never stopping, never deviating from their course with shells bursting all around them. We got through on good old American guts. Many of the men drove over forty consecutive hours.

He then made reference to the fact that the Allied deception plan in place before the Normandy landings included an imaginary formation called First US Army Group, or FUSAG for short, which was being held in reserve for operations elsewhere. He continued:

> *Don't forget, you don't know I'm here at all. No word of that fact is to be mentioned in any letter. The world is not supposed to know what the hell they did with me. I'm not supposed to be commanding this army. I'm not even supposed to be in England. Let the first bastards to find out be the goddamn Germans. Some day I want them to raise up on their hind legs and howl: 'Jesus Christ, it's that goddamn Third Army and that sonofabitch Patton again!'*

**Patton pays a morale-boosting
visit to US troops prior
to the Normandy landings**

ROUSING THE TROOPS

According to one observer: 'This
statement had real significance
behind it – much more than met
the eye – and the men instinctively
sensed the fact and the telling mark
that they themselves would play in
world history because of it, for they
were being told as much right now.
Deep sincerity and seriousness lay
behind the General's colourful
words, and well the men knew it,
but they loved the way he put it as only he could do it.' Patton went on:

> We want to get the hell over there. We want to get over there and clean the
> goddamn thing up. And then we'll have to take a little jaunt against the
> purple-pissing Japanese and clean their nest too, before the Marines get in and
> claim all the goddamn credit!

The men laughed at this, sincerely hoping that Patton was jesting. He would end by saying:

*Sure we all want to go home. We want this thing over with. But you can't win a war lying down.
The quickest way to get it over with is to get the bastards. The quicker they are whipped, the quicker
we go home. The shortest way home is through Berlin! Why if a man is lying down in a shell-hole, if
he just stays there all the day the Boche will get to him eventually, and probably get him first! There
is no such thing as a foxhole war any more. Foxholes only slow up the offensive. Keep moving! We
will win this war, but we will win it only by fighting and by showing guts.*

*There is one great thing you men will be able to say when you go home. You may all thank God
for it. Thank God that, thirty years from now, when you are sitting round the fireside with your
grandson on your knee and he asks you what you did in World War II, you won't have to say,
'I shovelled shit in Louisiana'.*

Patton's speeches were extremely offensive to some. On one occasion, local dignitaries and
citizens had turned up to hear Patton address US troops stationed near Armagh, Northern Ireland.

Patton's first words to the troops were: 'You men are not in the world's oldest profession: the women beat you to it'. The soldiers roared with laughter at this quip, while the outraged civilians walked away.

At the end of July 1944, Patton's United States Third Army was in Normandy poised to begin the breakout. He addressed his staff:

> *An ounce of sweat is worth a gallon of blood. The harder you push the Germans and the more you kill, the fewer American casualties. There's another thing I want you to remember. Forget this goddamn business of worrying about our flanks, but not to the extent we don't do anything else. Some Goddamned fool once said that flanks must be secured and since then sons of bitches all over the world have been going crazy guarding their flanks. We don't want any of that in the Third Army. Flanks are something for the enemy to worry about, not us. I don't want to get any messages saying that, 'We are holding our position.' We're not holding anything! Let the Hun do that. We are advancing constantly and we're not interested in holding on to anything except the enemy. We're going to hold on to him by the nose and we're going to kick him in the ass; we're going the kick the hell out of him all the time and we're going to go through him like crap through a goose … We have one motto, 'L'audace, l'audace, toujours l'audace!' Remember that gentlemen.*

THRIVING ON ADVERSITY

The Battle of the Bulge in the Ardennes in December 1944, when the Germans caught the Allies by surprise, driving the Americans back in a huge salient, saw Patton at the peak of his performance. He revelled in the fact that his Third Army was tasked with restoring the situation on the south flank of the 'bulge'. He also found much satisfaction in bailing out his superiors: Eisenhower and Bradley, both of whom he privately despised, and with good reason since the mess was of their making. Before attacking with his Third Army he issued an order to his troops, which read:

> *Everyone in this army must understand we are not fighting this battle in a half-cocked manner. It's either root hog – or die! Shoot the works. If those Hun bastards want war in the raw then that's the way we'll give it to them.*

To the staffs of three of his four corps, sensing that they were less than resolute:

> *I always seem to be a ray of sunshine, and, by God I always am. We can and will win. God helping. I wish it were this time tomorrow night. When one attacks it is the enemy who has to worry. Give us Victory Lord.*

Patton died in December 1945 as a result of injuries sustained in a motor accident. To this day he remains a controversial figure. Some people, including many of his fellow countrymen, thought him mad, while others, especially those close to him, admired him. Whatever one's view of him as a person, he was undoubtedly the outstanding exponent of armoured warfare produced by the Western Allies in the Second World War.

BRIGADIER GENERAL NORMAN COTA

'There are only two kinds of people on this beach: those who are dead and those who are going to die. Now let's get the hell out of here.'

BRIGADIER GENERAL NORMAN COTA ON D-DAY, 6 JUNE 1944

On 6 June 1944, Brigadier General Norman Cota (1893–1971) was the assistant divisional commander of the United States 29th Infantry Division at Omaha Beach, Normandy. The landing at Omaha has gone down in history as a near disaster. This reputation owes much to flawed planning and defective execution in the initial phase. In essence, the assault at Omaha was delivered by infantry in the first wave, in contrast to the landings on the British and Canadian beaches where the infantry was in the fourth wave preceded by three waves of specialized armour. The blame can be laid at the door of General Omar Bradley, commander of the United States First Army, who refused to use most of the specialized armour on offer. Bradley took only the swimming tanks ('DD's – duplex drive tanks that were driven by a propeller at sea and tracks on land), but crucially not the armoured engineer vehicles specifically designed to blast their way through obstacles (flame thrower tanks, explosive throwers and mine-clearing flail tanks). The result was a suicidal head-on infantry assault.

Unlike many of his fellow senior officers, Cota did not assure his men that the German defenders would be so pulverized by the massive air and sea bombardment that they would be incapable of offering much resistance. Addressing the soldiers of the 29th Infantry Division, he said:

> The little discrepancies that we tried to correct [in training] are going to be magnified and are going to give way to incidents that you might at first view as chaotic. The air and naval bombardment and artillery support are reassuring. But you're going to find confusion. The landing craft aren't going in on schedule and people are going to be landed in the wrong place. Some won't be landed at all. The enemy will ... prevent our gaining a lodgement. But we must improvise, carry on, not lose our heads.

Wise advice indeed and containing the same message that a British commander conveyed to his brigade on the eve of Normandy. Cota was right; chaos was the order of the day at Omaha to a greater degree than on any other of the Normandy beaches, and probably more than even he anticipated. The rocket ships opened fire too far from the shore, dropping most of their projectiles among the leading assault craft. The attempt to land artillery from DUKWs failed dismally and predictably, as these amphibious vehicles had no ramp, which made unloading even a light gun – all they could carry – virtually impossible. This was in stark contrast to the British and Canadian beaches, where self-propelled, tracked and armoured artillery was landed from tank landing craft (LCTs), driving down a ramp, having engaged targets on the run-in. The crews of the LCTs carrying the 32 DD tanks bound for Omaha Beach launched them in rough water too far offshore. Most of the tanks, their canvas buoyancy skirts collapsing in the choppy sea, sank like stones. Five made it to the beach, but long after the leading wave of infantry.

Cota landed in the second wave on Dog White Beach. Three of his headquarters group were killed almost instantly. Encountering some men of the 5th Rangers huddled beneath a bank where they had remained for two hours, Cota asked:

What outfit is this?

Rangers, replied the men.

Well, goddamn it then, Rangers, get up and lead the way! ordered Cota.

The rangers grabbed the lengths of Bangalore torpedo with which they had landed, and began to blow holes in the wire.

All afternoon, Cota was up with the leading troops urging soldiers to get on inland. Coming across another group of Rangers pinned down, he calmly walked ahead of them to demonstrate that they could move. By nightfall the Omaha beachhead was secure.

BRIGADIER JAMES HILL

The task given to the British 6th Airborne Division for the Normandy invasion in June 1944, was to seize and hold the left flank of the Allied Lodgement area, by taking the bridges over the River Orne and the Caen Canal and denying the vital ground east of the Orne to the enemy. Within the divisional plan, the tasks assigned to the 3rd Parachute Brigade were to destroy four bridges over the River Dives, and the battery at Merville; after achieving these objectives they were to take up a defensive position on the Bois de Bavent Ridge.

The commander of the 3rd Parachute Brigade, James Hill (1911–2006), was an experienced soldier who had taken part in the retreat to Dunkirk in 1940, and commanded the 1st Parachute Battalion in North Africa in 1942. Before the Normandy operation, he addressed his brigade:

> *Gentlemen, in spite of your excellent training and orders, do not be dismayed
> if chaos reigns, it undoubtedly will.*

It might strike some people as odd that a commander on the eve of battle should speak thus. But James Hill was a charismatic leader, totally trusted by his men, most of whom had never been in battle before, and by warning them in these stark terms, he was preparing them to face the shocks to come. And shocks there were.

The drop of the division was carried out during the night of 5–6 June 1944. The turbulence generated by the mass of aircraft carrying the 3rd Parachute Brigade to its three Dropping Zones, plus a strong westerly wind, caused the sticks of parachutists to drop wide. This was exacerbated by the loss of all beacons for DZ V, and the party of pathfinders for DZ K dropping on DZ N without realizing it and setting up the beacons and lights giving out the signal for DZ K. Many soldiers found themselves on the wrong DZ and some in the flooded valley of the River Dives. In the area where the 3rd Parachute Brigade dropped were deep, water-filled ditches, in which some men drowned. A few soldiers landed miles east of the lodgement area. Some were killed fighting lonely battles, or were captured. For weeks after D Day, airborne soldiers trickled in to the brigade lines.

Despite these setbacks, the 3rd Parachute Brigade carried out nearly all its tasks. The 9th Parachute Battalion tasked with destroying the guns in the Merville Battery was unable to do so. Thanks to a scattered drop over some 130 square kilometres (50 sq mi), it arrived with no means of destroying the guns. But despite arriving with less than a quarter of its men, the battalion attacked and distracted the enemy from firing on the Caen Canal bridge while it was being taken by glider troops of the 6th Air Landing Brigade.

James Hill did not join his brigade until 4 p.m. on the afternoon of D-Day. He dropped in the flooded valley of the River Dives, where the water was about a metre (4 ft) deep. The enemy had wired it before flooding and there were numerous deep ditches. After four hours of wading through the flood, he and a party of men he had collected together struck dry land. Walking towards the Merville Battery, the party was bombed by Allied aircraft, mistaking them for Germans. All except three men were killed, and Hill had one side of his buttocks blown off.

Hobbling his way to the 9th Battalion, he was patched up by their medical officer, and was immensely cheered by the news of the battalion's efforts that night. When Hill reported to divisional headquarters, the division's senior doctor insisted on operating on him there and then, but promised to return him to his own brigade headquarters as soon as he recovered from the anaesthetic.

The MO was as good as his word. Unable to sit down, James Hill arrived at his headquarters standing in the medical officer's jeep and holding a saline drip in one hand. Driving past a slit trench, and peering down into it from his elevated position, he upbraided its unfortunate occupant:

Square off the sides of that slit, and polish your boots!

James Hill had arrived, and soon everybody knew it and was greatly uplifted by his presence. In the subsequent days he personally led two counter-attacks, and his greatly reduced brigade held the Bois de Bavent ridge against everything the Germans could throw at it in the ensuing weeks.

VICE ADMIRAL CHUICHI NAGUMO

On 7 December 1941, Vice Admiral Chuichi Nagumo (1887–1944) commanded the Imperial Japanese Navy's élite carrier striking force that attacked Pearl Harbor. His carriers supported the capture of the Netherlands East Indies, and sent aircraft to raid Darwin in Australia and Ceylon (Sri Lanka). After his crushing defeat at the Battle of Midway in June 1942, Nagumo won tactical victories at Tassafaronga and Santa Cruz off Guadalcanal. In early 1943 he was sent to command the Central Pacific Area Fleet based at Saipan in the Mariana Islands.

The Marianas were key strategic islands straddling Japan's sea lines of communications and offering bases from which American B-29 bombers could strike Japan. Admiral Chester Nimitz, commander-in-chief of the US Pacific Fleet and Pacific Ocean Area, determined to capture them,

starting with Saipan. The Americans deployed a massive force based around the Fifth Fleet. The carrier force alone consisted of 15 carriers with over 900 aircraft embarked, seven battleships, 21 cruisers and 69 destroyers. The 77,000 strong landing force consisted of the 2nd and 4th Marine Divisions and the US Army's 27th Infantry Division.

American intelligence had underestimated the strength of the defence of Saipan. Instead of 19,000 defenders, there were around 30,000; about three-quarters army personnel commanded by Lieutenant General Yoshitsugu Saito, and the rest naval personnel under Nagumo. The latter were concentrated around Tanapag Harbour in the northwest of the island. The Japanese were sited in caves and bunkers, in rugged, mountainous terrain, covered with thick undergrowth.

The American landings began on 15 June 1944. The preliminary bombardment was inadequate and the US Marines took 4000 casualties in the first 48 hours, but carved out a beachhead, which they held against furious Japanese attacks. Saito and Nagumo hoped to stall the US Marines at the beachhead while the Japanese Mobile Fleet of 9 carriers, 5 battleships and 13 cruisers destroyed the transports offshore. But the US Fifth Fleet sortied from Saipan and destroyed the Mobile Fleet in the Battle of the Philippine Sea on 19 June, forcing Saito to conclude that his only option was to withdraw to the centre of the island and fight a delaying action, supported by Nagumo's naval defence force. The Japanese defence was so tenacious that the capture of the island took three weeks instead of the three days allocated for the operation.

Near the end, as the Japanese launched *banzai* charges down the Tanapag Plain, Nagumo declared:

> *Whether we attack, or whether we stay where we are is only death. But realizing that in death there is life, let us take this opportunity to exalt Japanese manhood. I shall advance upon the Americans to deliver still another blow and leave my bones upon Saipan as a bulwark of the Pacific.*

Before the final assault, Saito, after a farewell feast of sake and tinned crabmeat, stabbed himself with his sword before his adjutant shot him in the head with a pistol. On 3 July, the last *banzai* charge by 2500 troops was halted by artillery firing point-blank at the massed ranks of screaming Japanese. The next day, Vice Admiral Nagumo shot himself.

Saipan cost the Americans 16,525 casualties, including 3426 dead. The emperor Hirohito greeted the news of the capture of the island by saying: 'Hell is on us'. Vice Admiral Shigeyoshi Miwa concurred: 'Our war was lost with the loss of Saipan. I feel it was a decisive battle.'

LIEUTENANT GENERAL WALTON H. WALKER

❛You can live without food, but you cannot last long without ammunition.❜

LIEUTENANT GENERAL WALTON H. WALKER, REMARK TO A SENIOR COMMANDER IN KOREA, JULY 1950

The North Korean army invaded South Korea at 4 a.m. on 25 June 1950, striking without warning in the half-light before sunrise, gaining complete tactical surprise. The ill-equipped and badly trained forces of the Southern Republic of Korea (ROK) were overwhelmed and pushed back. The Security Council of the United Nations condemned the attack, and authorized a United Nations force to eject the North Koreans from the south of the 38th Parallel, the border between the two countries. The Russians had been boycotting the meetings of the Security Council, and were not present to exercise their veto.

The first United Nations troops to arrive in South Korea were part of the United States 24th Infantry Division, from the US Eighth Army of occupation in Japan. Although a United Nations operation, with eventually some 23 countries participating, by far the greatest proportion of the air, sea and land forces were provided by the USA, which was in all respects the 'lead nation', dictating policy and running the war.

As the American troops fought a series of delaying actions, it became apparent to General Douglas MacArthur, the American commander-in-chief, based in Japan, that the Eighth Army would have to take over the running of the war in Korea. The commander of the Eighth Army, Lieutenant General Walton Walker (1889–1950) was appointed commander of land forces.

Few of the officers and soldiers of the US Eighth Army were fit for war-fighting. Occupation duty among the fleshpots of Japan

was a poor preparation for fighting North Koreans, and later the Chinese, whose soldiers were tough, fanatically brave and masters of camouflage and fieldcraft. The occupation divisions in Japan were not trained, equipped or ready for battle. The great majority of enlisted men were young and not really interested in being soldiers. The recruiting posters that had induced most of these men to enter the army mentioned all conceivable advantages and promised many good things, but never suggested that the principal business of an army is to fight. Although Walker, when he took over the Eighth Army in Japan the previous year had instituted a training programme to shake the soldiers out of the comfortable ways they had acquired on occupation duty, there was still a long way to go before they could be considered fit to fight. Some of their equipment was obsolescent, while many of the more up-to-date items of kit had arrived only as the units left Japan. On the whole the soldiers of the Eighth Army performed badly. As always in such situations, this was not their fault, but that of their senior commanders and of politicians. Because of the poor state of readiness of the US Army, the burden for keeping the show on the road in the early days of the war in Korea was borne by battalion and company commanders, and senior non-commissioned officers, many of whom had seen much fighting in the Second World War, which had ended just under five years before. In consequence, a high proportion of those killed or wounded in the early battles were the experienced battalion-level commanders, leaving the young soldiers leaderless.

THE TENACIOUS BULLDOG

Walker was short and stocky, looked rather like a bulldog and was similarly brave and tenacious. Indeed, he had already acquired this nickname in the US Army (admittedly an improvement on 'fat Walker', Patton's name for him when he commanded XX Corps in the US Third Army in northwest Europe in 1944–5). To give Patton his due, he did more often call Walker a 'fighting sonofabitch'. By the time he came to Korea, Walker had seen a considerable amount of combat, beginning with the Veracruz expedition of 1914, and both World Wars. He was a tough, thrusting general, and to have survived under Patton was recommendation enough.

As soon as he arrived in Korea, he was to be seen right up in the front encouraging and cajoling, and instructing one senior officer:

> *I only want to see you in the rear in your coffin.*

As the Americans and South Koreans pulled back into a perimeter around the southern port of Pusan, he wanted to make sure that everyone realized that there could be no evacuation from Korea. On 29 July he told the commander and staff of the 25th Division:

> *General MacArthur was over here two days ago; he is thoroughly conversant with the situation. He knows where we are and what we have to fight with. He knows our needs and where the enemy is hitting the hardest. General MacArthur is doing everything possible to send reinforcements. A Marine unit and two regiments are expected in the next few days to reinforce us. Additional units are being sent over as quickly as possible. We are fighting a battle against time. There will be no more retreating, withdrawal, or readjustment of the lines or any other term you choose. There is no line behind us to which we retreat. Every unit must counter-attack to keep the enemy in a state of confusion and off balance. There will be no Dunkirk, no Bataan. A retreat to Pusan would be one of the greatest butcheries in history. We must fight until the end. Capture by these people is worse than death itself. We will fight as a team. If some of us must die, we will die fighting together. Any man who gives ground may be personally responsible for the death of thousands of his comrades.*
>
> *I want you to put this out to all men in the Division. I want everybody to understand that we are going to hold this line. We are going to win.*

A similar exhortation was given to the other divisions, and passed down to everyone in the fighting units. In fact, withdrawal did not suddenly come to an end. But Walker's message did the trick, and resistance was more stubborn and the momentum of the Northern attack slowed. It eventually stopped after Walker's army crossed the Naktong river on 31 July. The river was to become part of the Pusan perimeter.

The North Koreans tried again and again to smash through to the Port of Pusan, but were held in weeks of bitter fighting. Again, Walker seemed to be everywhere. On one occasion a party of reinforcements, halting on their way forward to join their unit to fill their water bottles in a stream, were accosted by Walker, who drove up in a jeep. On discovering what they were doing, he yelled:

> *What are you thinking of? I want your asses forward!*

By early September, just as even Walker was beginning to wonder if the perimeter could be held much longer, the North Korean offensive began to run out of steam. Then, on 15 September, the weary troops around Pusan heard the news of MacArthur's master stroke, the amphibious hook at Inchon. The spirits of the Eighth Army rose, and they began to see that they owed their survival to 'Bulldog' Walker. Despite being saddled with the least professional, worst trained army America had ever sent to war, filled with callow unmotivated soldiers, Walker had kept them up to the mark. Without him and a small handful of first-class officers and units, such as the United States Marine Brigade, the Pusan perimeter would have folded and the war would have been lost, with incalculable consequences, which might have echoed down to the present.

The Inchon landing cut the North Korean lines of communication, and they fell back in haste. Walker broke out of the Pusan perimeter, and pushed north to the border with China. When the Chinese attacked at the end of November 1950, the Eighth Army was driven back. By mid-December UN forces, including the Eighth Army was back along the general line of the 38th Parallel. In the space of three months Walker's men had advanced 350 miles (560 km), only to be driven back nearly 200 miles (320 km). On 23 December, Walker was killed when his jeep collided with a truck. He was tired and depressed, and sensed that MacArthur was planning to relieve him for the Eighth Army's poor showing in the withdrawal from the Chinese border. It was a tragic end for the man who had contributed so much to the defeat of the North Korean invaders in the early part of the war.

GENERAL NORMAN SCHWARZKOPF

'We are going to destroy the Republican Guard.'

GENERAL NORMAN SCHWARZKOPF ADDRESSING HIS SENIOR COMMANDERS, 14 NOVEMBER 1990

On 17 January 1991, General Norman Schwarzkopf (b.1934), commander of the United States Central Command and of the Coalition Forces in Saudi Arabia and the Arabian Gulf addressed his staff in the war room in Riyadh:

> *Soldiers, sailors, airmen, and Marines of United States Central Command:*
> *This morning at 0300 we launched Operation Desert Storm, an offensive*
> *campaign that will enforce United Nations resolutions that Iraq must cease its*
> *rape and pillage of its weaker neighbour and withdraw its forces from Kuwait.*
> *The President, the Congress, the American people, and indeed the world*
> *stand united in their support for your actions. You are a member of the most*
> *powerful force our country, in coalition with our allies, has ever assembled in*
> *a single theatre to face such an aggressor. You have trained hard for this battle*
> *and you are ready. During my visits with you, I have seen in your eyes a fire*
> *of determination to get this job done quickly so that we may return to the*
> *shores of our great nation. My confidence in you is total. Our cause is just!*
> *Now you must be the thunder and lightning of Desert Storm. May God be*
> *with you, your loved ones at home, and our country.*

Norman Schwarzkopf, a West Point graduate, first saw action in Vietnam in 1965 as a senior adviser to the South Vietnamese Airborne Brigade. He saw much fighting especially in the Ia Drang Valley, the siege of Duc Co and the Battle of Bong Son. In 1970 he returned to command the 1st Battalion, 6th Infantry in the US American Division. By now Vietnam was a deeply unpopular war in the United States, the morale of the soldiers was low and racial tension was widespread in the army. By his leadership, Norman Schwarzkopf transformed his battalion into an effective fighting unit.

In the late 1970s and early 1980s, Schwarzkopf helped restore the self-worth of the US Army whose morale had taken such a battering in Vietnam. When the Iraqi leader Saddam Hussein

invaded Kuwait in August 1990, he was commanding US Central Command, a joint headquarters responsible for US operations in the Middle East. The task of ejecting the invaders was placed on the shoulders of Norman Schwarzkopf. He was to command a naval, air and land coalition of 10 major and 12 minor participants, fighting the first true air-land battle in history.

Iraq had 42 divisions in the Kuwait theatre of operations, some 450,000 men, 4280 tanks, 3100 guns, and 500 tactical aircraft. The Iraqi army was deployed in three layers along the border with Saudi Arabia, with the élite Republican Guard held back in reserve. The doom-mongers in Europe, including ex-prime minister Edward Heath, predicted massive slaughter among the Coalition Forces at the hands of the mighty Iraqi Army. Norman Schwarzkopf set out to prove them wrong.

He addressed his senior commanders on 14 November 1990:

> *My written orders from Washington are still to deter Iraq from attacking*
> *Saudi Arabia. But there is no doubt about the fact that we are getting ready to*

go on the offensive. That's what we are here to talk about today. Forget the defensive bullshit, we are now talking offensive. And we are going to talk offensive until the day we go home.

There are a hell of a lot of them – 450,000 right now in the Kuwait theatre, so they've got mass on their side. Another strength is their chemical capability. They have used it in the past and there is no doubt in my mind that they're going to use it on us.

The first thing we're going to have to do is, I don't like to use the word 'decapitate', so I think I'll use the word 'attack' [their] leadership, and go after his command and control. Number two, we need to cut totally his supply lines. We also need to destroy his chemical, biological, and nuclear capability. And finally, all you tankers [armoured formation commanders], listen to this. We need to destroy – not attack, not damage, not surround – I want you to destroy the Republican Guard. When you've done with them, I don't want them to be an effective fighting force anymore. I don't want them to exist as a military organization.

General Norman Schwarzkopf (centre) meeting with Richard Cheney, secretary of defence, and other American commanders in preparation for the liberation of Kuwait

Conscious that many of those he was addressing had fought in Vietnam, a war lost by the United States because of self-imposed limitations placed on the use of military power, Schwarzkopf stressed:

> *We are not going into this with one arm tied behind our backs. We're not gonna say we want to be as nice as we possibly can, and if they draw back across the border that's fine with us. That's bullshit!*

Schwarzkopf outlined his plan, pinning the Iraqis in Kuwait by a United States Marine attack, followed by a wide outflanking sweep through the desert with the bulk of his armoured formations to pin the Republican Guard against the sea. The effect on his commanders was electric.

Following a massive air campaign, the ground assault starting on 24 February 1991 went like clockwork, and by the end of the fourth day the Iraqi army had collapsed. A ceasefire came into effect on 28 February. The Iraqis lost at least 25,000 dead, and large numbers of tanks and other equipment destroyed. The Coalition losses were 4 tanks, 37 aircraft and 139 soldiers killed in action.

Norman Schwarzkopf retired in August 1991, having refused the post of chief of staff because of his opposition to impending defence cuts. Before he retired he addressed the cadets at West Point:

> *Out there among you are the cynics, the people who scoff at what you're learning here. The people who scoff at character, the people that scoff at hard work. But they don't know what they're talking about, let me tell you. I can assure you that when the going gets tough and their country needs them, they're not going to be there. They will not be there, but you will. After Vietnam, we had a whole cottage industry develop basically in Washington DC, that consisted of a bunch of military fairies that had never been shot at in anger, who felt fully qualified to comment on the leadership ability of all the leaders of the United States Army. They were not Monday-morning quarterbacks, they were the worst of all possible kind, they were the Friday-afternoon quarterbacks. They felt qualified to criticize us even before the game was played. And they are the same people who are saying, my goodness, we have terrible problems with our armed forces because there are no leaders out there, there are no more combat leaders. Where are the Eisenhowers? Where are the Bradleys? Where are the MacArthurs? Where are the Audie Murphys? Coming from a guy who's never been shot at in his life, that's a pretty bold statement.*

LIEUTENANT COLONEL TIM COLLINS

On Wednesday 19 March 2003, just before the Coalition Forces led by the United States invaded Iraq, Lieutenant Colonel Tim Collins (b.1960), commanding officer of the 1st Battalion The Royal Irish Regiment addressed his men at Blair Mayne Camp in Kuwait:

We go to liberate, not to conquer. We will not fly our flags in their country. We are entering Iraq to free a people and the only flag which will be flown in that ancient land is their own. Show respect for them.

There are some who are alive at this moment who will not be alive shortly. Those who do not wish to go on that journey, we will not send. As for the others, I expect you to rock their world. Wipe them out if that is what they choose. But if you are ferocious in battle remember to be magnanimous in victory.

Iraq is steeped in history. It is the site of the Garden of Eden, of the Great Flood and the birthplace of Abraham. Tread lightly there.

You will see things that no man could pay to see – and you will have to go a long way to find a more decent, generous and upright people than the Iraqis. You will be embarrassed by their hospitality even though they have nothing.

Don't treat them as refugees for they are in their own country. Their children will be poor, in years to come they will know that the light of liberation in their lives was brought by you.

If there are casualties of war then remember that when they woke up and got dressed in the morning they did not plan to die this day. Allow them dignity in death. Bury them properly and mark their graves.

It is my foremost intention to bring every single one of you out alive. But there may be people among us who will not see the end of this campaign. We will put them in their sleeping bags and send them back. There will be no time for sorrow.

The enemy should be in no doubt that we are his nemesis and that we are bringing about his rightful destruction. There are many regional commanders who have stains on their souls and they are stoking the fires of hell for Saddam. He and his forces will be destroyed by this coalition for what they have done. As they die they will know their deeds have brought them to this place. Show them no pity.

It is a big step to take another human life. It is not to be done lightly. I know of men who have taken life needlessly in other conflicts. I can assure you they live with the mark of Cain upon them.

If someone surrenders to you then remember they have that right in international law and ensure that one day they go home to their family. The ones who wish to fight, well, we aim to please.

If you harm the regiment or its history by over-enthusiasm in killing or in cowardice, know it is your family who will suffer. You will be shunned unless your conduct is of the highest – for your deeds will follow you down through history. We will bring shame on neither our uniform or our nation.

Concerning Saddam's deployment of chemical and biological weapons, Collins stated:

> *It is not a question of if, it's a question of when. We know he has already devolved the decision to lower commanders, and that means he has already taken the decision himself. If we survive the first strike we will survive the attack.*
>
> *As for ourselves, let's bring everyone home and leave Iraq a better place for us having been there. Our business now is north.*

The speech was written down by a journalist at the time, and is an accurate record of what Lieutenant Colonel Collins said. Unlike some pre-battle speeches, it has not been embroidered or amended in the light of subsequent events. It is, therefore, a perfect reflection of the circumstances in which it was delivered, to young Irish soldiers, most of whom had never been in battle before, with all the apprehension that facing the unknown brings, and fully aware that what they were about to do did not have the full-hearted support of many of the public in Great Britain and Ireland.

As with most battles, events did not progress as planned, and the aftermath of the invasion was not as happy as those who took part would have wished. This was not their fault. The guilty ones are the politicians who ordered the invasion, who lied to provide a reason for their decision, and who did not plan properly for the post-invasion phase.

As so often before, British soldiers by their bravery, devotion to duty and professionalism did their best to make up for the incompetence and mendacity of their political leaders. They continue to do so to this day.

INDEX

PICTURE CREDITS